MILLENNIUM

THE GIRL WHO KICKED THE HORNET'S NEST

TITAN
COMICS

ALSO FROM TITAN COMICS AND HARD CASE CRIME

GRAPHIC NOVELS

THE ASSIGNMENT

BABYLON BERLIN

MILLENNIUM: THE GIRL WITH THE DRAGON TATTOO

MILLENNIUM: THE GIRL WHO PLAYED WITH FIRE

MILLENNIUM: THE GIRL WHO KICKED THE HORNET'S NEST

MINKY WOODCOCK: THE GIRL WHO HANDCUFFED HOUDINI

NORMANDY GOLD

PEEPLAND

QUARRY'S WAR

TRIGGERMAN

NOVELS

361

A DIET OF TREACLE

A TOUCH OF DEATH

A WALK AMONG THE TOMBSTONES

BABY MOLL

BINARY

BLACKMAILER

BLOOD ON THE MINK

BORDERLINE

BRAINQUAKE

BRANDED WOMAN

BUST

CASINO MOON

CHOKE HOLD

THE COCKTAIL WAITRESS

THE COMEDY IS FINISHED

THE CONFESSION

THE CONSUMMATA

THE CORPSE WORE PASTIES

CUT ME IN

THE CUTIE

DEAD STREET

DEADLY BELOVED

THE DEAD MAN'S BROTHER

DRUG OF CHOICE

DUTCH UNCLE

EASY DEATH

EASY GO

FADE TO BLONDE

FAKE I.D.

FALSE NEGATIVE

FIFTY-TO-ONE

FOREVER AND A DEATH

GETTING OFF: A NOVEL OF SEX AND VIOLENCE

THE GIRL WITH THE DEEP BLUE EYES

THE GIRL WITH THE LONG GREEN HEART

GRAVE DESCEND

GRIFTER'S GAME

GUN WORK

THE GUTTER AND THE GRAVE

HELP I AM BEING HELD PRISONER

HOME IS THE SAILOR

HONEY IN HIS MOUTH

HOUSE DICK

JOYLAND

KILL NOW PAY LATER

KILLING CASTRO

THE KNIFE SLIPPED

THE LAST MATCH

THE LAST STAND

LEMONS NEVER LIE

LITTLE GIRL LOST

LOSERS LIVE LONGER

LUCKY AT CARDS

THE MAX

MEMORY

MONEY SHOT

MURDER IS MY BUSINESS

THE MURDERER VINE

THE NICE GUYS

NIGHT WALKER

NO HOUSE LIMIT

NOBODY'S ANGEL

ODDS ON

PASSPORT TO PERIL

THE PEDDLER

PIMP

PLUNDER OF THE SUN

ROBBIE'S WIFE

SAY IT WITH BULLETS

SCRATCH ONE

THE SCRET LIVES OF MARRIED WOMEN

SEDUCTION OF THE INNOCENT

SHOOTING STAR/SPIDERWEB

SINNER MAN

SLIDE

SNATCH

SO NUDE, SO DEAD

SOHO SINS

SOMEBODY OWES ME MONEY

SONGS OF INNOCENCE

STOP THIS MAN!

STRAIGHT CUT

THIEVES FALL OUT

TOP OF THE HEAP

TURN ON THE HEAT

THE TWENTY-YEAR DEATH

TWO FOR THE MONEY

THE VALLEY OF FEAR

THE VENGEFUL VIRGIN

THE VENOM BUSINESS

WEB OF THE CITY

THE WOUNDED AND THE SLAIN

ZERO COOL

QUARRY

THE FIRST QUARRY

THE LAST QUARRY

QUARRY

QUARRY'S CHOICE

QUARRY'S CLIMAX

QUARRY'S CUT

QUARRY'S DEAL

QUARRY'S EX

QUARRY IN THE BLACK

QUARRY IN THE MIDDLE

QUARRY'S LIST

QUARRY'S VOTE

THE WRONG QUARRY

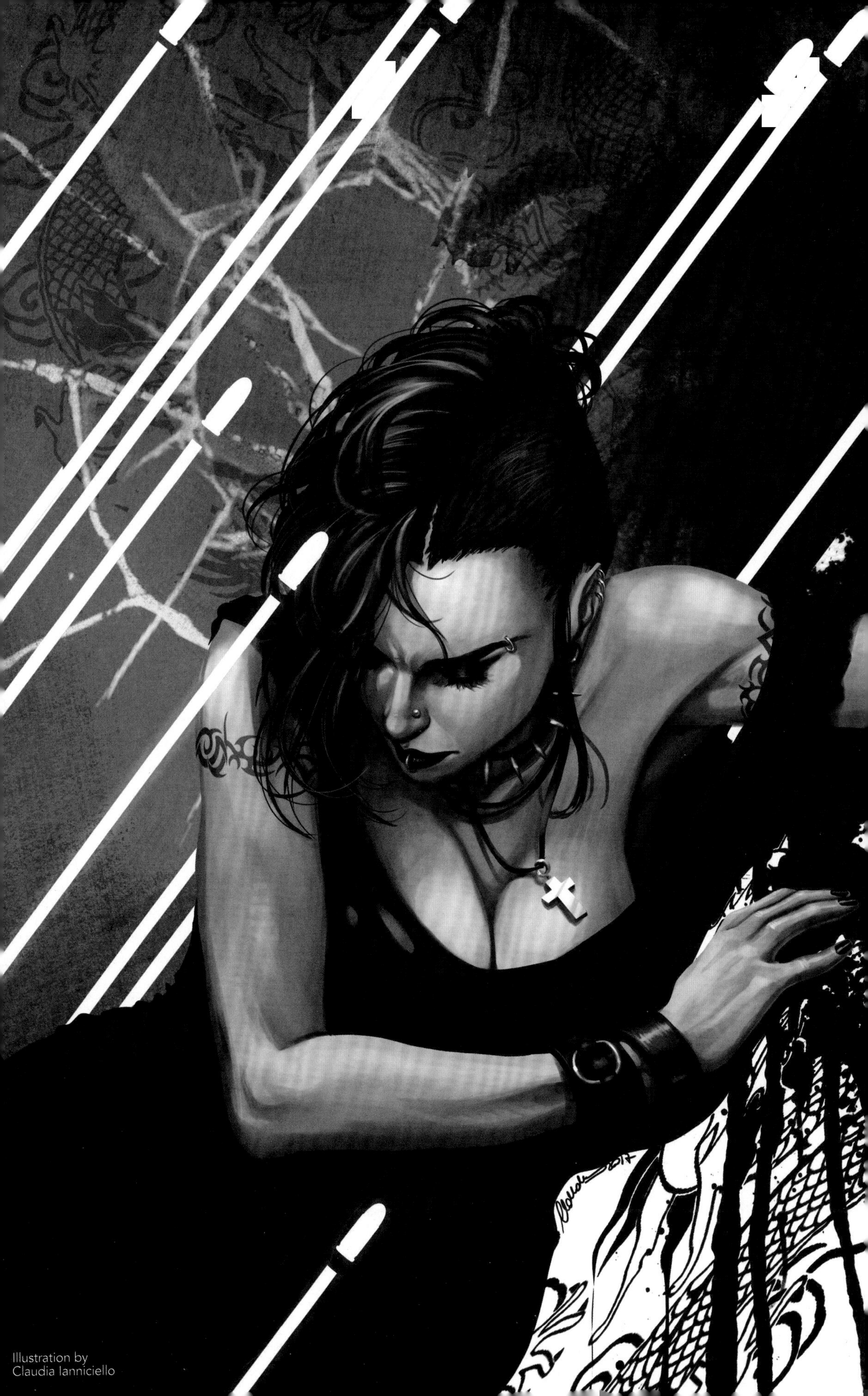

Illustration by
Claudia Ianniciello

THE GIRL WHO KICKED THE HORNET'S NEST

TITAN COMICS

EDITOR: LAUREN BOWES
DESIGNER: OZ BROWNE

Consulting Editor: Charles Ardai
Line Editor: Tom Williams
Managing & Launch Editor: Andrew James
Senior Production Controller: Jackie Flook
Production Supervisor: Maria Pearson
Production Controller: Peter James
Production Assistant: Natalie Bolger
Art Director: Oz Browne
Senior Sales Manager: Steve Tothill
Press Officer: Will O'Mullane
Direct Sales & Marketing Manager: Ricky Claydon
Commercial Manager: Michelle Fairlamb
Ads & Marketing Assistant: Tom Miller
Publishing Manager: Darryl Tothill
Publishing Director: Chris Teather
Operations Director: Leigh Baulch
Executive Director: Vivian Cheung
Publisher: Nick Landau

MILLENNIUM: THE GIRL WHO KICKED THE HORNET'S NEST
9781785863455
Published by Titan Comics
A division of Titan Publishing Group Ltd.
144 Southwark St., London, SE1 0UP

A CIP catalogue record for this title is available from the British Library

10 9 8 7 6 5 4 3 2 1
First Published May 2018
Printed in China.
Titan Comics.

WWW.TITAN-COMICS.COM
Follow us on Twitter @ComicsTitan
Visit us at facebook.com/comicstitan

MILLENNIUM

THE GIRL WHO KICKED THE HORNET'S NEST

WRITTEN BY

SYLVAIN RUNBERG

ARTWORK BY

JOSÉ HOMS & MANOLO CAROT

TRANSLATED BY

RACHEL ZERNER

BASED ON THE NOVEL
TRILOGY BY
STIEG LARSSON

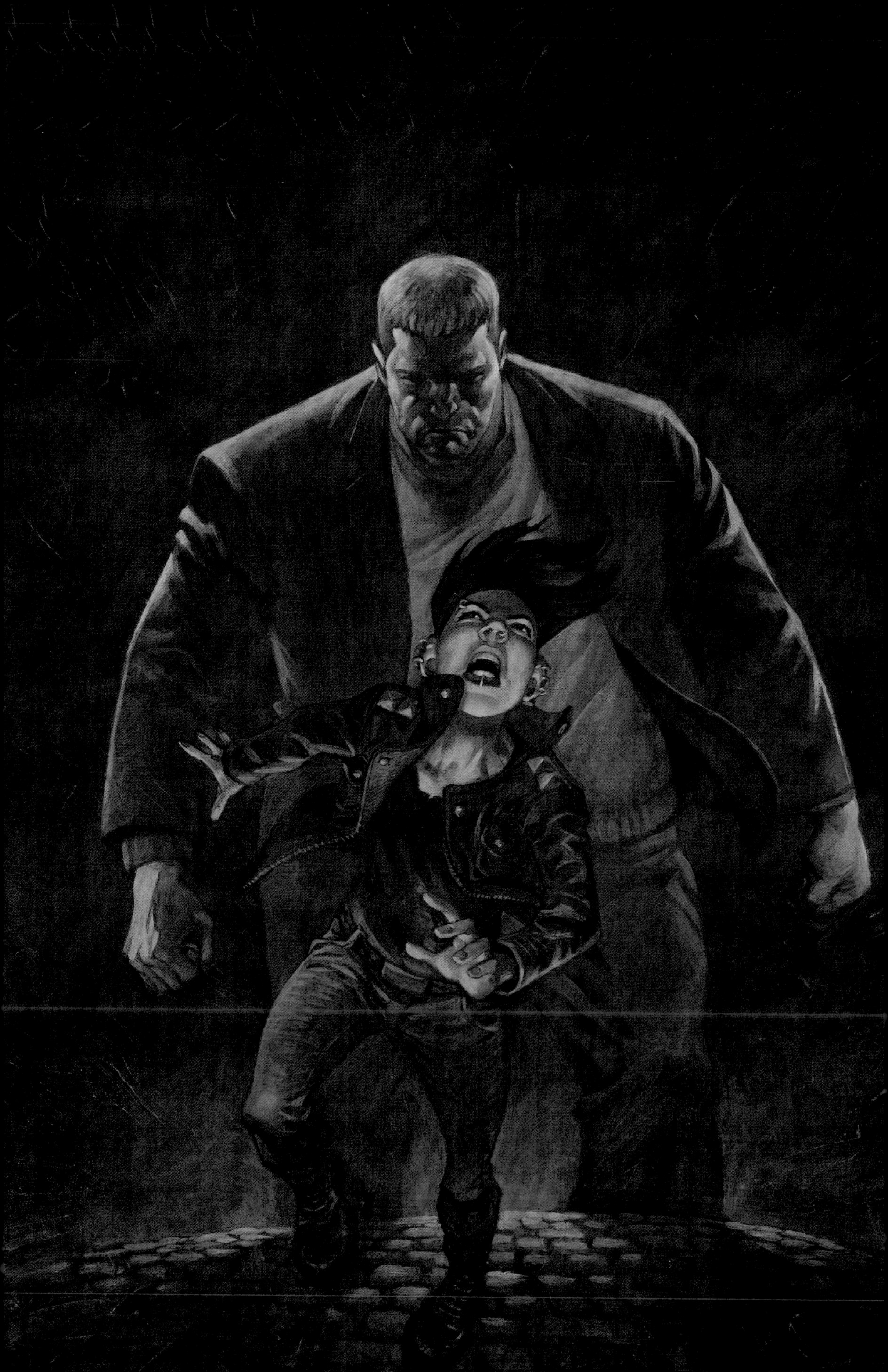

Illustration by Homs

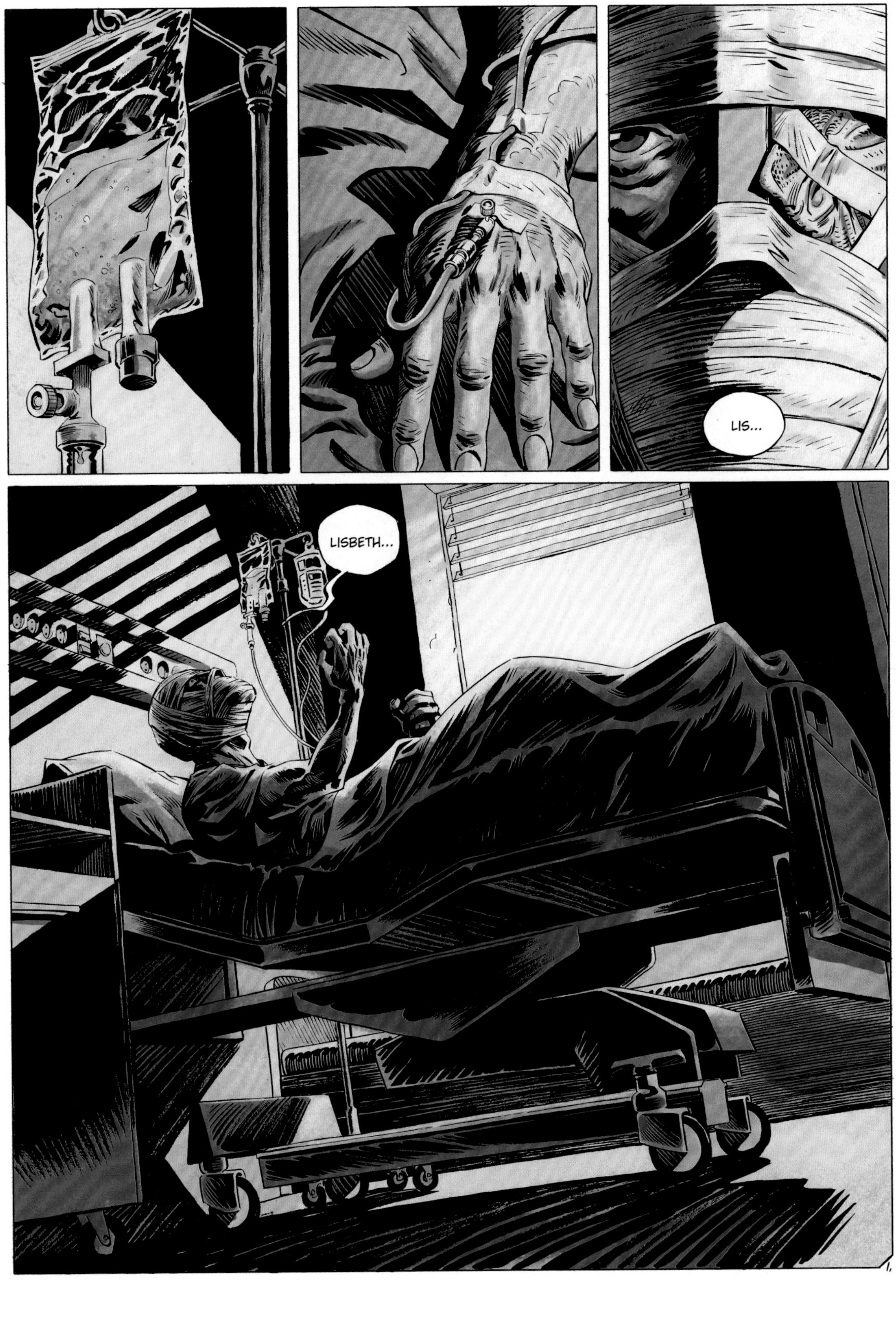
LIS...
LISBETH...

HERE, WE JUST GOT THIS IN -- THE SPECIAL ISSUE DEDICATED TO SEX TRAFFICKING IN SWEDEN.

IT'LL BE HITTING NEWSSTANDS WITHIN A COUPLE WEEKS... LIKE A BOMBSHELL.

NATURALLY, IT'S DEDICATED IN MEMORY OF DAG AND MIA.

A FINE PIECE OF WORK. CONG- RATS.

WHAT ABOUT YOU? HOW'S IT GOING? RUNNING THE COUNTRY'S MOST POPULAR MAGAZINE?

I'D LOVE TO HEAR -- WE'VE HARDLY TALKED SINCE YOU LEFT MILLENNIUM!

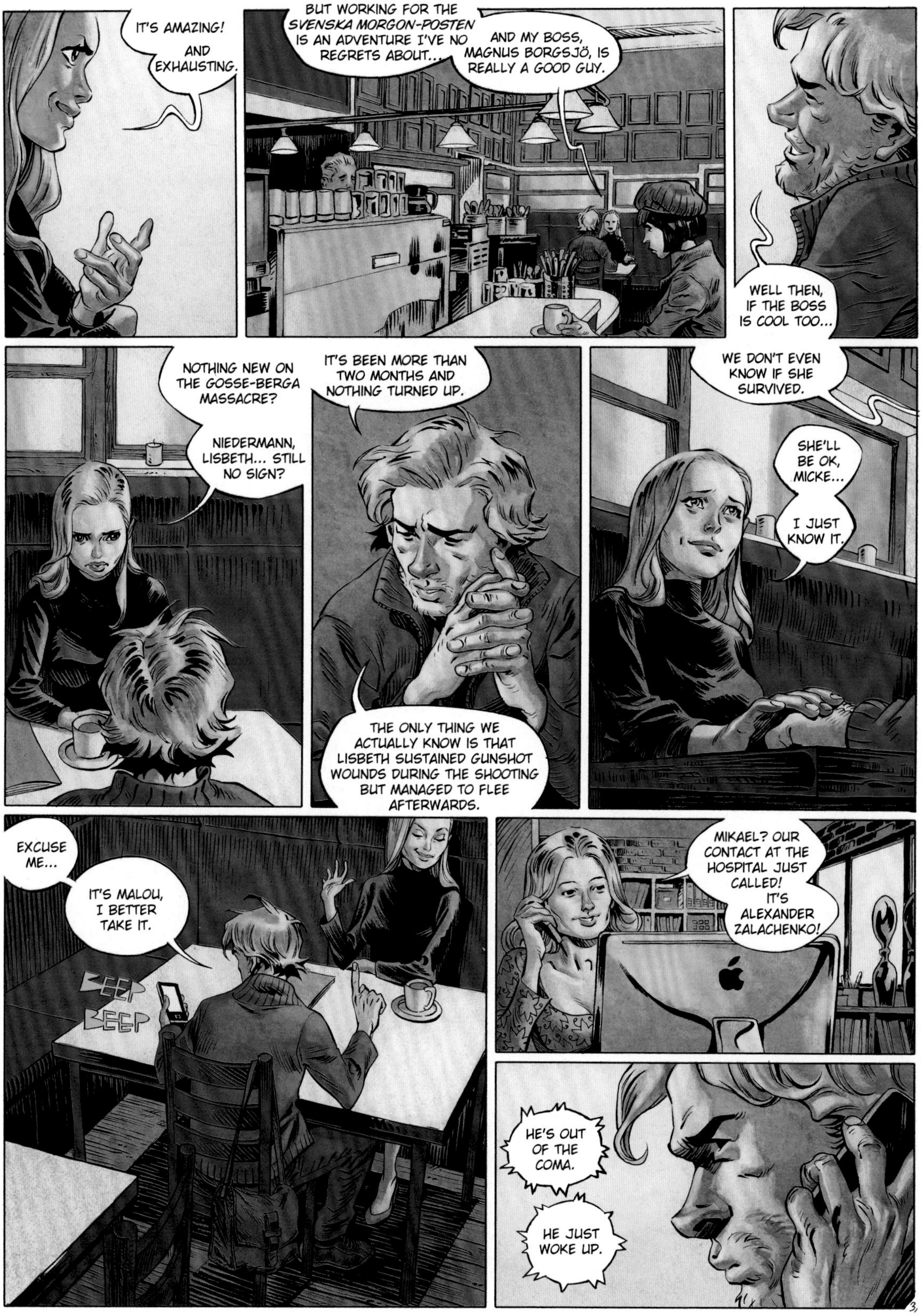
IT'S AMAZING!
AND EXHAUSTING.
BUT WORKING FOR THE *SVENSKA MORGON-POSTEN* IS AN ADVENTURE I'VE NO REGRETS ABOUT...
AND MY BOSS, MAGNUS BORGSJÖ, IS REALLY A GOOD GUY.
WELL THEN, IF THE BOSS IS COOL TOO...
NOTHING NEW ON THE GOSSE-BERGA MASSACRE?
NIEDERMANN, LISBETH... STILL NO SIGN?
IT'S BEEN MORE THAN TWO MONTHS AND NOTHING TURNED UP.
THE ONLY THING WE ACTUALLY KNOW IS THAT LISBETH SUSTAINED GUNSHOT WOUNDS DURING THE SHOOTING BUT MANAGED TO FLEE AFTERWARDS.
WE DON'T EVEN KNOW IF SHE SURVIVED.
SHE'LL BE OK, MICKE...
I JUST KNOW IT.
EXCUSE ME...
BEEP
BEEP
IT'S MALOU, I BETTER TAKE IT.
MIKAEL? OUR CONTACT AT THE HOSPITAL JUST CALLED! IT'S ALEXANDER ZALACHENKO!
HE'S OUT OF THE COMA.
HE JUST WOKE UP.

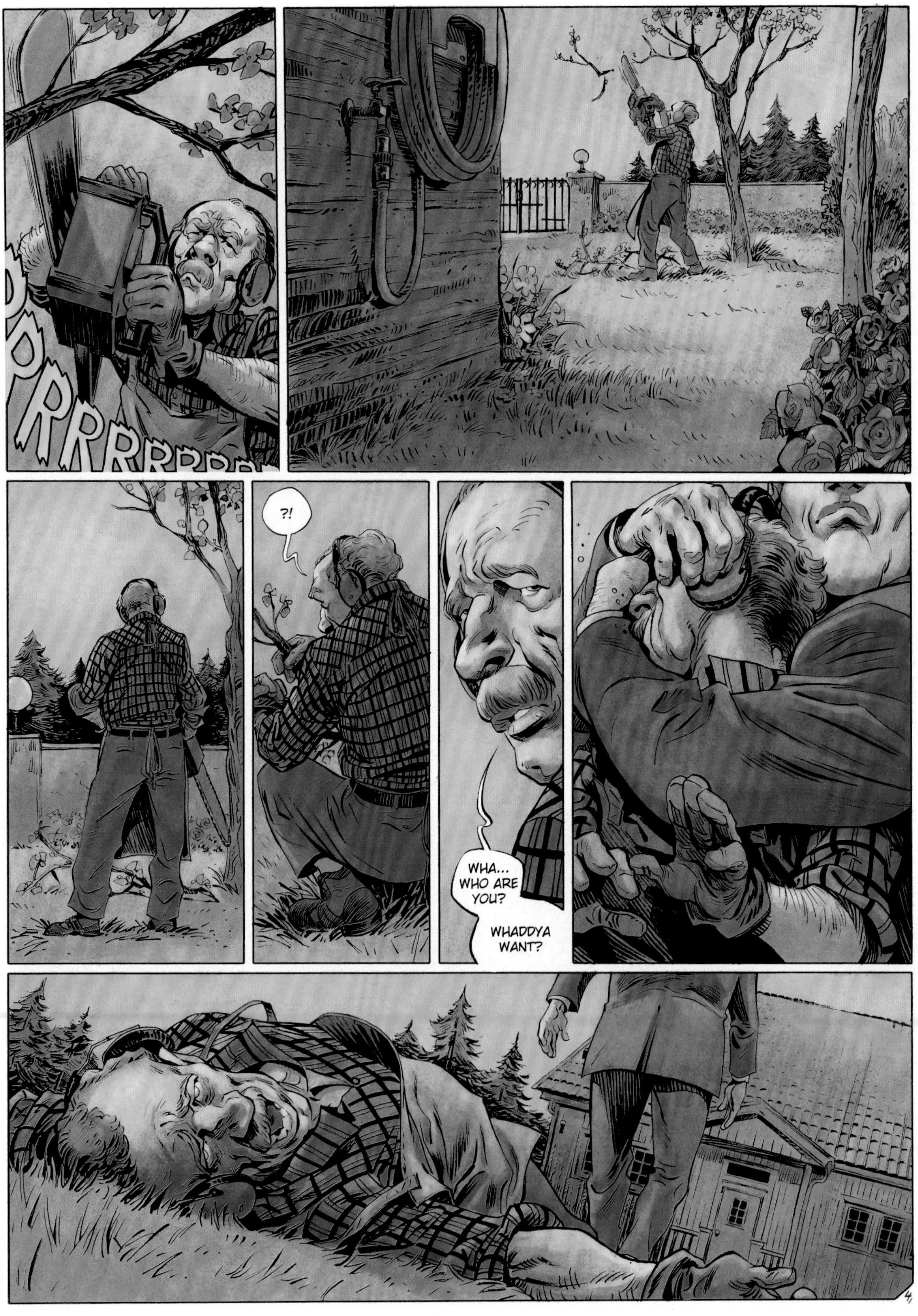
PRRRRRRR
?!
WHA... WHO ARE YOU?
WHADDYA WANT?

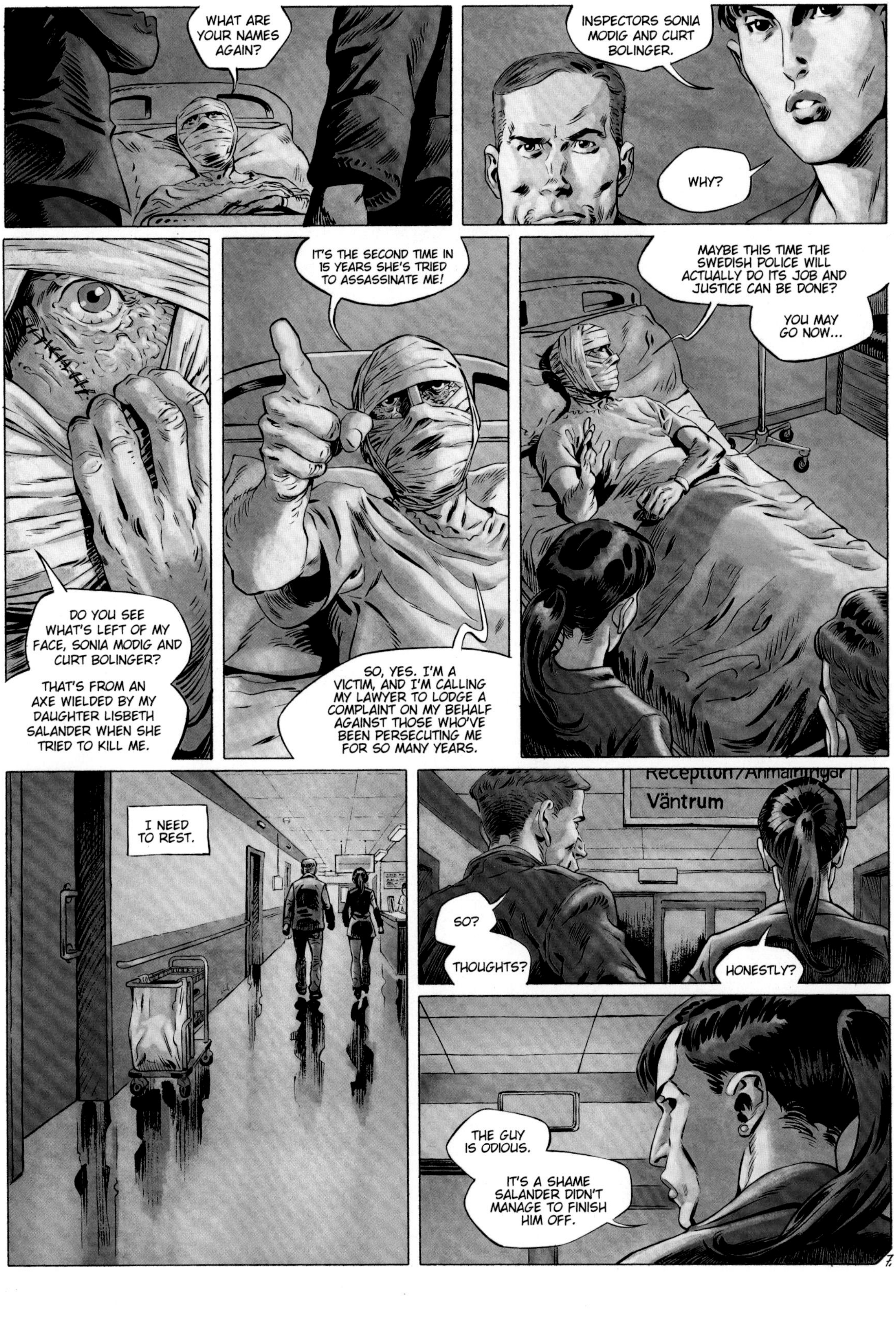
WHAT ARE YOUR NAMES AGAIN?
INSPECTORS SONIA MODIG AND CURT BOLINGER.
WHY?
DO YOU SEE WHAT'S LEFT OF MY FACE, SONIA MODIG AND CURT BOLINGER?
THAT'S FROM AN AXE WIELDED BY MY DAUGHTER LISBETH SALANDER WHEN SHE TRIED TO KILL ME.
IT'S THE SECOND TIME IN 15 YEARS SHE'S TRIED TO ASSASSINATE ME!
SO, YES. I'M A VICTIM, AND I'M CALLING MY LAWYER TO LODGE A COMPLAINT ON MY BEHALF AGAINST THOSE WHO'VE BEEN PERSECUTING ME FOR SO MANY YEARS.
MAYBE THIS TIME THE SWEDISH POLICE WILL ACTUALLY DO ITS JOB AND JUSTICE CAN BE DONE?
YOU MAY GO NOW...
I NEED TO REST.
Väntrum
SO?
THOUGHTS?
HONESTLY?
THE GUY IS ODIOUS.
IT'S A SHAME SALANDER DIDN'T MANAGE TO FINISH HIM OFF.

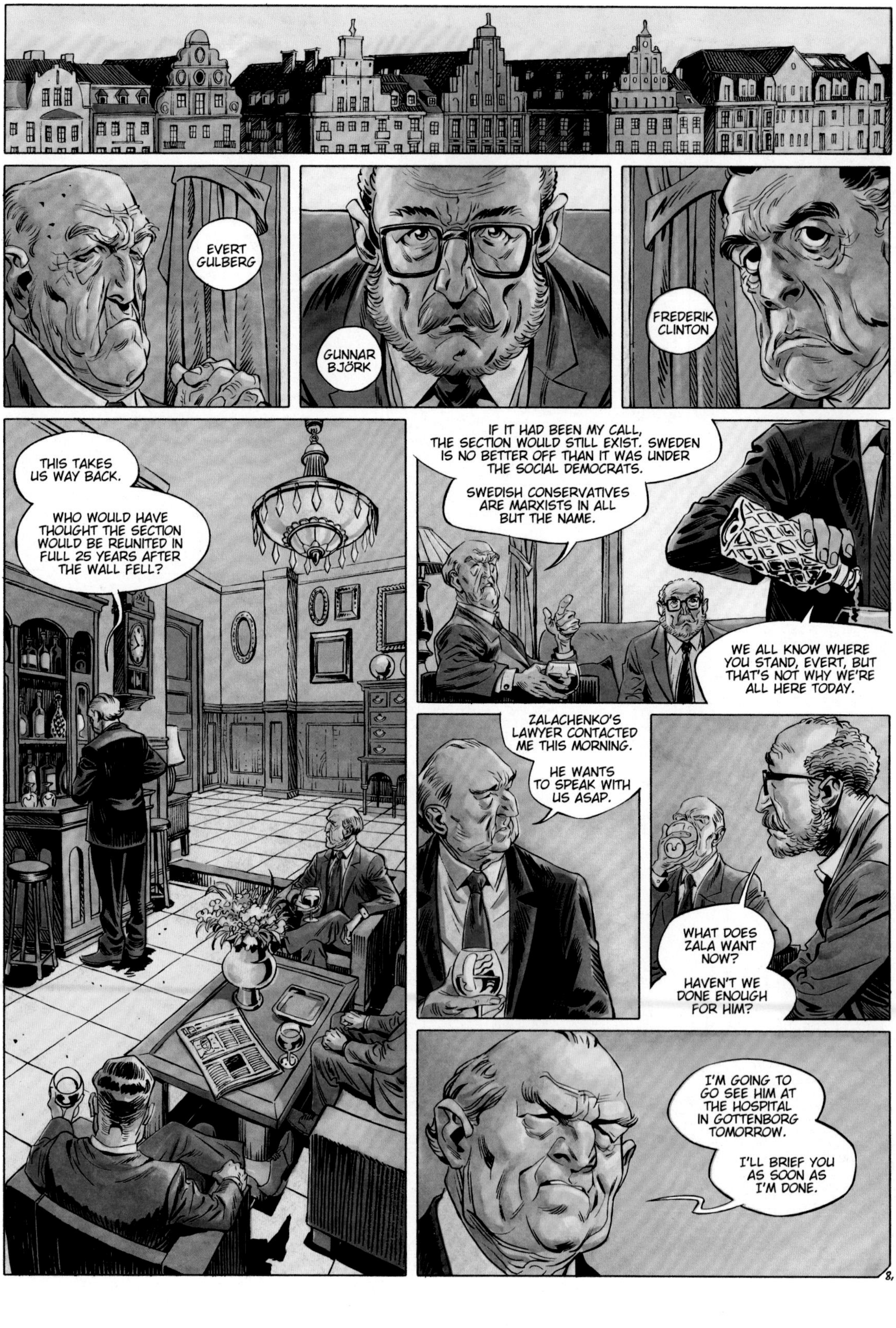
EVERT GULBERG
GUNNAR BJÖRK
FREDERIK CLINTON
THIS TAKES US WAY BACK.
WHO WOULD HAVE THOUGHT THE SECTION WOULD BE REUNITED IN FULL 25 YEARS AFTER THE WALL FELL?
IF IT HAD BEEN MY CALL, THE SECTION WOULD STILL EXIST. SWEDEN IS NO BETTER OFF THAN IT WAS UNDER THE SOCIAL DEMOCRATS.
SWEDISH CONSERVATIVES ARE MARXISTS IN ALL BUT THE NAME.
WE ALL KNOW WHERE YOU STAND, EVERT, BUT THAT'S NOT WHY WE'RE ALL HERE TODAY.
ZALACHENKO'S LAWYER CONTACTED ME THIS MORNING.
HE WANTS TO SPEAK WITH US ASAP.
WHAT DOES ZALA WANT NOW?
HAVEN'T WE DONE ENOUGH FOR HIM?
I'M GOING TO GO SEE HIM AT THE HOSPITAL IN GOTTENBORG TOMORROW.
I'LL BRIEF YOU AS SOON AS I'M DONE.

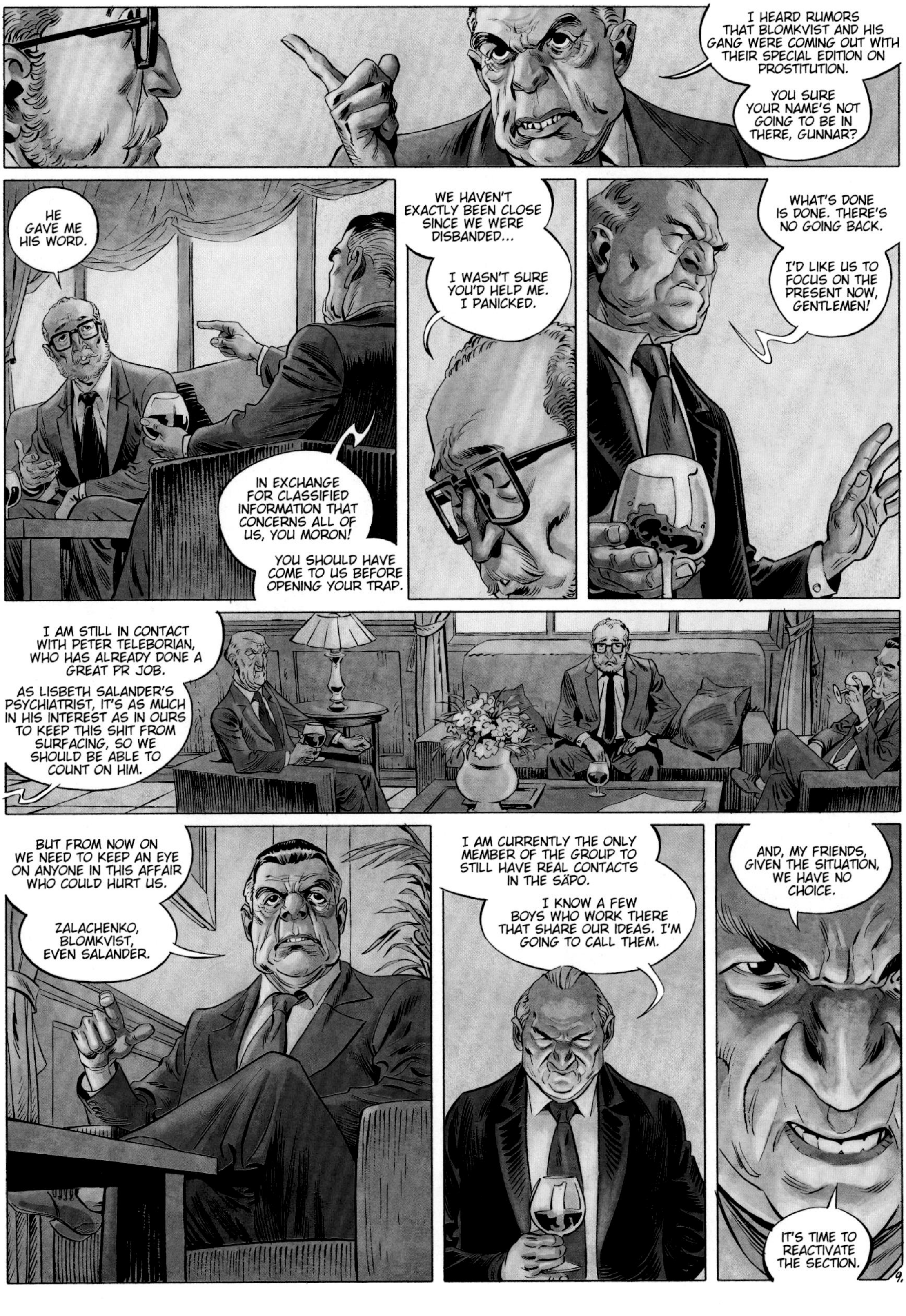
I HEARD RUMORS THAT BLOMKVIST AND HIS GANG WERE COMING OUT WITH THEIR SPECIAL EDITION ON PROSTITUTION.
YOU SURE YOUR NAME'S NOT GOING TO BE IN THERE, GUNNAR?
HE GAVE ME HIS WORD.
IN EXCHANGE FOR CLASSIFIED INFORMATION THAT CONCERNS ALL OF US, YOU MORON!
YOU SHOULD HAVE COME TO US BEFORE OPENING YOUR TRAP.
WE HAVEN'T EXACTLY BEEN CLOSE SINCE WE WERE DISBANDED...
I WASN'T SURE YOU'D HELP ME. I PANICKED.
WHAT'S DONE IS DONE. THERE'S NO GOING BACK.
I'D LIKE US TO FOCUS ON THE PRESENT NOW, GENTLEMEN!
I AM STILL IN CONTACT WITH PETER TELEBORIAN, WHO HAS ALREADY DONE A GREAT PR JOB.
AS LISBETH SALANDER'S PSYCHIATRIST, IT'S AS MUCH IN HIS INTEREST AS IN OURS TO KEEP THIS SHIT FROM SURFACING, SO WE SHOULD BE ABLE TO COUNT ON HIM.
BUT FROM NOW ON WE NEED TO KEEP AN EYE ON ANYONE IN THIS AFFAIR WHO COULD HURT US.
ZALACHENKO, BLOMKVIST, EVEN SALANDER.
I AM CURRENTLY THE ONLY MEMBER OF THE GROUP TO STILL HAVE REAL CONTACTS IN THE SÄPO.
I KNOW A FEW BOYS WHO WORK THERE THAT SHARE OUR IDEAS. I'M GOING TO CALL THEM.
AND, MY FRIENDS, GIVEN THE SITUATION, WE HAVE NO CHOICE.
IT'S TIME TO REACTIVATE THE SECTION.
9.

PLAGUE.

PUNCTUAL AS EVER!

HOW GOES IT, ANDERS?

DAY OFF, SO, ALL GOOD.

ANY PROGRESS?

YES, LOTS. BUT WHAT I SEE IN THE MEDIA BOTHERS ME.

HAS HACKER REPUBLIC EVER ASKED YOU TO HELP SOMEONE WHO DIDN'T DESERVE IT, ANDERS?

SERIOUSLY?

NO. YOU KNOW I TRUST YOU, AND TO BE HONEST, I'M GROWING ATTACHED.

BUT, YOU MUST ADMIT, IT'S A BIT OF A DIFFERENT SITUATION FROM THE PEOPLE I USUALLY AGREE TO HELP.

IT'S NOT LIKE SHE'S A POLITICAL EXILE ESCAPING TORTURE, OR A TEENAGER BEING MARRIED OFF TO SOME OLD GEEZER BY HER PARENTS.

DON'T WORRY.

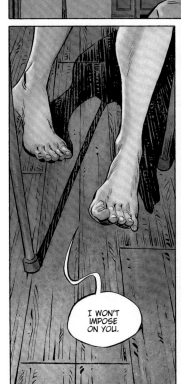

I WON'T IMPOSE ON YOU.

AS SOON AS I CAN WALK WITHOUT FALLING OVER...

I'LL CLEAR OUT.

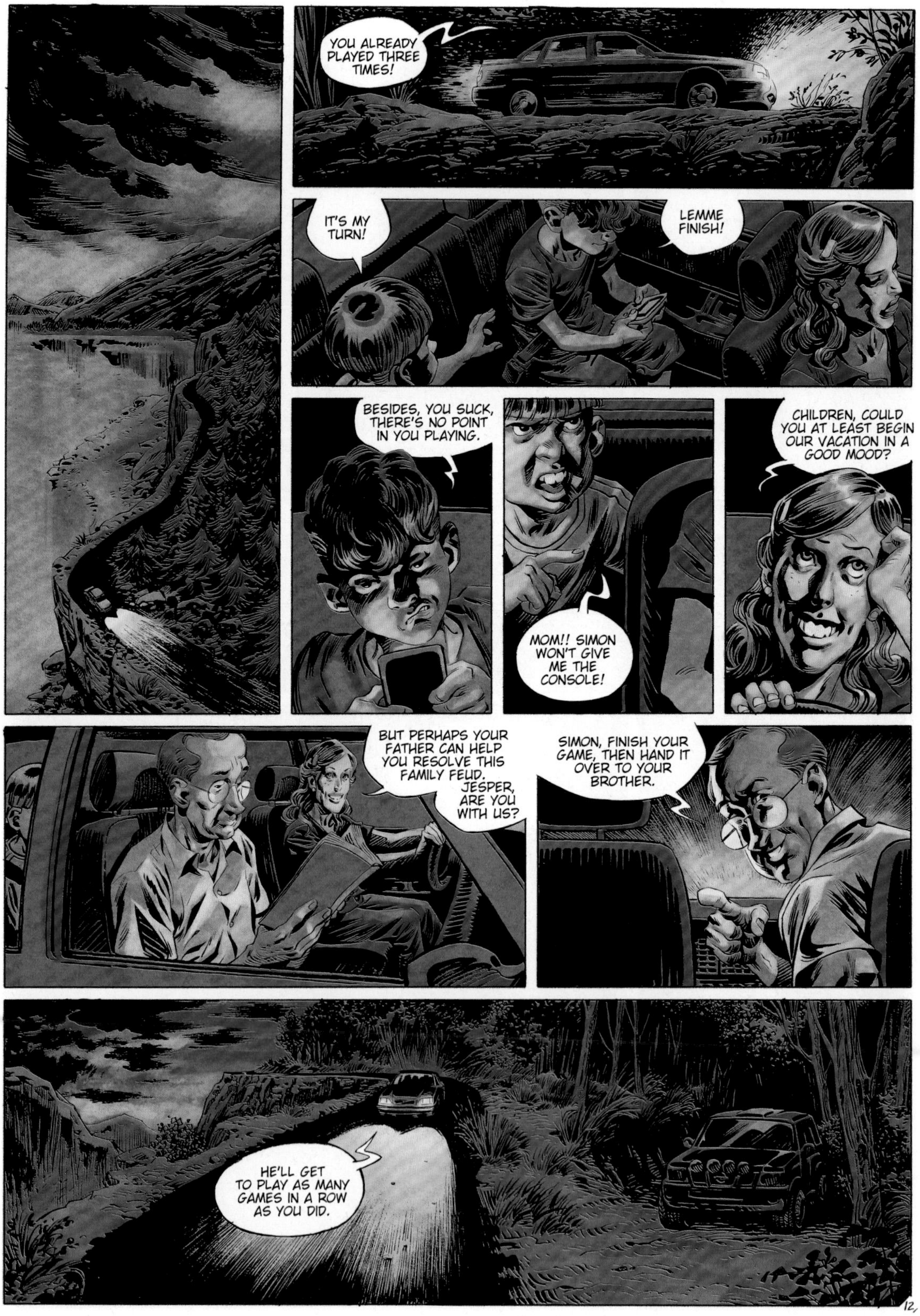
YOU ALREADY PLAYED THREE TIMES!
IT'S MY TURN!
LEMME FINISH!
BESIDES, YOU SUCK, THERE'S NO POINT IN YOU PLAYING.
MOM!! SIMON WON'T GIVE ME THE CONSOLE!
CHILDREN, COULD YOU AT LEAST BEGIN OUR VACATION IN A GOOD MOOD?
BUT PERHAPS YOUR FATHER CAN HELP YOU RESOLVE THIS FAMILY FEUD.
JESPER, ARE YOU WITH US?
SIMON, FINISH YOUR GAME, THEN HAND IT OVER TO YOUR BROTHER.
HE'LL GET TO PLAY AS MANY GAMES IN A ROW AS YOU DID.

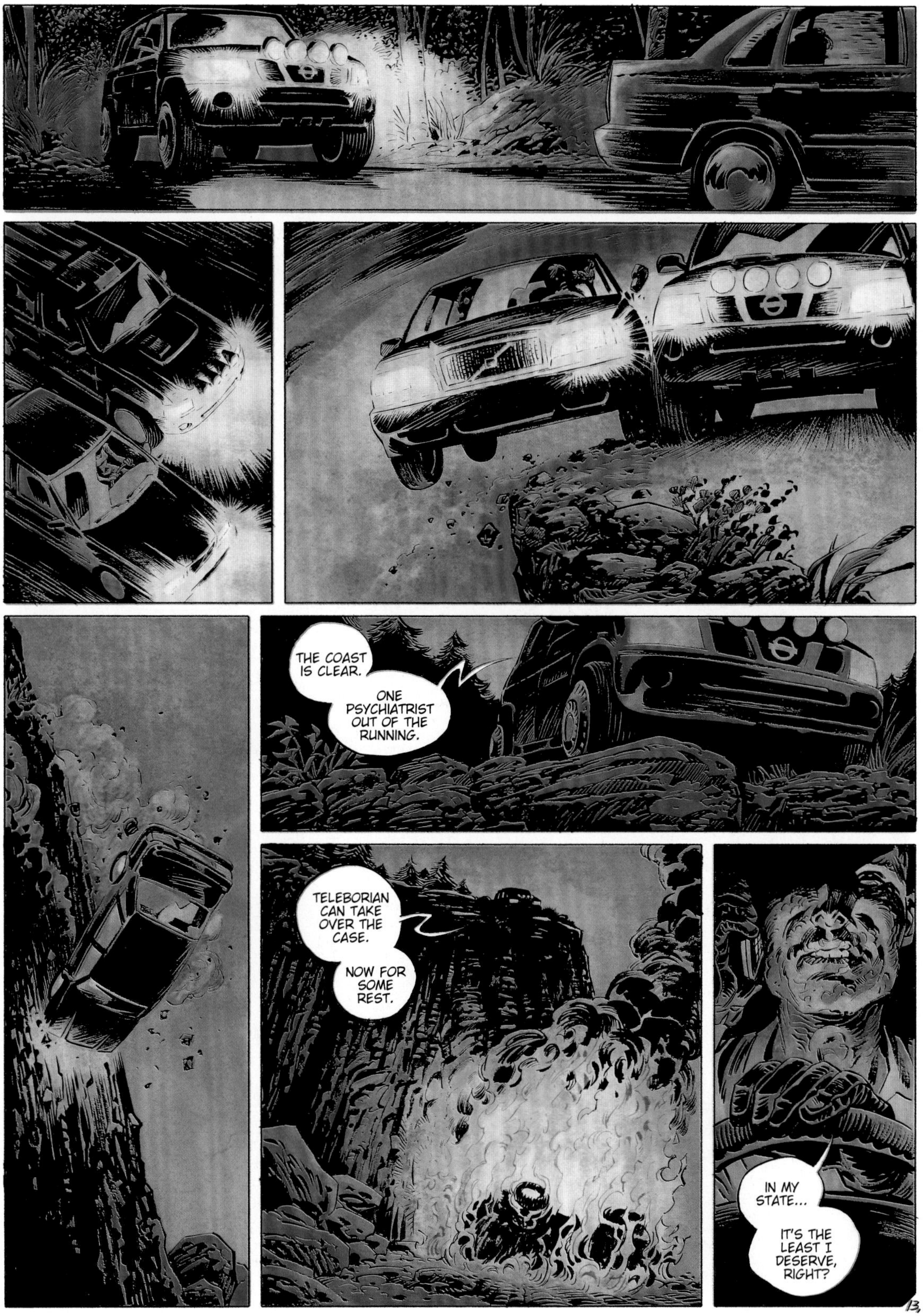
THE COAST IS CLEAR.
ONE PSYCHIATRIST OUT OF THE RUNNING.
TELEBORIAN CAN TAKE OVER THE CASE.
NOW FOR SOME REST.
IN MY STATE...
IT'S THE LEAST I DESERVE, RIGHT?

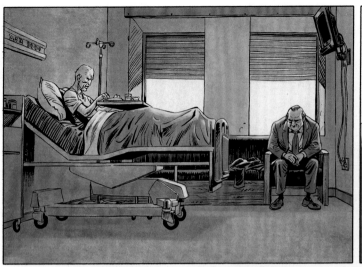

MY OLD FRIEND WADENSJÖÖ.

IT WARMS MY HEART TO HAVE YOU VISIT, YOU KNOW?

WHAT DO YOU WANT?

FOR THE COPS TO LEAVE ME THE FUCK ALONE. AND FOR YOU TO FIND NIEDERMANN AND SALANDER.

THAT MORON FREAKED OUT WHEN HE SAW HER COME OUT OF THE CELLAR, BUT HE'S STILL DANGEROUS! AND UNPREDICTABLE. WHO KNOWS WHAT GOES ON IN HIS MIND? AS FOR SALANDER, BEFORE SHE TRIED TO KILL ME, SHE CLAIMED SHE'D GOT HOLD OF BJURMAN'S FILE.

TELEBORIAN'S FALSE DIAGNOSIS OF HER...

SHE KNOWS.

YOU NEED TO FIND THEM BEFORE THE POLICE DO. THEY KNOW TOO MUCH.

AND GET RID OF THEM FOR GOOD.

YOU OF ALL PEOPLE SHOULD KNOW THE SECTION IS LONG DEFUNCT. YOU'RE ASSUMING CAPABILITIES WE JUST DON'T HAVE ANYMORE.

SURE, BACK IN THE DAY, THE DIRTY WORK ALWAYS CAME MY WAY, EVEN WHEN I SHOULD HAVE BEEN IN REHAB...

AND NOT DRIVING A 4X4.

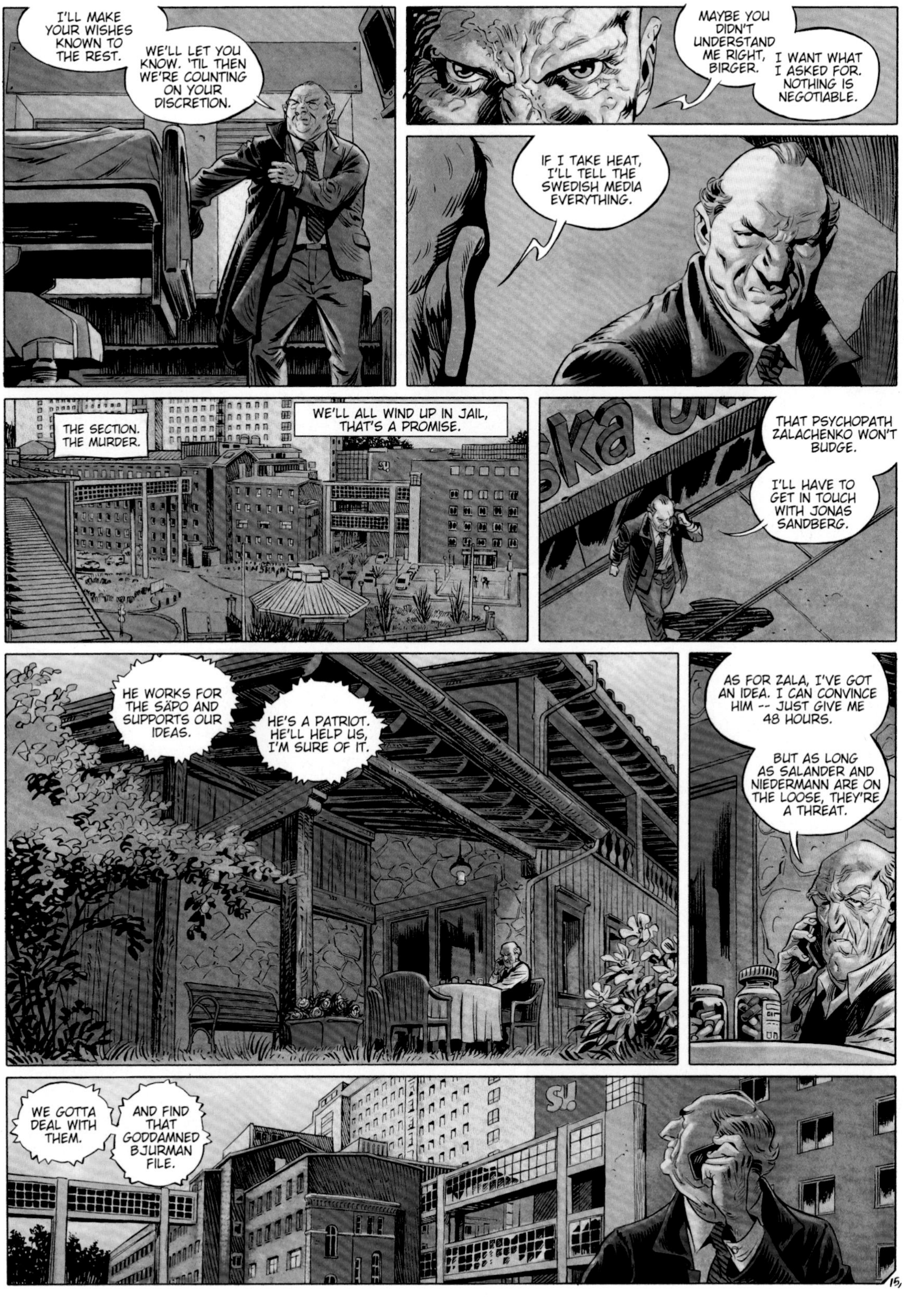
I'LL MAKE YOUR WISHES KNOWN TO THE REST.
WE'LL LET YOU KNOW. 'TIL THEN WE'RE COUNTING ON YOUR DISCRETION.
MAYBE YOU DIDN'T UNDERSTAND ME RIGHT, BIRGER.
I WANT WHAT I ASKED FOR. NOTHING IS NEGOTIABLE.
IF I TAKE HEAT, I'LL TELL THE SWEDISH MEDIA EVERYTHING.
THE SECTION. THE MURDER.
WE'LL ALL WIND UP IN JAIL, THAT'S A PROMISE.
THAT PSYCHOPATH ZALACHENKO WON'T BUDGE.
I'LL HAVE TO GET IN TOUCH WITH JONAS SANDBERG.
HE WORKS FOR THE SÄPO AND SUPPORTS OUR IDEAS.
HE'S A PATRIOT. HE'LL HELP US, I'M SURE OF IT.
AS FOR ZALA, I'VE GOT AN IDEA. I CAN CONVINCE HIM -- JUST GIVE ME 48 HOURS.
BUT AS LONG AS SALANDER AND NIEDERMANN ARE ON THE LOOSE, THEY'RE A THREAT.
WE GOTTA DEAL WITH THEM.
AND FIND THAT GODDAMNED BJURMAN FILE.

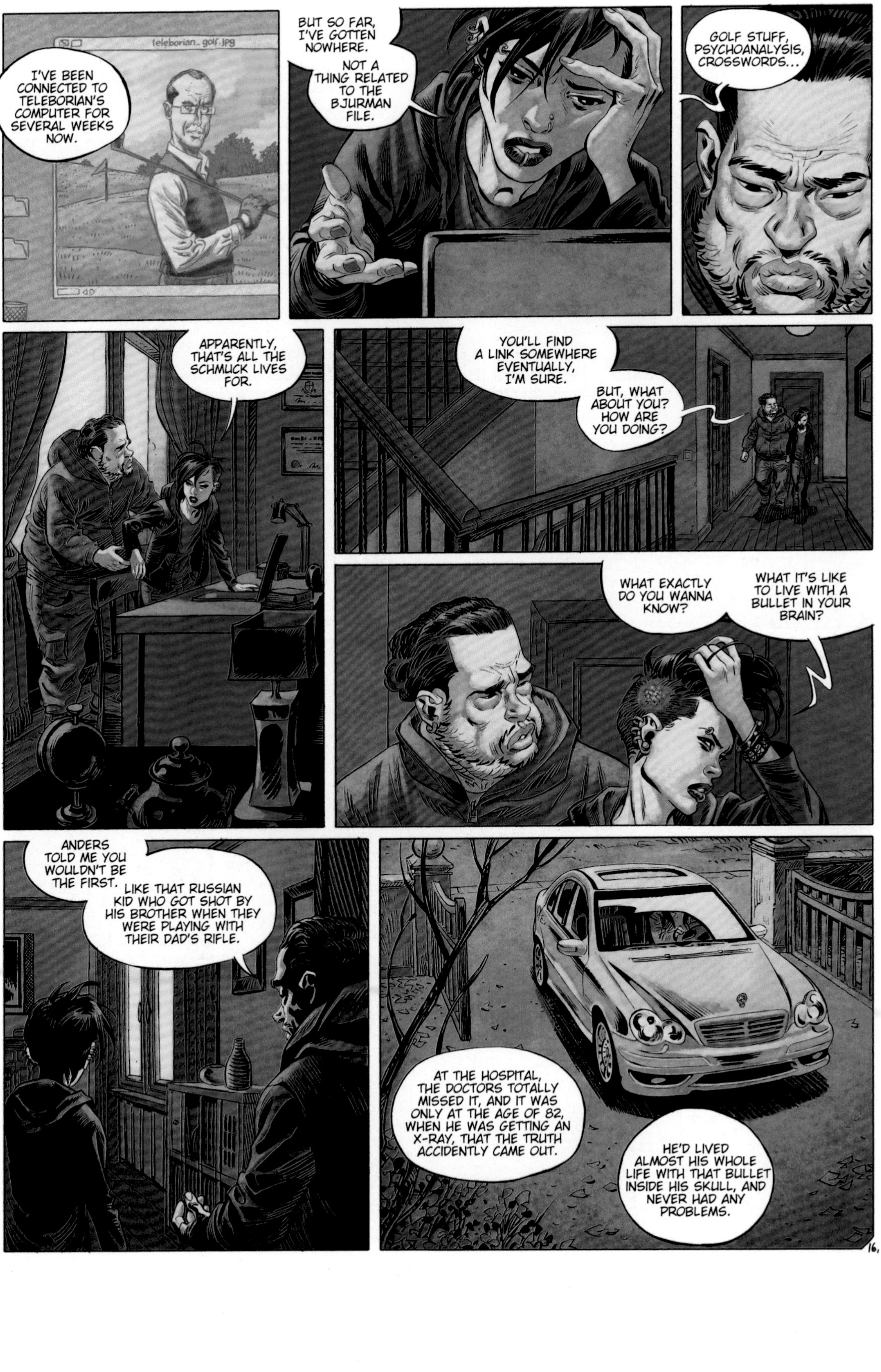
teleborian_golf.jpg
I'VE BEEN CONNECTED TO TELEBORIAN'S COMPUTER FOR SEVERAL WEEKS NOW.
BUT SO FAR, I'VE GOTTEN NOWHERE.
NOT A THING RELATED TO THE BJURMAN FILE.
GOLF STUFF, PSYCHOANALYSIS, CROSSWORDS...
APPARENTLY, THAT'S ALL THE SCHMUCK LIVES FOR.
YOU'LL FIND A LINK SOMEWHERE EVENTUALLY, I'M SURE.
BUT, WHAT ABOUT YOU? HOW ARE YOU DOING?
WHAT EXACTLY DO YOU WANNA KNOW?
WHAT IT'S LIKE TO LIVE WITH A BULLET IN YOUR BRAIN?
ANDERS TOLD ME YOU WOULDN'T BE THE FIRST.
LIKE THAT RUSSIAN KID WHO GOT SHOT BY HIS BROTHER WHEN THEY WERE PLAYING WITH THEIR DAD'S RIFLE.
AT THE HOSPITAL, THE DOCTORS TOTALLY MISSED IT, AND IT WAS ONLY AT THE AGE OF 82, WHEN HE WAS GETTING AN X-RAY, THAT THE TRUTH ACCIDENTLY CAME OUT.
HE'D LIVED ALMOST HIS WHOLE LIFE WITH THAT BULLET INSIDE HIS SKULL, AND NEVER HAD ANY PROBLEMS.

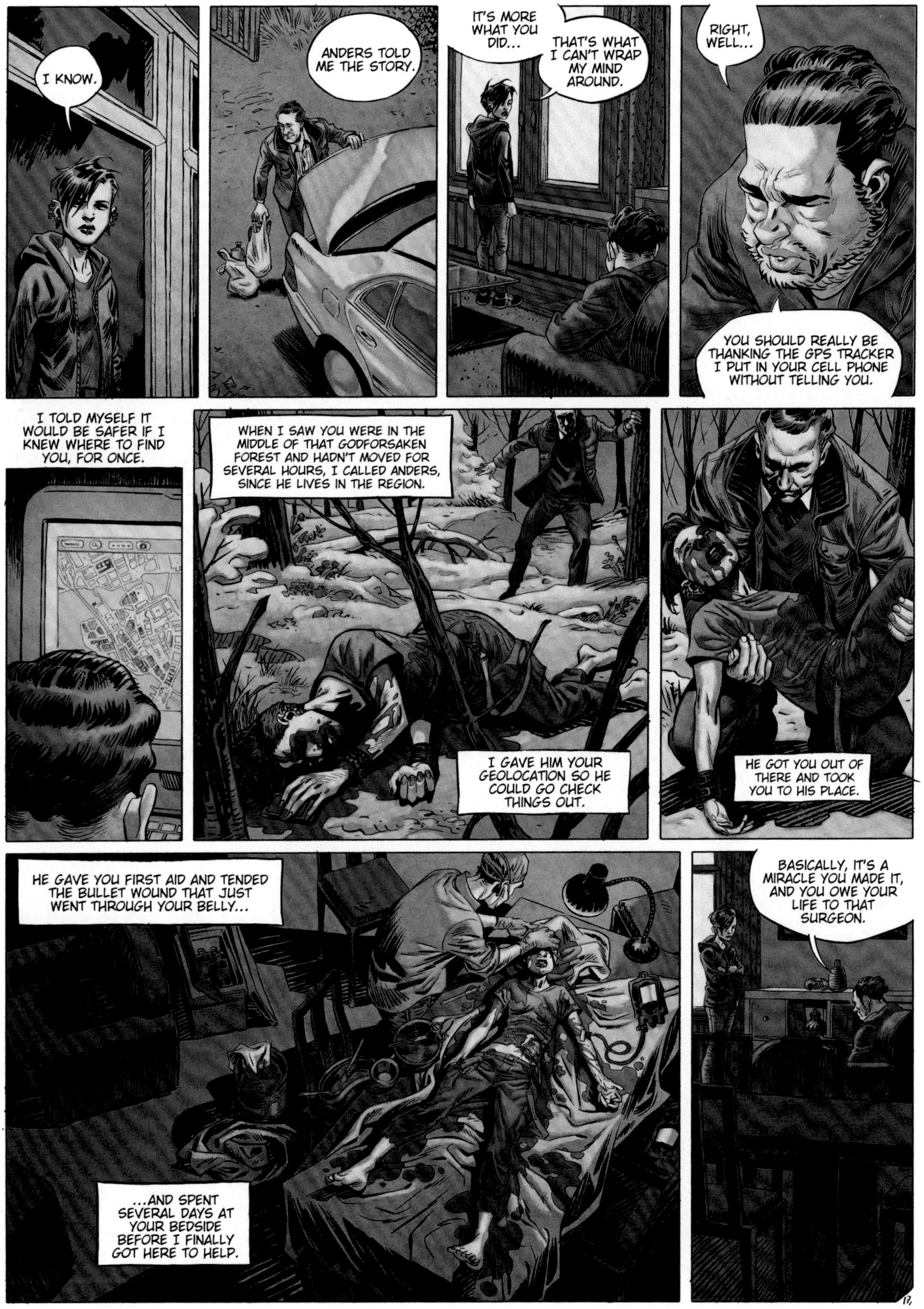
I KNOW.
ANDERS TOLD ME THE STORY.
IT'S MORE WHAT YOU DID...
THAT'S WHAT I CAN'T WRAP MY MIND AROUND.
RIGHT, WELL...
YOU SHOULD REALLY BE THANKING THE GPS TRACKER I PUT IN YOUR CELL PHONE WITHOUT TELLING YOU.
I TOLD MYSELF IT WOULD BE SAFER IF I KNEW WHERE TO FIND YOU, FOR ONCE.
WHEN I SAW YOU WERE IN THE MIDDLE OF THAT GODFORSAKEN FOREST AND HADN'T MOVED FOR SEVERAL HOURS, I CALLED ANDERS, SINCE HE LIVES IN THE REGION.
I GAVE HIM YOUR GEOLOCATION SO HE COULD GO CHECK THINGS OUT.
HE GOT YOU OUT OF THERE AND TOOK YOU TO HIS PLACE.
HE GAVE YOU FIRST AID AND TENDED THE BULLET WOUND THAT JUST WENT THROUGH YOUR BELLY...
...AND SPENT SEVERAL DAYS AT YOUR BEDSIDE BEFORE I FINALLY GOT HERE TO HELP.
BASICALLY, IT'S A MIRACLE YOU MADE IT, AND YOU OWE YOUR LIFE TO THAT SURGEON.

I REMEMBER THE NIGHT HE TOOK ME TO THE HOSPITAL.

WHERE HE WORKS.

WHERE MY ASSHOLE FATHER IS.

HE EVEN COVERED ME SO NO ONE WOULD RECOGNIZE ME.

THAT'S WHEN HE SAW THE BULLET WAS LODGED IN MY SKULL AND THERE WAS NOTHING TO BE DONE.

IT HADN'T DONE MUCH DAMAGE, BUT IT WAS THERE TO STAY.

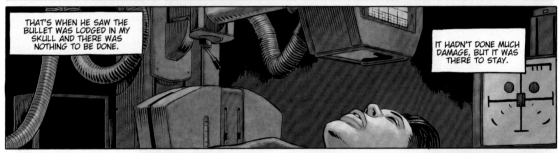

THAT MAN RISKED HIS CAREER, AND MAYBE HIS LIFE, BY HELPING ME.

WHY DID HE DO THAT?

HACKER REPUBLIC HAS BEEN IN TOUCH WITH HIM FOR SEVERAL YEARS.

FOR YEARS, HE'S TREATED ILLEGALS, POLITICAL AND ECONOMIC REFUGEES, ALL FOR FREE.

HIS MOTHER WAS CHILEAN. HER PARENTS WERE CAPTURED BY THE ARMY AFTER PINOCHET'S COUP WHEN SHE WAS ONLY 10. THEY WERE NEVER SEEN AGAIN.

SHE WOUND UP FLEEING THE DICTATORSHIP WITH ONE OF HER UNCLES AND THEY WOUND UP IN SWEDEN, WHERE SHE STARTED A NEW LIFE.

THAT'S WHY HE HELPS STRANGERS.

FLIGHT, REPRESSION, THE UNDERGROUND... HIS FAMILY EXPERIENCED IT.

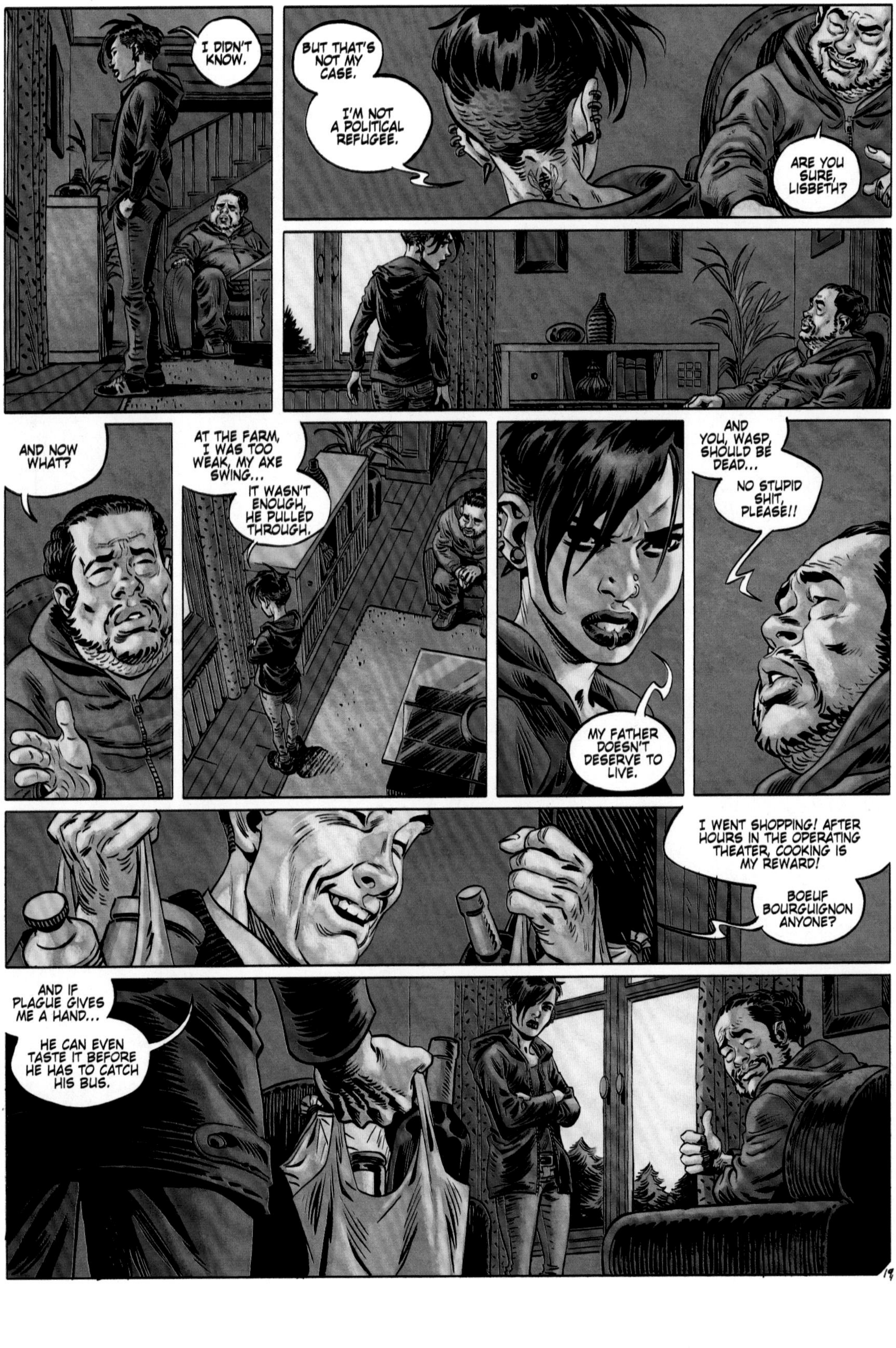
I DIDN'T KNOW.
BUT THAT'S NOT MY CASE.
I'M NOT A POLITICAL REFUGEE.
ARE YOU SURE, LISBETH?
AND NOW WHAT?
AT THE FARM, I WAS TOO WEAK, MY AXE SWING...
IT WASN'T ENOUGH, HE PULLED THROUGH.
MY FATHER DOESN'T DESERVE TO LIVE.
AND YOU, WASP, SHOULD BE DEAD...
NO STUPID SHIT, PLEASE!!
I WENT SHOPPING! AFTER HOURS IN THE OPERATING THEATER, COOKING IS MY REWARD!
BOEUF BOURGUIGNON ANYONE?
AND IF PLAGUE GIVES ME A HAND...
HE CAN EVEN TASTE IT BEFORE HE HAS TO CATCH HIS BUS.

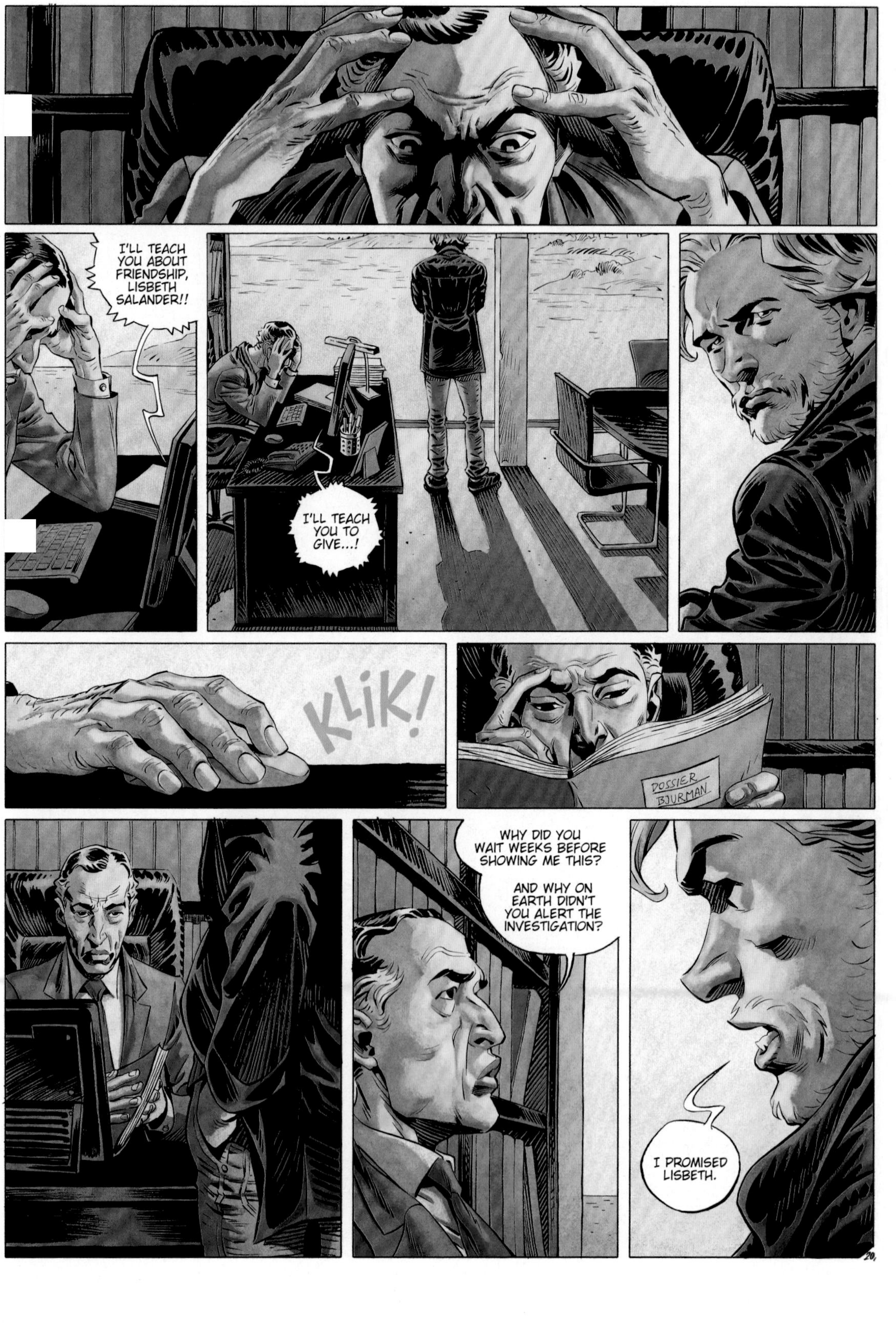
I'LL TEACH YOU ABOUT FRIENDSHIP, LISBETH SALANDER!!
I'LL TEACH YOU TO GIVE...!
KLIK!
DOSSIER BJURMAN
WHY DID YOU WAIT WEEKS BEFORE SHOWING ME THIS?
AND WHY ON EARTH DIDN'T YOU ALERT THE INVESTIGATION?
I PROMISED LISBETH.

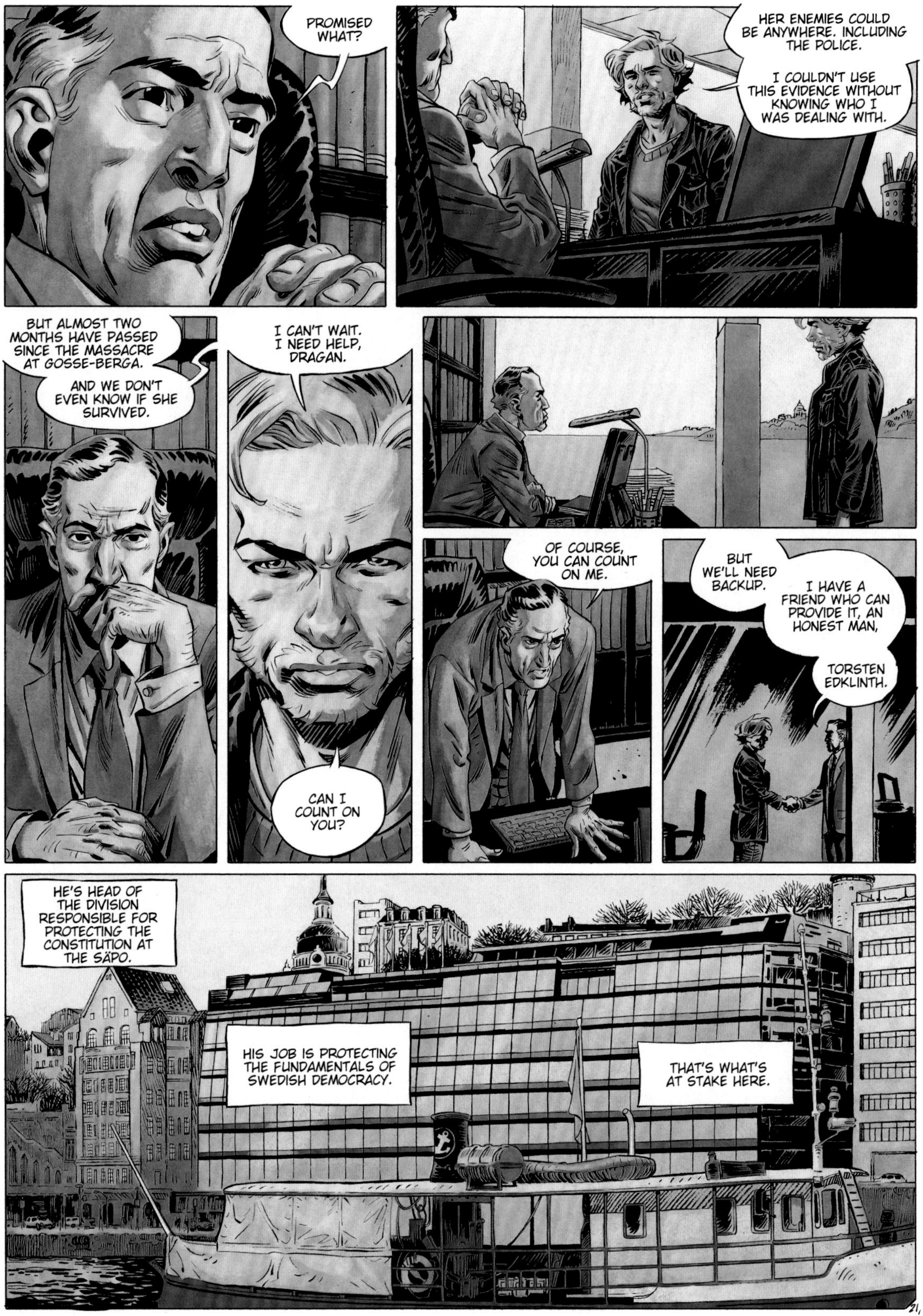
PROMISED WHAT?
HER ENEMIES COULD BE ANYWHERE. INCLUDING THE POLICE.
I COULDN'T USE THIS EVIDENCE WITHOUT KNOWING WHO I WAS DEALING WITH.
BUT ALMOST TWO MONTHS HAVE PASSED SINCE THE MASSACRE AT GOSSE-BERGA.
AND WE DON'T EVEN KNOW IF SHE SURVIVED.
I CAN'T WAIT. I NEED HELP, DRAGAN.
CAN I COUNT ON YOU?
OF COURSE, YOU CAN COUNT ON ME.
BUT WE'LL NEED BACKUP.
I HAVE A FRIEND WHO CAN PROVIDE IT, AN HONEST MAN,
TORSTEN EDKLINTH.
HE'S HEAD OF THE DIVISION RESPONSIBLE FOR PROTECTING THE CONSTITUTION AT THE SÄPO.
HIS JOB IS PROTECTING THE FUNDAMENTALS OF SWEDISH DEMOCRACY.
THAT'S WHAT'S AT STAKE HERE.

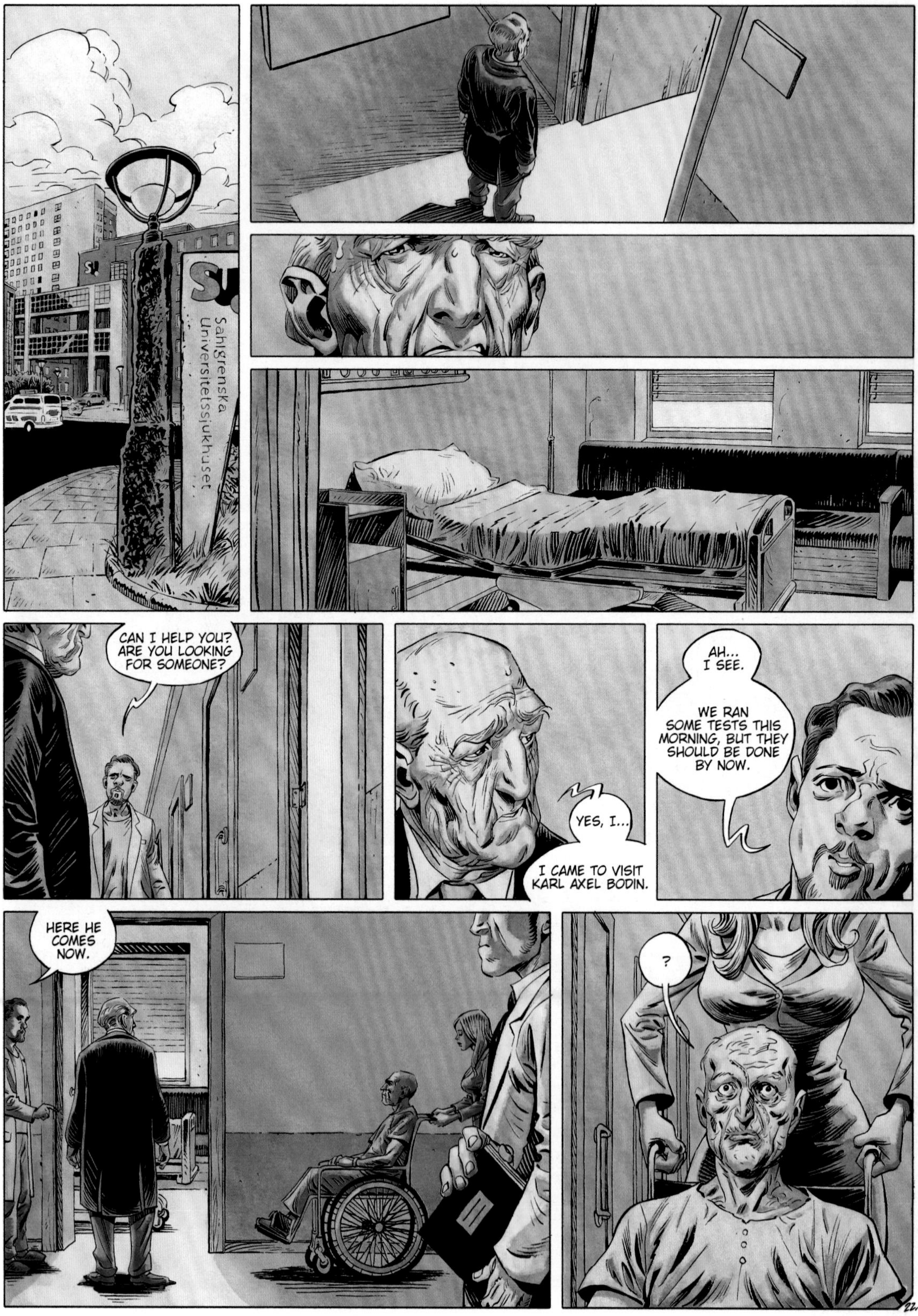
SU
Sahlgrenska Universitetssjukhuset
CAN I HELP YOU? ARE YOU LOOKING FOR SOMEONE?
YES, I...
I CAME TO VISIT KARL AXEL BODIN.
AH... I SEE.
WE RAN SOME TESTS THIS MORNING, BUT THEY SHOULD BE DONE BY NOW.
HERE HE COMES NOW.
?

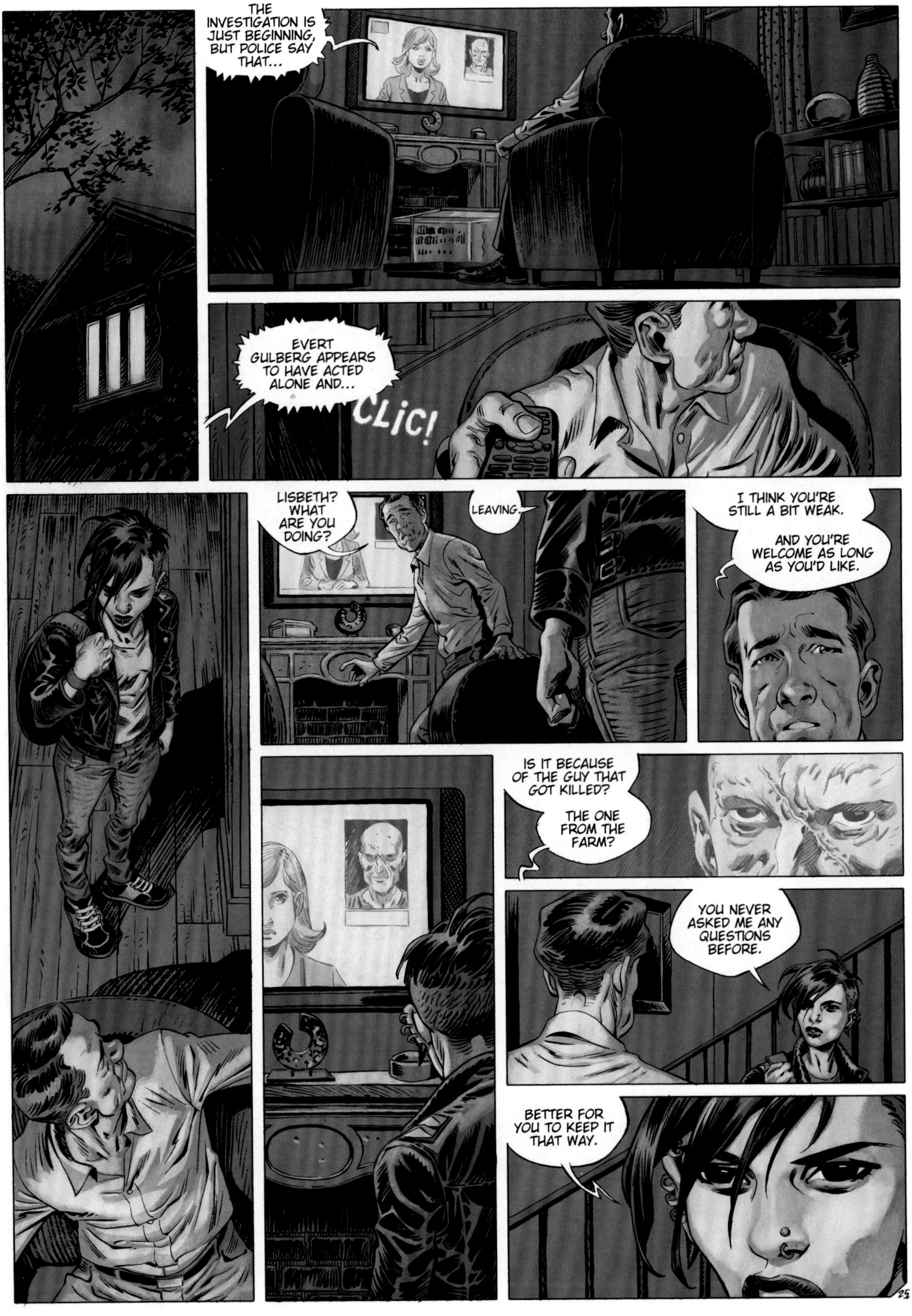

THE INVESTIGATION IS JUST BEGINNING, BUT POLICE SAY THAT...
EVERT GULBERG APPEARS TO HAVE ACTED ALONE AND...
CLIC!
LISBETH? WHAT ARE YOU DOING?
LEAVING.
I THINK YOU'RE STILL A BIT WEAK.
AND YOU'RE WELCOME AS LONG AS YOU'D LIKE.
IS IT BECAUSE OF THE GUY THAT GOT KILLED?
THE ONE FROM THE FARM?
YOU NEVER ASKED ME ANY QUESTIONS BEFORE.
BETTER FOR YOU TO KEEP IT THAT WAY.

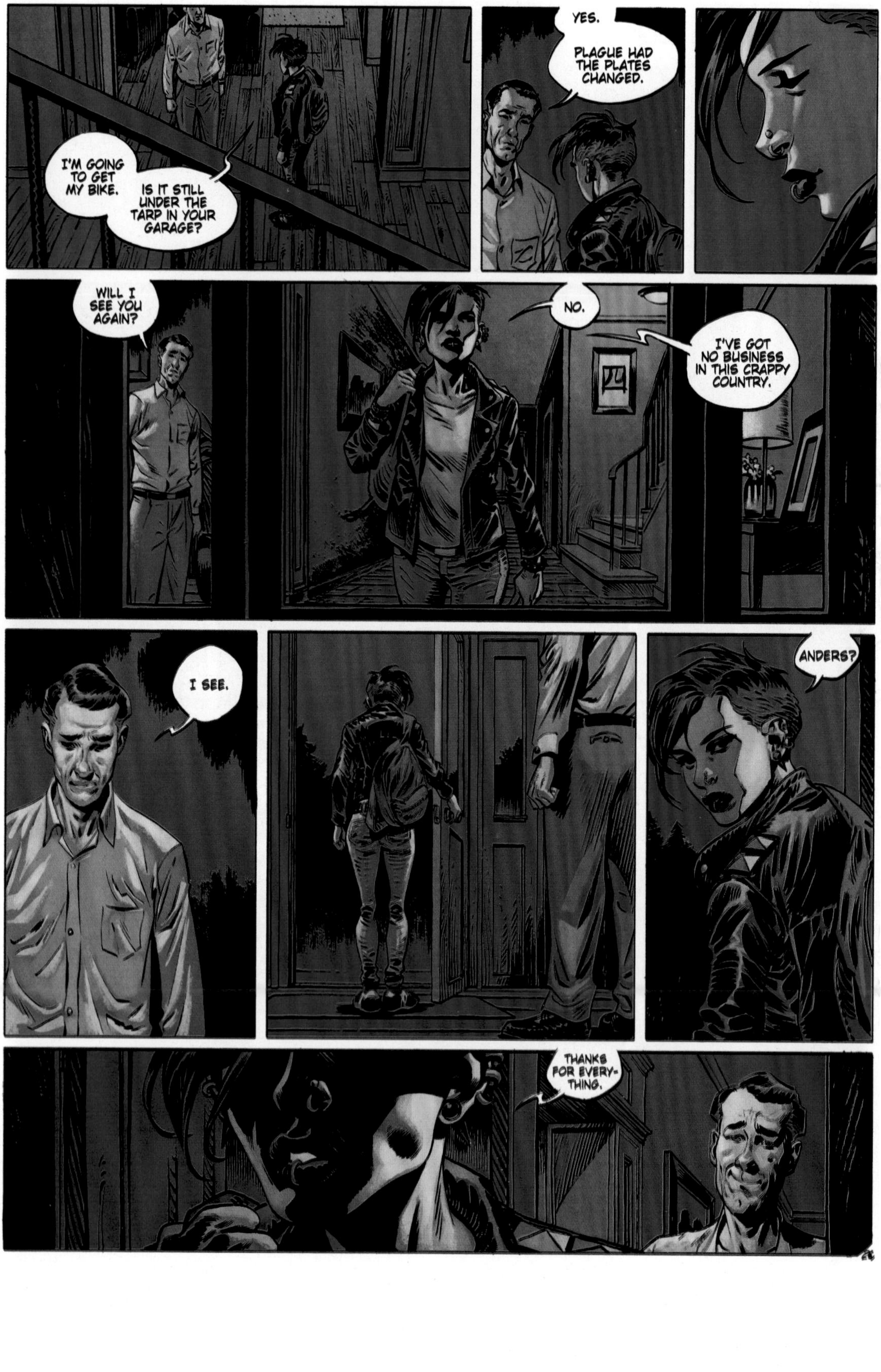
I'M GOING TO GET MY BIKE.
IS IT STILL UNDER THE TARP IN YOUR GARAGE?
YES.
PLAGUE HAD THE PLATES CHANGED.
WILL I SEE YOU AGAIN?
NO.
I'VE GOT NO BUSINESS IN THIS CRAPPY COUNTRY.
I SEE.
ANDERS?
THANKS FOR EVERY-THING.

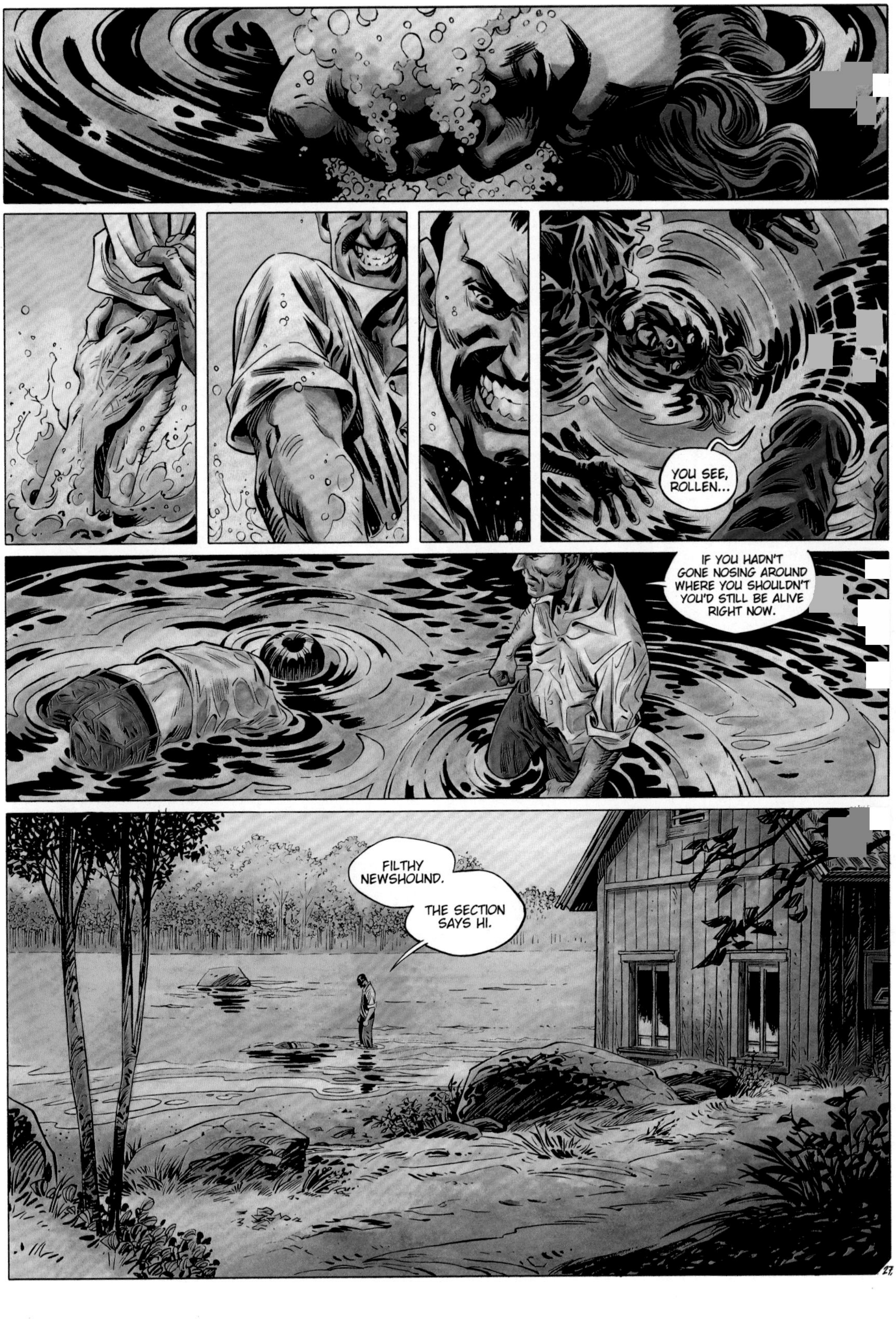
YOU SEE, ROLLEN...
IF YOU HADN'T GONE NOSING AROUND WHERE YOU SHOULDN'T YOU'D STILL BE ALIVE RIGHT NOW.
FILTHY NEWSHOUND.
THE SECTION SAYS HI.

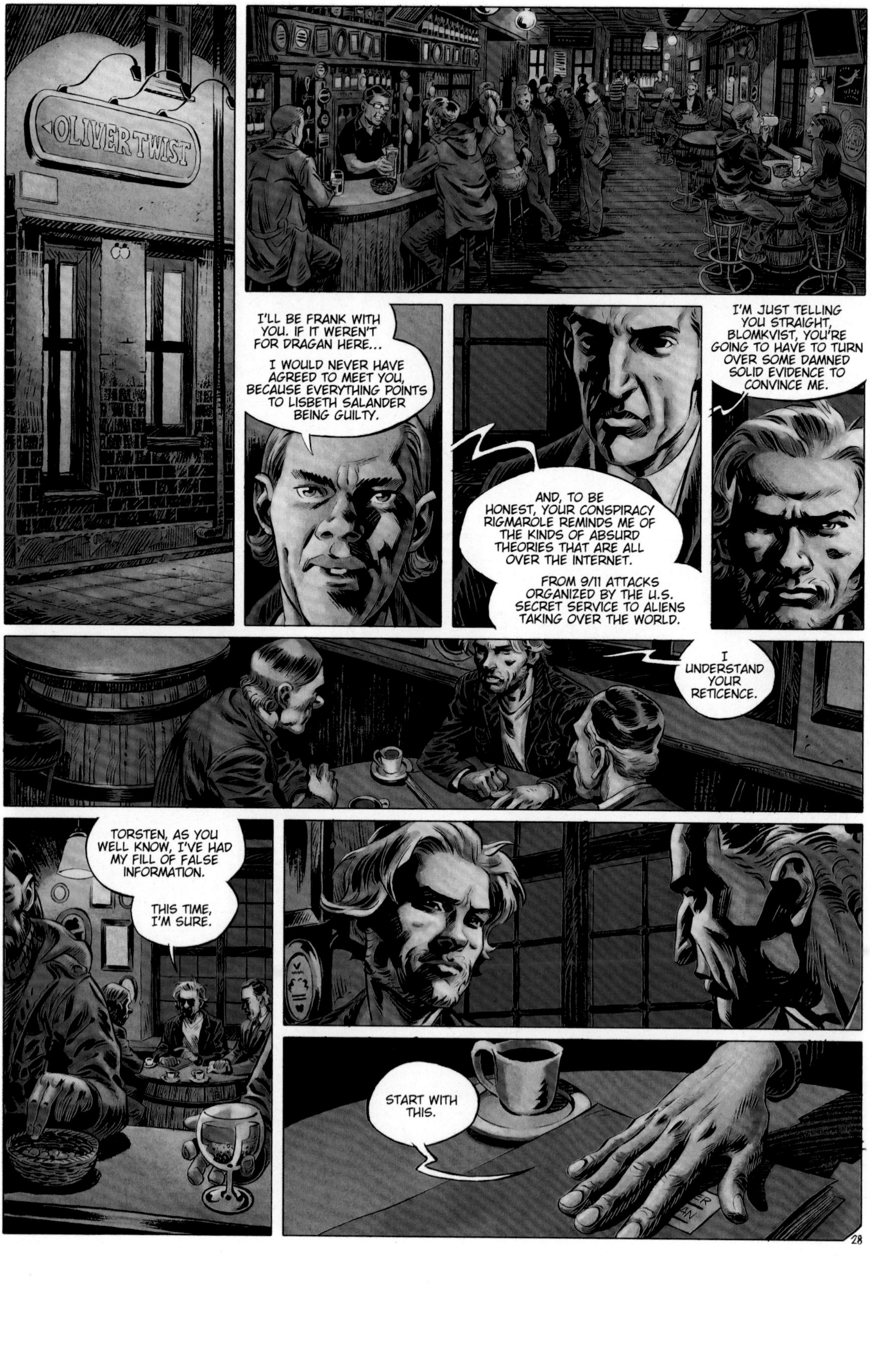
OLIVER TWIST
I'LL BE FRANK WITH YOU. IF IT WEREN'T FOR DRAGAN HERE...
I WOULD NEVER HAVE AGREED TO MEET YOU, BECAUSE EVERYTHING POINTS TO LISBETH SALANDER BEING GUILTY.
AND, TO BE HONEST, YOUR CONSPIRACY RIGMAROLE REMINDS ME OF THE KINDS OF ABSURD THEORIES THAT ARE ALL OVER THE INTERNET.
FROM 9/11 ATTACKS ORGANIZED BY THE U.S. SECRET SERVICE TO ALIENS TAKING OVER THE WORLD.
I'M JUST TELLING YOU STRAIGHT, BLOMKVIST, YOU'RE GOING TO HAVE TO TURN OVER SOME DAMNED SOLID EVIDENCE TO CONVINCE ME.
I UNDERSTAND YOUR RETICENCE.
TORSTEN, AS YOU WELL KNOW, I'VE HAD MY FILL OF FALSE INFORMATION.
THIS TIME, I'M SURE.
START WITH THIS.

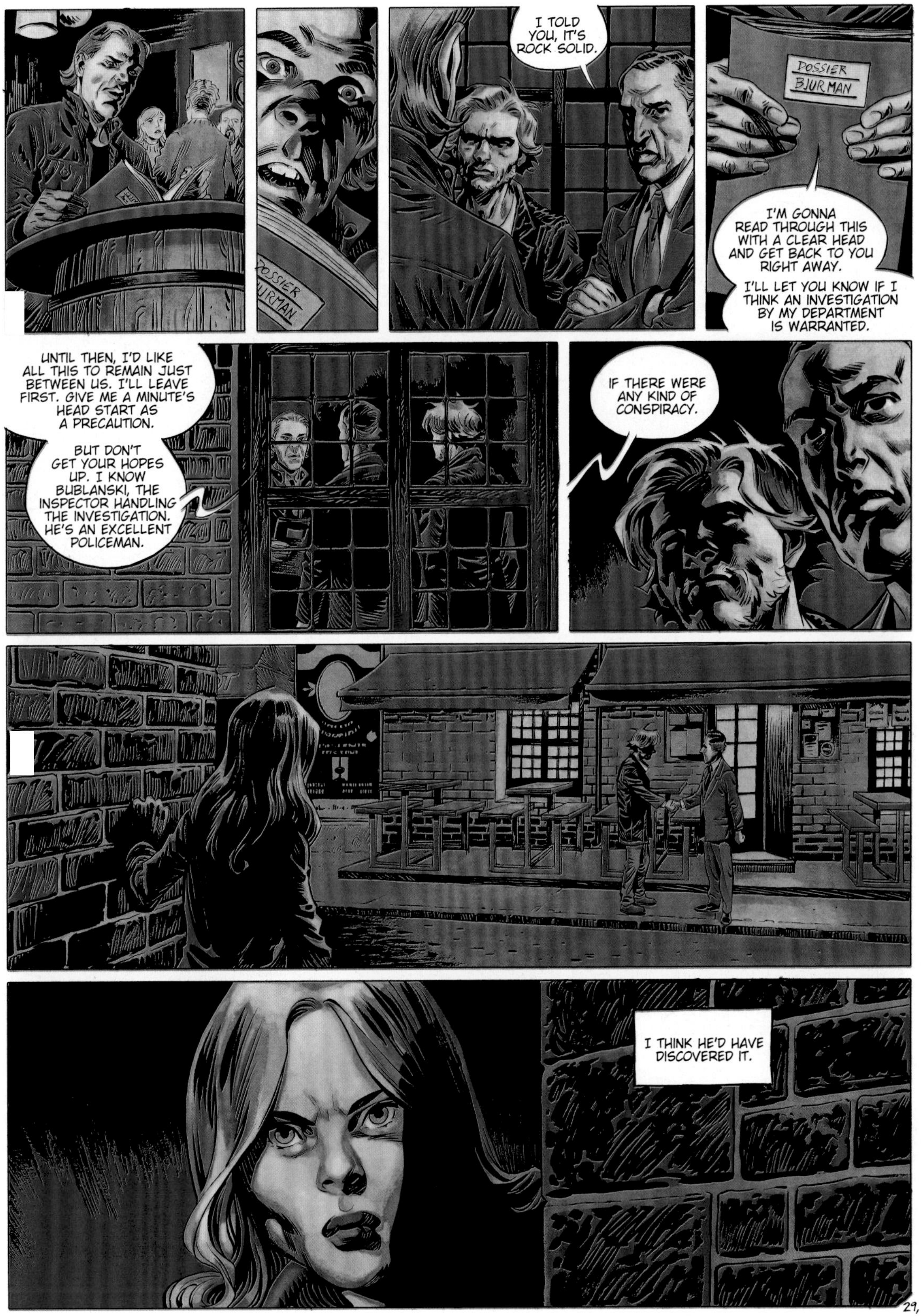
DOSSIER BJURMAN
I TOLD YOU, IT'S ROCK SOLID.
DOSSIER BJURMAN
I'M GONNA READ THROUGH THIS WITH A CLEAR HEAD AND GET BACK TO YOU RIGHT AWAY.
I'LL LET YOU KNOW IF I THINK AN INVESTIGATION BY MY DEPARTMENT IS WARRANTED.
UNTIL THEN, I'D LIKE ALL THIS TO REMAIN JUST BETWEEN US. I'LL LEAVE FIRST. GIVE ME A MINUTE'S HEAD START AS A PRECAUTION.
BUT DON'T GET YOUR HOPES UP. I KNOW BUBLANSKI, THE INSPECTOR HANDLING THE INVESTIGATION. HE'S AN EXCELLENT POLICEMAN.
IF THERE WERE ANY KIND OF CONSPIRACY.
I THINK HE'D HAVE DISCOVERED IT.

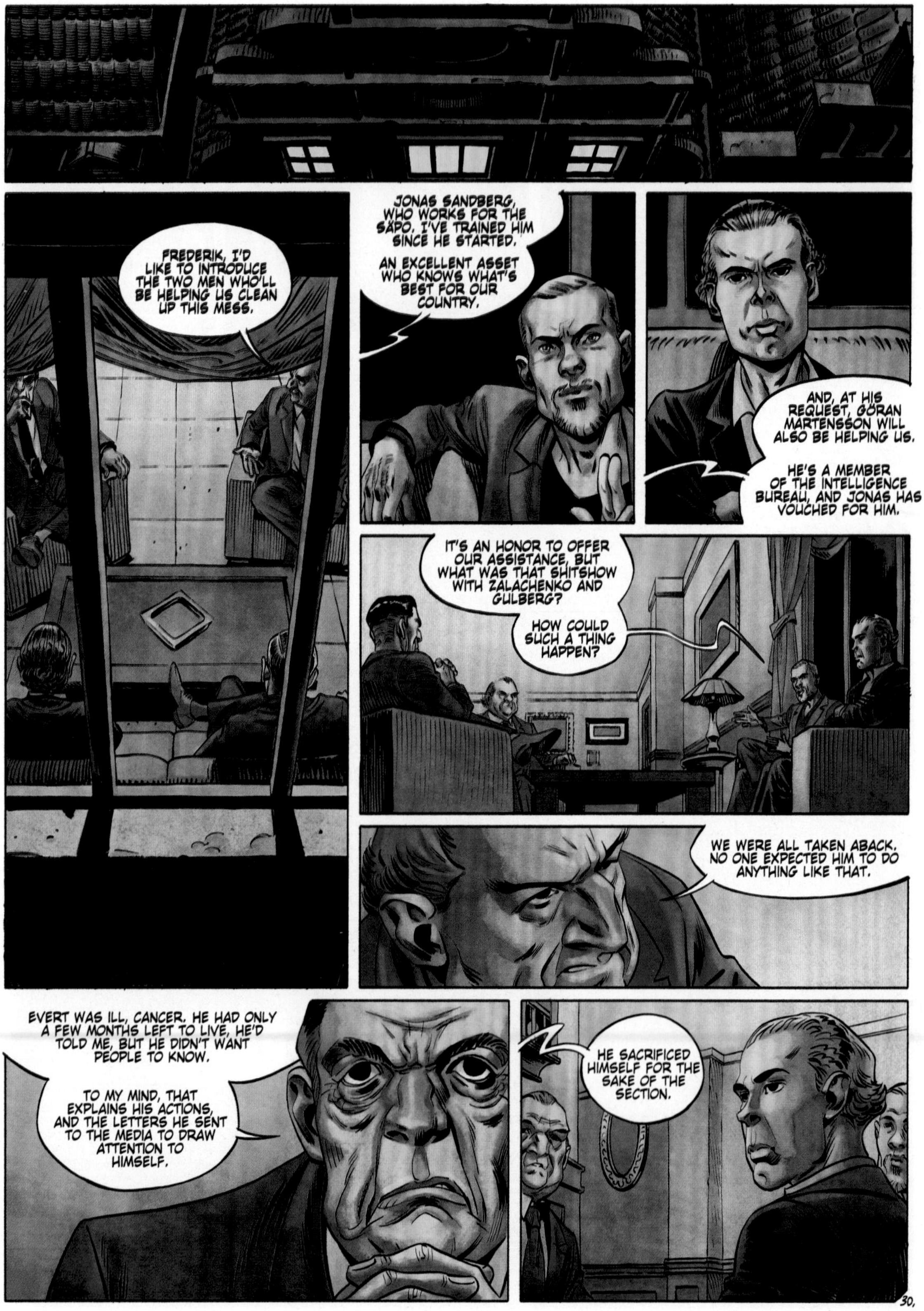

FREDERIK, I'D LIKE TO INTRODUCE THE TWO MEN WHO'LL BE HELPING US CLEAN UP THIS MESS.
JONAS SANDBERG, WHO WORKS FOR THE SÄPO. I'VE TRAINED HIM SINCE HE STARTED.
AN EXCELLENT ASSET WHO KNOWS WHAT'S BEST FOR OUR COUNTRY.
AND, AT HIS REQUEST, GÖRAN MARTENSSON WILL ALSO BE HELPING US.
HE'S A MEMBER OF THE INTELLIGENCE BUREAU, AND JONAS HAS VOUCHED FOR HIM.
IT'S AN HONOR TO OFFER OUR ASSISTANCE, BUT WHAT WAS THAT SHITSHOW WITH ZALACHENKO AND GULBERG?
HOW COULD SUCH A THING HAPPEN?
WE WERE ALL TAKEN ABACK. NO ONE EXPECTED HIM TO DO ANYTHING LIKE THAT.
EVERT WAS ILL, CANCER. HE HAD ONLY A FEW MONTHS LEFT TO LIVE, HE'D TOLD ME, BUT HE DIDN'T WANT PEOPLE TO KNOW.
TO MY MIND, THAT EXPLAINS HIS ACTIONS, AND THE LETTERS HE SENT TO THE MEDIA TO DRAW ATTENTION TO HIMSELF.
HE SACRIFICED HIMSELF FOR THE SAKE OF THE SECTION.

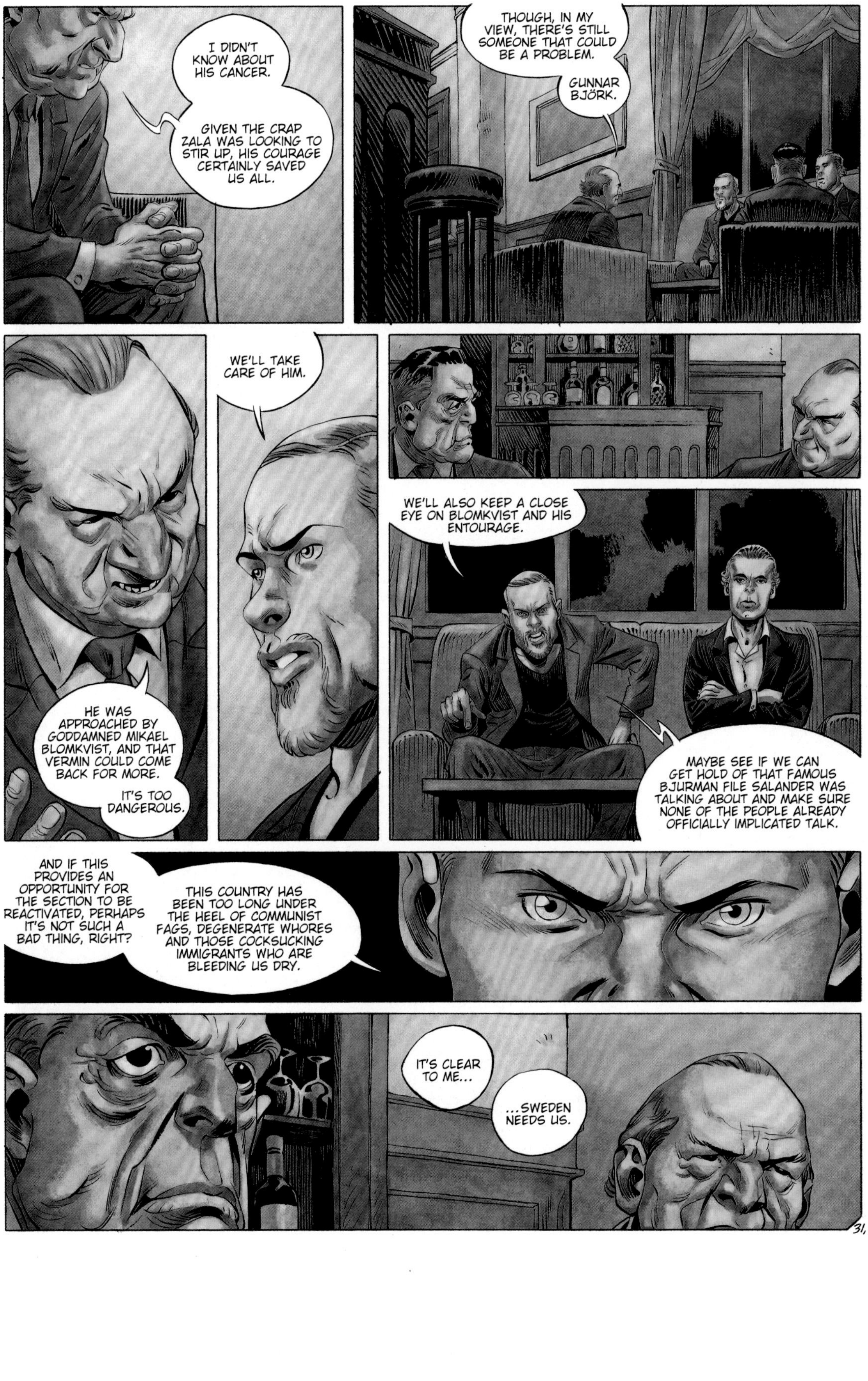
I DIDN'T KNOW ABOUT HIS CANCER.
GIVEN THE CRAP ZALA WAS LOOKING TO STIR UP, HIS COURAGE CERTAINLY SAVED US ALL.
THOUGH, IN MY VIEW, THERE'S STILL SOMEONE THAT COULD BE A PROBLEM.
GUNNAR BJÖRK.
HE WAS APPROACHED BY GODDAMNED MIKAEL BLOMKVIST, AND THAT VERMIN COULD COME BACK FOR MORE.
IT'S TOO DANGEROUS.
WE'LL TAKE CARE OF HIM.
WE'LL ALSO KEEP A CLOSE EYE ON BLOMKVIST AND HIS ENTOURAGE.
MAYBE SEE IF WE CAN GET HOLD OF THAT FAMOUS BJURMAN FILE SALANDER WAS TALKING ABOUT AND MAKE SURE NONE OF THE PEOPLE ALREADY OFFICIALLY IMPLICATED TALK.
AND IF THIS PROVIDES AN OPPORTUNITY FOR THE SECTION TO BE REACTIVATED, PERHAPS IT'S NOT SUCH A BAD THING, RIGHT?
THIS COUNTRY HAS BEEN TOO LONG UNDER THE HEEL OF COMMUNIST FAGS, DEGENERATE WHORES AND THOSE COCKSUCKING IMMIGRANTS WHO ARE BLEEDING US DRY.
IT'S CLEAR TO ME...
...SWEDEN NEEDS US.

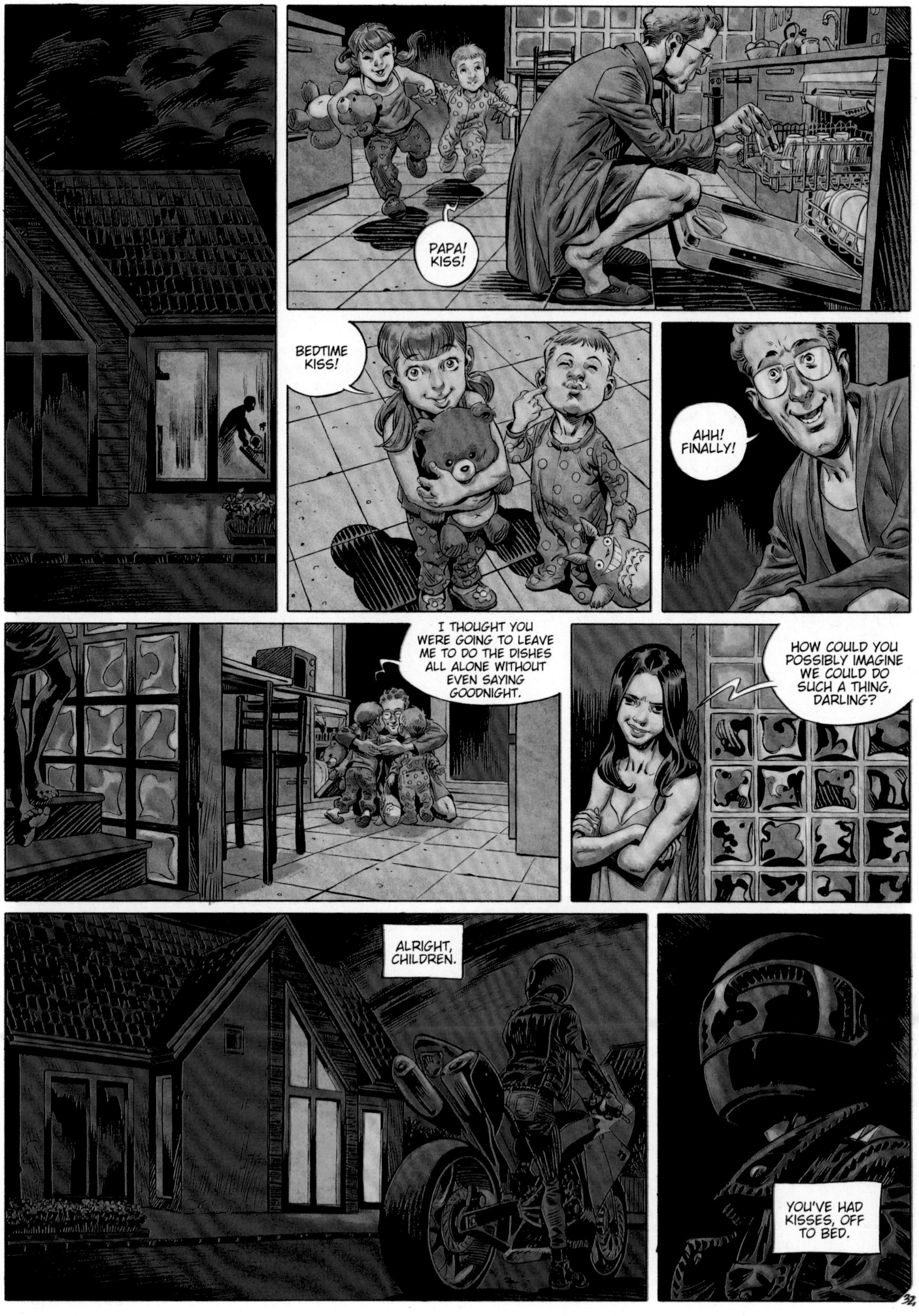
PAPA! KISS!
BEDTIME KISS!
AHH! FINALLY!
I THOUGHT YOU WERE GOING TO LEAVE ME TO DO THE DISHES ALL ALONE WITHOUT EVEN SAYING GOODNIGHT.
HOW COULD YOU POSSIBLY IMAGINE WE COULD DO SUCH A THING, DARLING?
ALRIGHT, CHILDREN.
YOU'VE HAD KISSES, OFF TO BED.

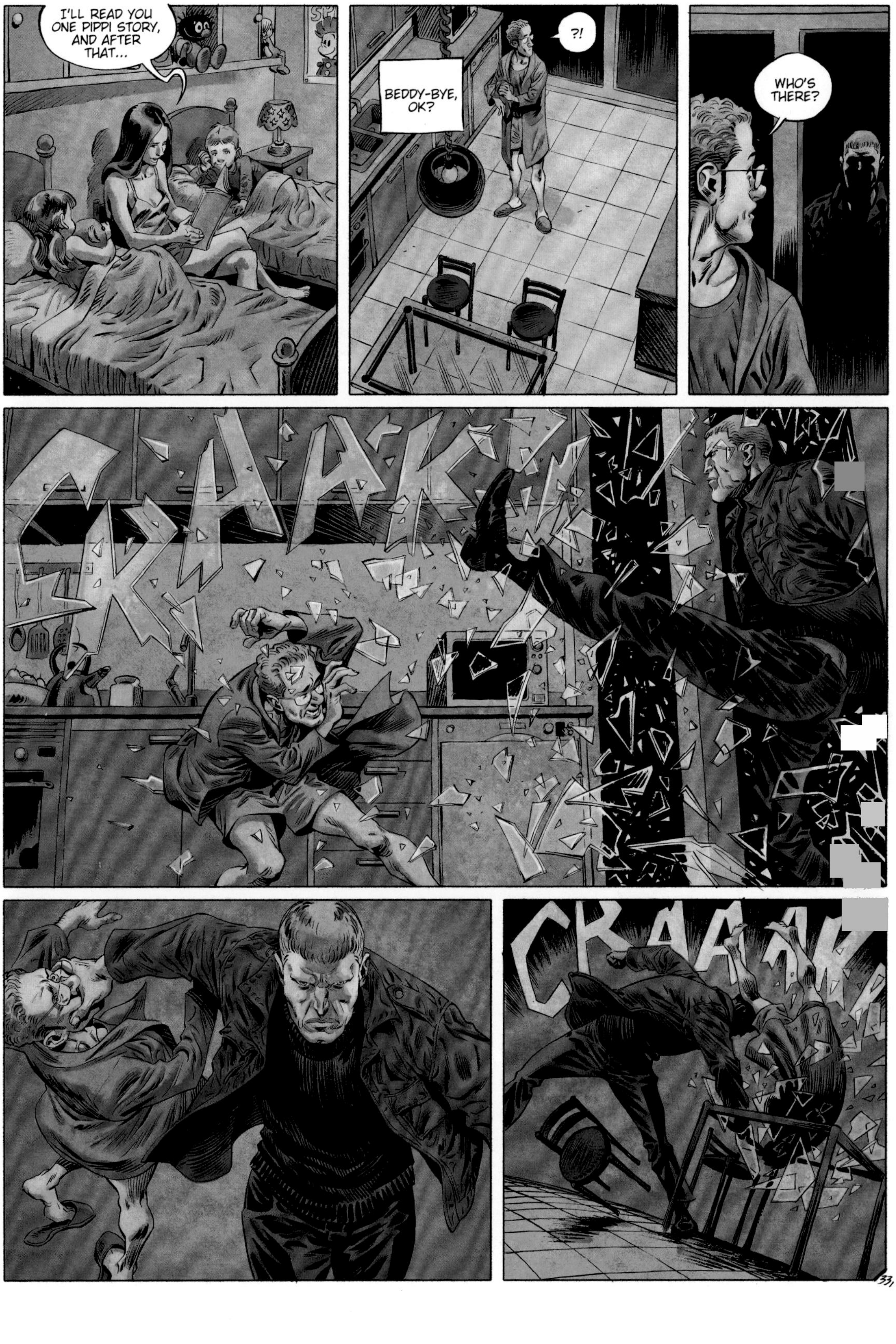
I'LL READ YOU ONE PIPPI STORY, AND AFTER THAT...
BEDDY-BYE, OK?
?!
WHO'S THERE?

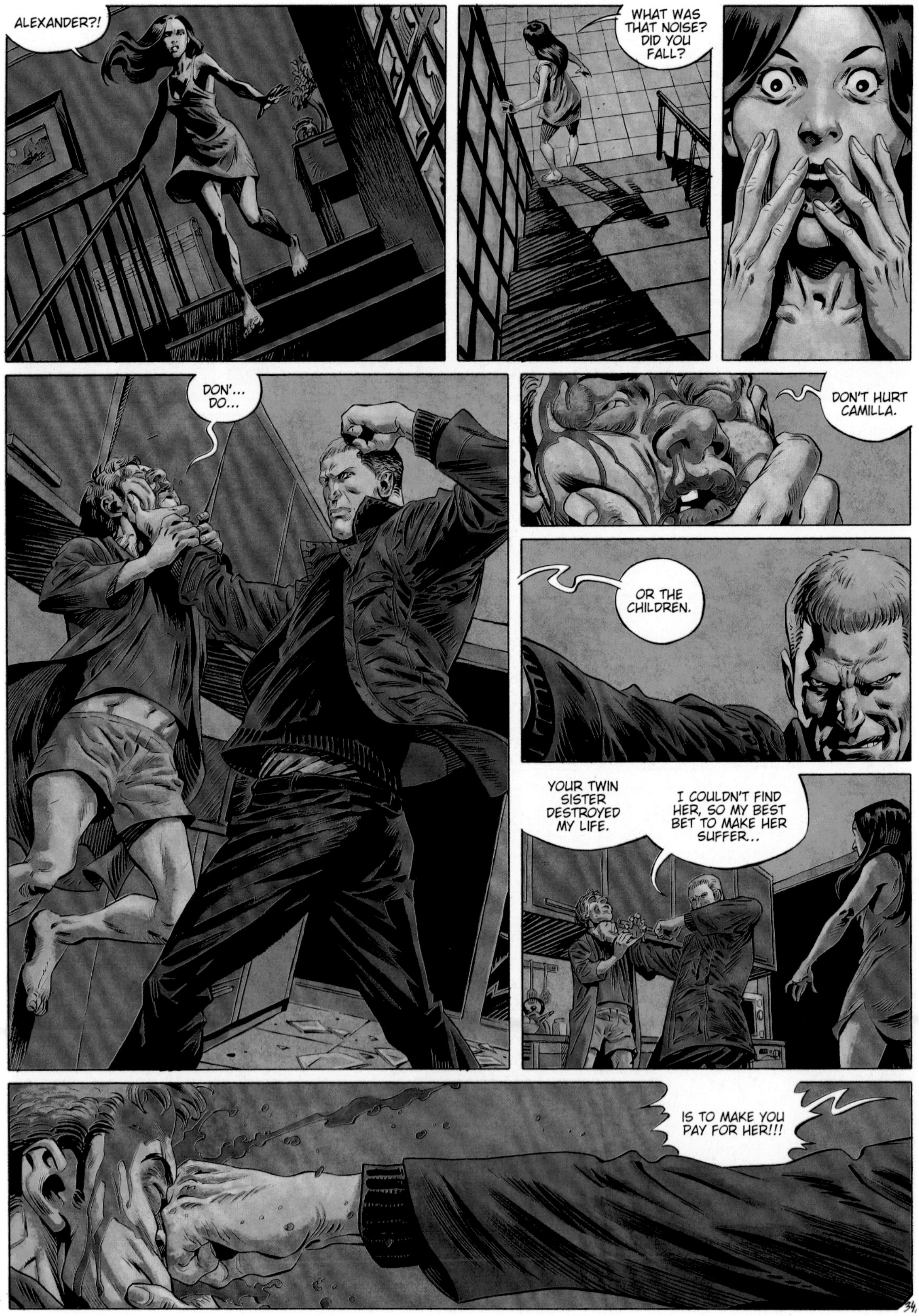
ALEXANDER?!
WHAT WAS THAT NOISE? DID YOU FALL?
DON'... DO...
DON'T HURT CAMILLA.
OR THE CHILDREN.
YOUR TWIN SISTER DESTROYED MY LIFE.
I COULDN'T FIND HER, SO MY BEST BET TO MAKE HER SUFFER...
IS TO MAKE YOU PAY FOR HER!!!

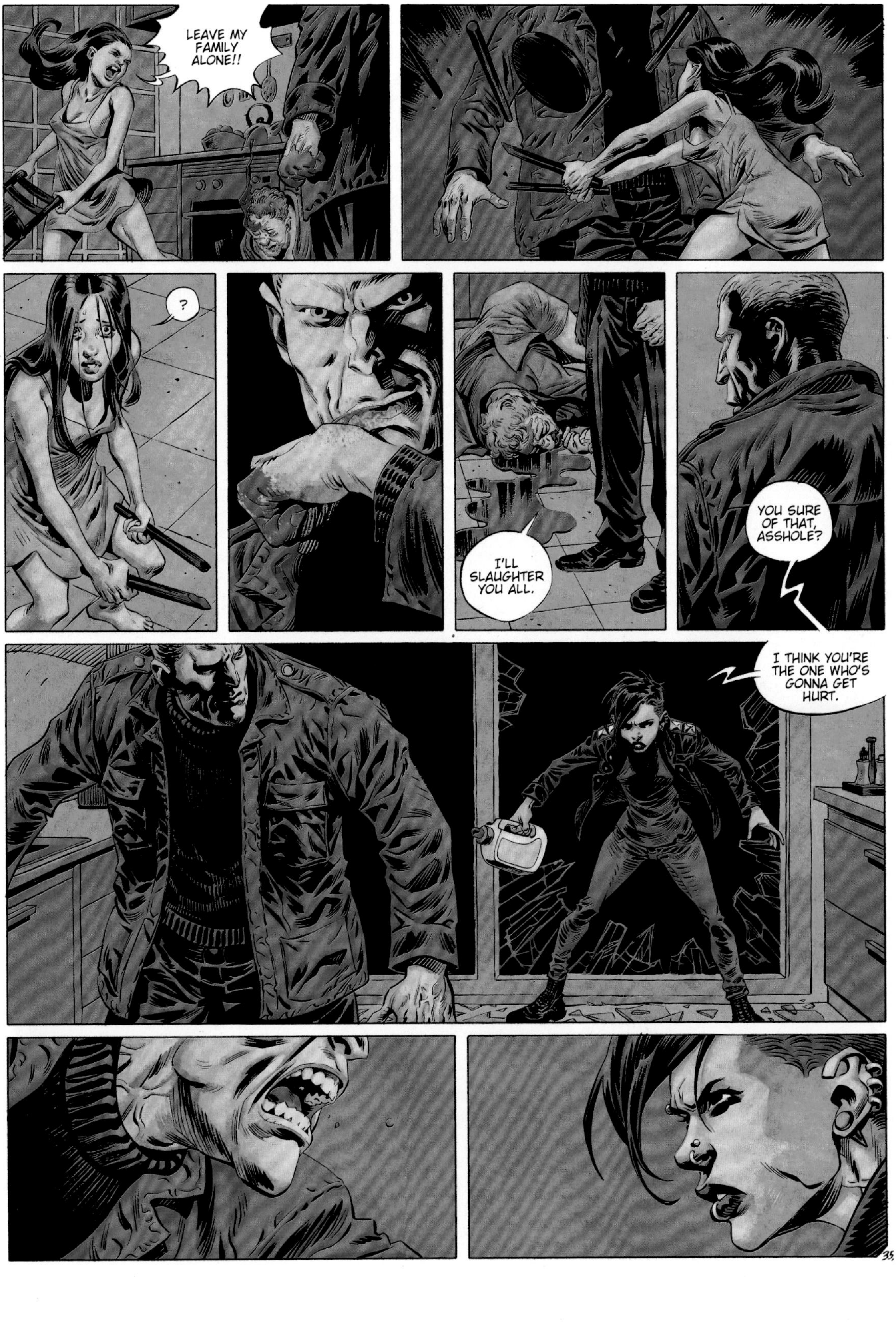
LEAVE MY FAMILY ALONE!!
?
I'LL SLAUGHTER YOU ALL.
YOU SURE OF THAT, ASSHOLE?
I THINK YOU'RE THE ONE WHO'S GONNA GET HURT.

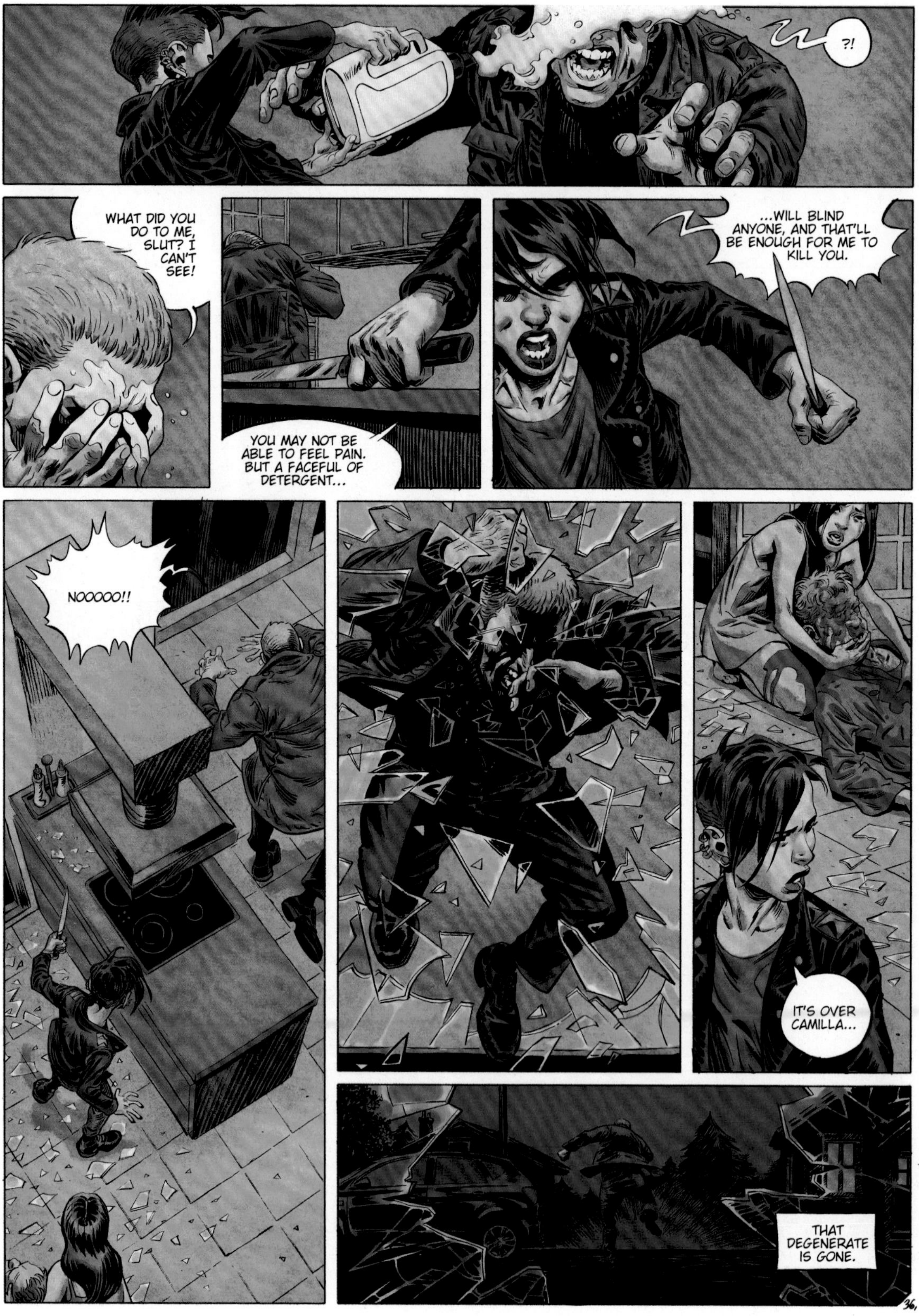
?!
WHAT DID YOU DO TO ME, SLUT? I CAN'T SEE!
YOU MAY NOT BE ABLE TO FEEL PAIN. BUT A FACEFUL OF DETERGENT...
...WILL BLIND ANYONE, AND THAT'LL BE ENOUGH FOR ME TO KILL YOU.
NOOOOO!!
IT'S OVER CAMILLA...
THAT DEGENERATE IS GONE.

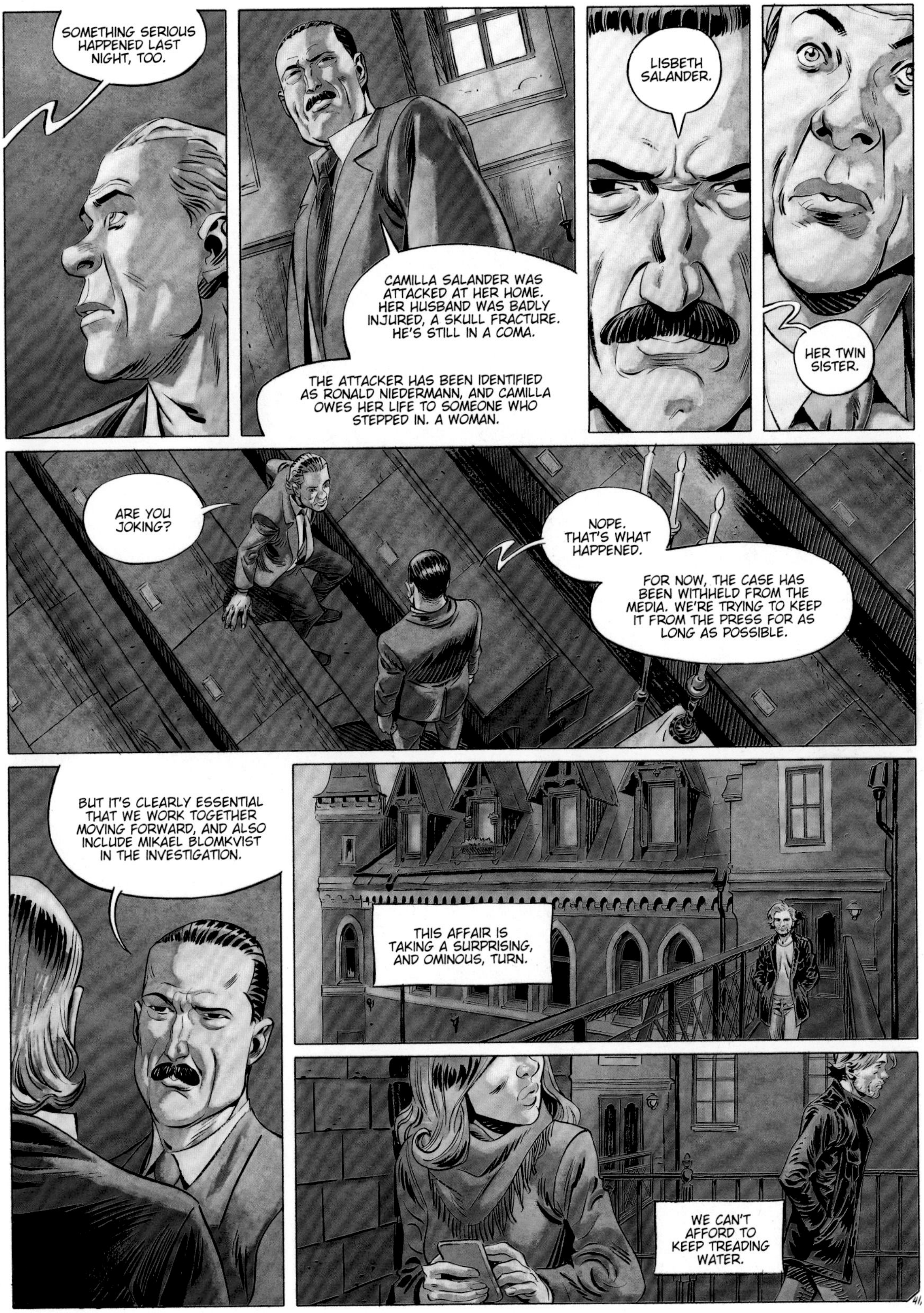
SOMETHING SERIOUS HAPPENED LAST NIGHT, TOO.
CAMILLA SALANDER WAS ATTACKED AT HER HOME. HER HUSBAND WAS BADLY INJURED, A SKULL FRACTURE. HE'S STILL IN A COMA.
THE ATTACKER HAS BEEN IDENTIFIED AS RONALD NIEDERMANN, AND CAMILLA OWES HER LIFE TO SOMEONE WHO STEPPED IN. A WOMAN.
LISBETH SALANDER.
HER TWIN SISTER.
ARE YOU JOKING?
NOPE. THAT'S WHAT HAPPENED.
FOR NOW, THE CASE HAS BEEN WITHHELD FROM THE MEDIA. WE'RE TRYING TO KEEP IT FROM THE PRESS FOR AS LONG AS POSSIBLE.
BUT IT'S CLEARLY ESSENTIAL THAT WE WORK TOGETHER MOVING FORWARD, AND ALSO INCLUDE MIKAEL BLOMKVIST IN THE INVESTIGATION.
THIS AFFAIR IS TAKING A SURPRISING, AND OMINOUS, TURN.
WE CAN'T AFFORD TO KEEP TREADING WATER.

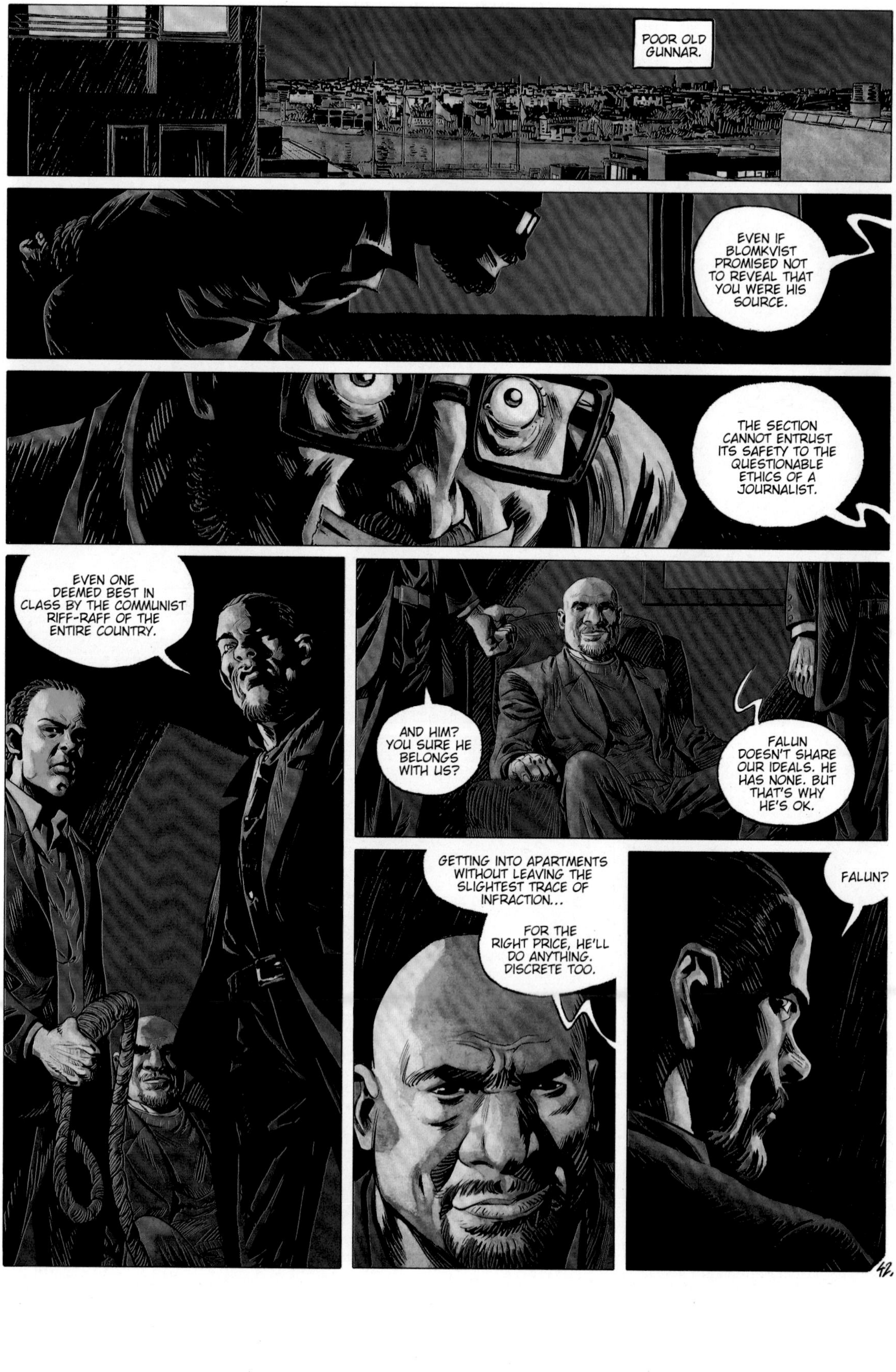
POOR OLD GUNNAR.
EVEN IF BLOMKVIST PROMISED NOT TO REVEAL THAT YOU WERE HIS SOURCE.
THE SECTION CANNOT ENTRUST ITS SAFETY TO THE QUESTIONABLE ETHICS OF A JOURNALIST.
EVEN ONE DEEMED BEST IN CLASS BY THE COMMUNIST RIFF-RAFF OF THE ENTIRE COUNTRY.
AND HIM? YOU SURE HE BELONGS WITH US?
FALUN DOESN'T SHARE OUR IDEALS. HE HAS NONE. BUT THAT'S WHY HE'S OK.
GETTING INTO APARTMENTS WITHOUT LEAVING THE SLIGHTEST TRACE OF INFRACTION...
FOR THE RIGHT PRICE, HE'LL DO ANYTHING. DISCRETE TOO.
FALUN?
42.

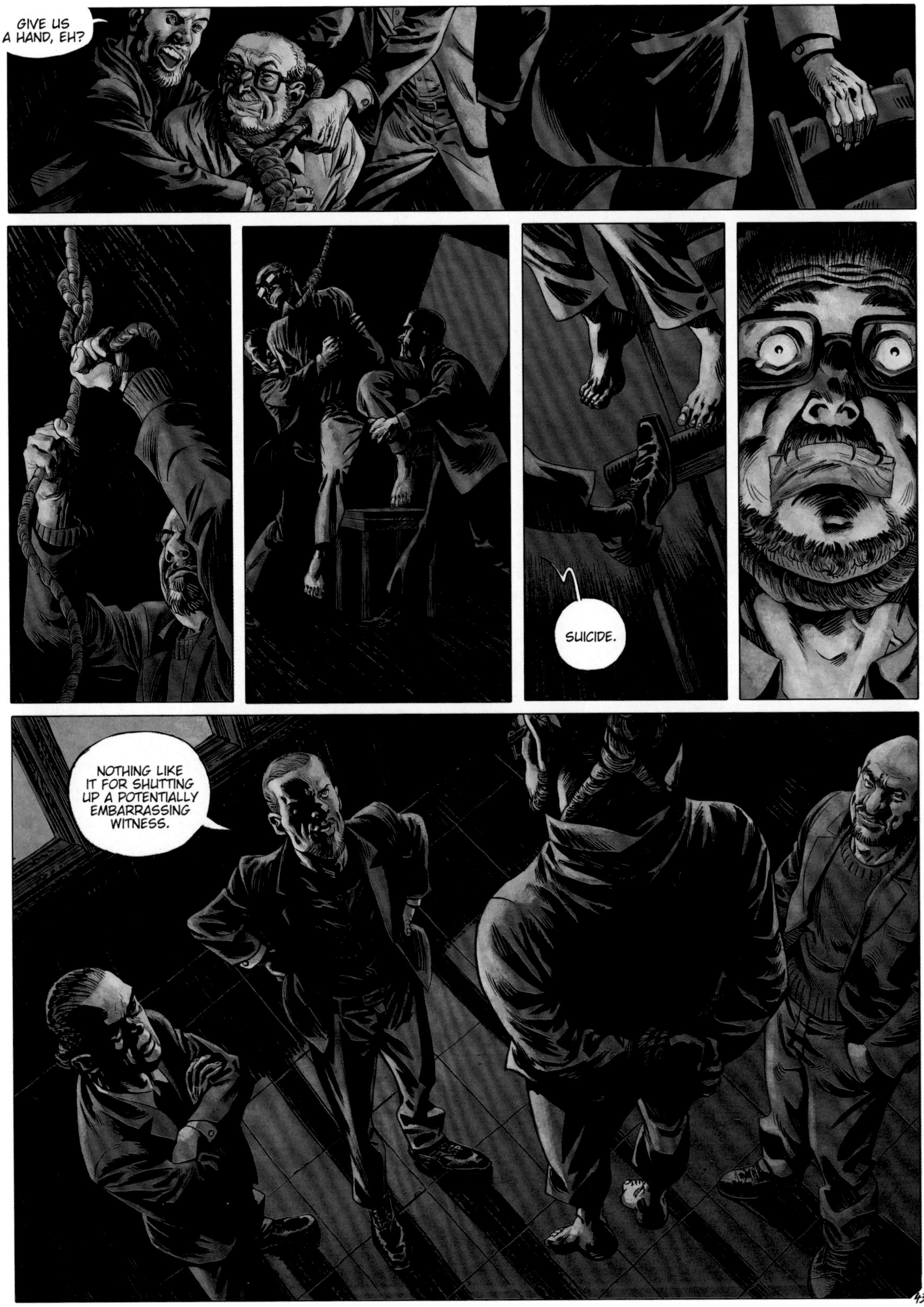
GIVE US A HAND, EH?
SUICIDE.
NOTHING LIKE IT FOR SHUTTING UP A POTENTIALLY EMBARRASSING WITNESS.

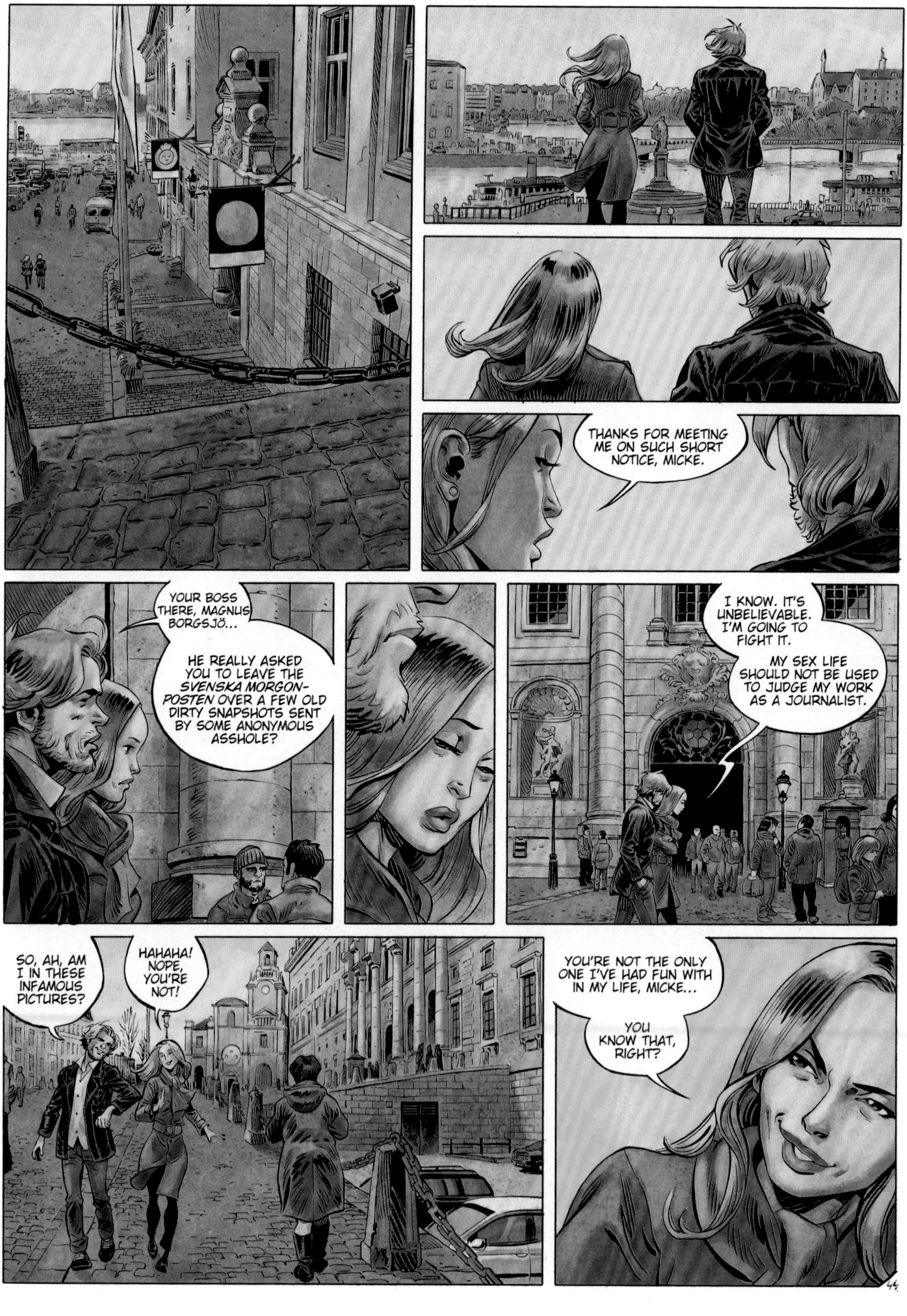
THANKS FOR MEETING ME ON SUCH SHORT NOTICE, MICKE.
YOUR BOSS THERE, MAGNUS BORGSJÖ...
HE REALLY ASKED YOU TO LEAVE THE *SVENSKA MORGON-POSTEN* OVER A FEW OLD DIRTY SNAPSHOTS SENT BY SOME ANONYMOUS ASSHOLE?
I KNOW. IT'S UNBELIEVABLE. I'M GOING TO FIGHT IT.
MY SEX LIFE SHOULD NOT BE USED TO JUDGE MY WORK AS A JOURNALIST.
SO, AH, AM I IN THESE INFAMOUS PICTURES?
HAHAHA! NOPE, YOU'RE NOT!
YOU'RE NOT THE ONLY ONE I'VE HAD FUN WITH IN MY LIFE, MICKE...
YOU KNOW THAT, RIGHT?

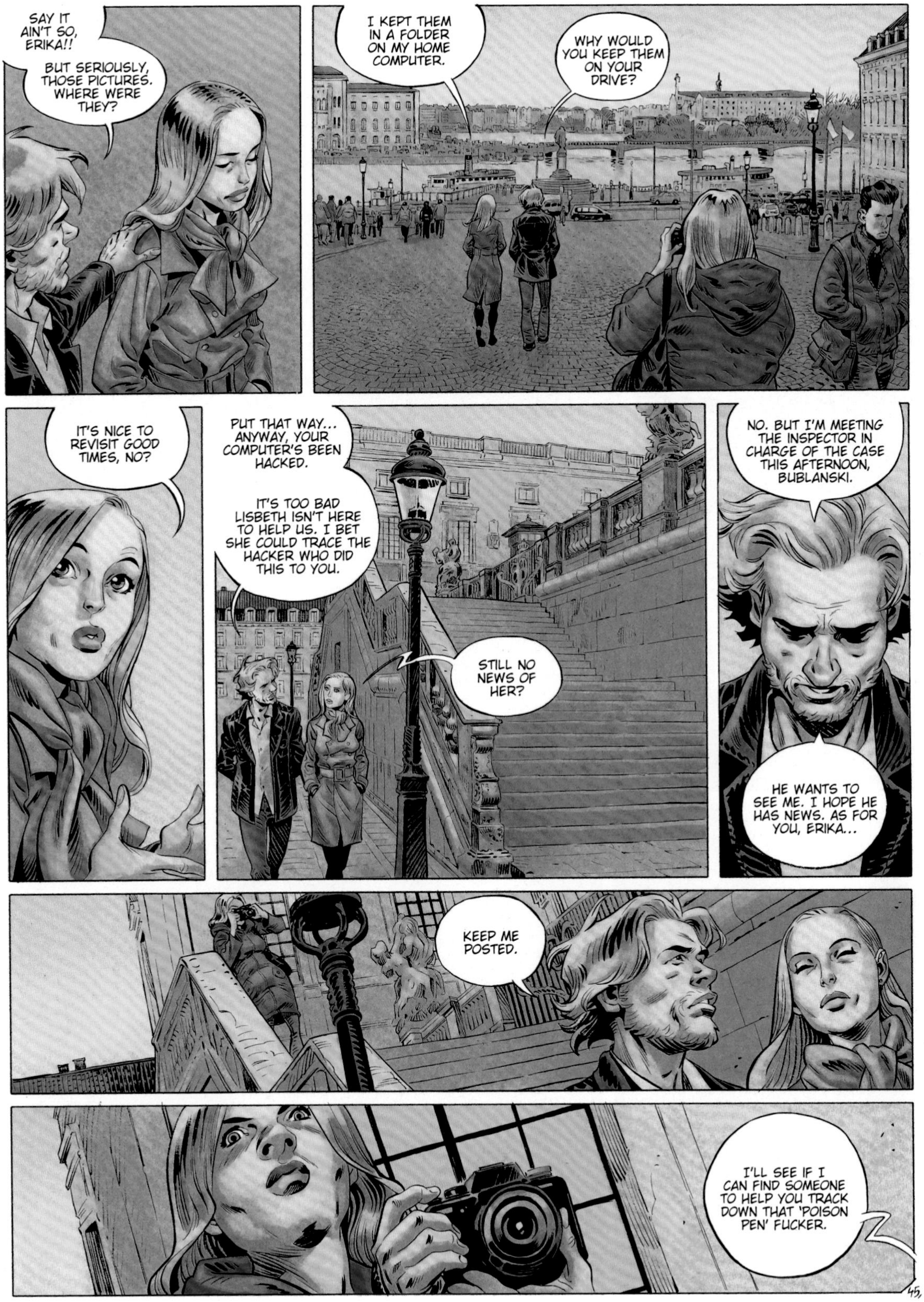
SAY IT AIN'T SO, ERIKA!!
BUT SERIOUSLY, THOSE PICTURES. WHERE WERE THEY?
I KEPT THEM IN A FOLDER ON MY HOME COMPUTER.
WHY WOULD YOU KEEP THEM ON YOUR DRIVE?
IT'S NICE TO REVISIT GOOD TIMES, NO?
PUT THAT WAY... ANYWAY, YOUR COMPUTER'S BEEN HACKED.
IT'S TOO BAD LISBETH ISN'T HERE TO HELP US. I BET SHE COULD TRACE THE HACKER WHO DID THIS TO YOU.
STILL NO NEWS OF HER?
NO. BUT I'M MEETING THE INSPECTOR IN CHARGE OF THE CASE THIS AFTERNOON, BUBLANSKI.
HE WANTS TO SEE ME. I HOPE HE HAS NEWS. AS FOR YOU, ERIKA...
KEEP ME POSTED.
I'LL SEE IF I CAN FIND SOMEONE TO HELP YOU TRACK DOWN THAT 'POISON PEN' FUCKER.
45

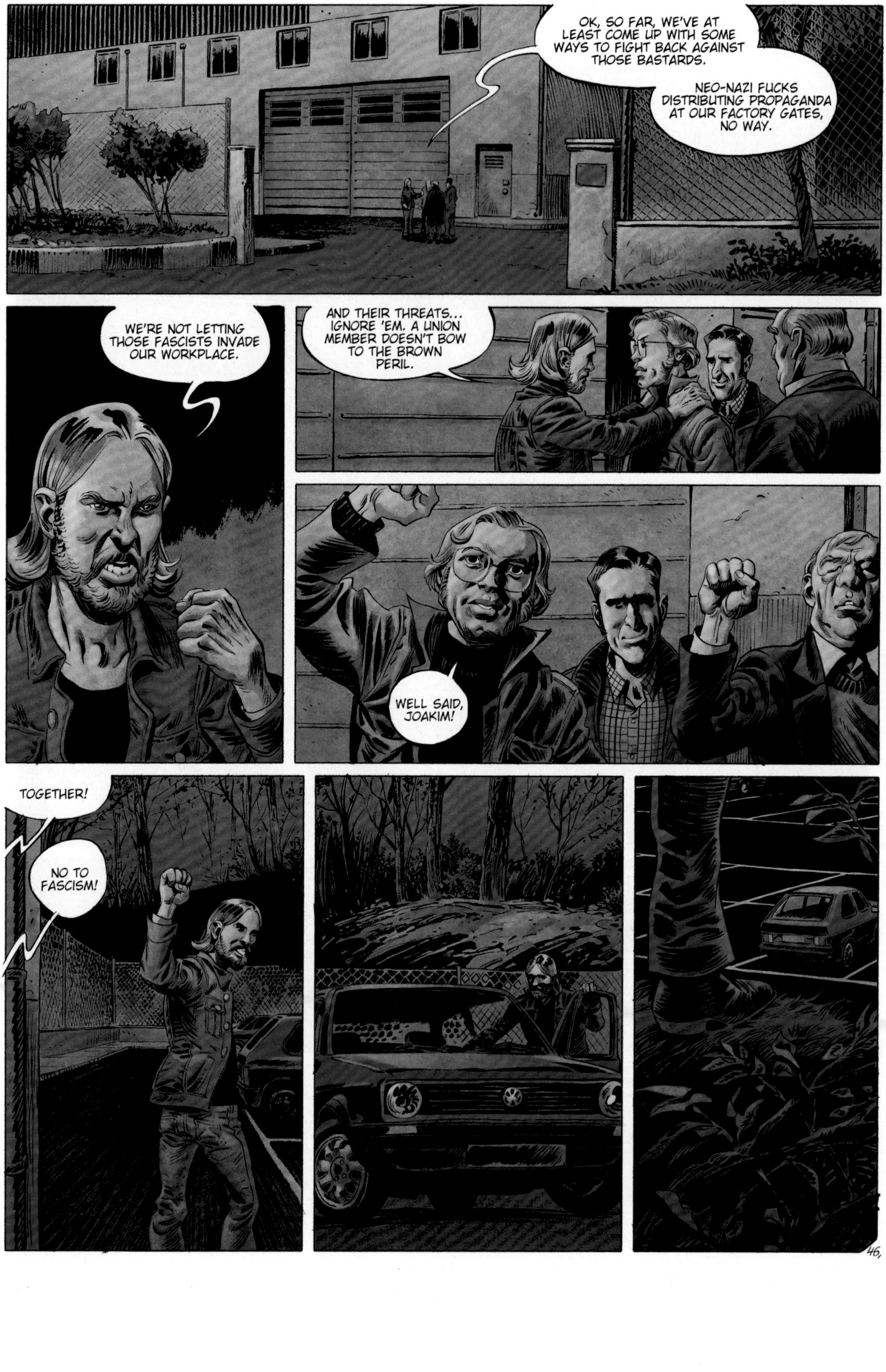
OK, SO FAR, WE'VE AT LEAST COME UP WITH SOME WAYS TO FIGHT BACK AGAINST THOSE BASTARDS.
NEO-NAZI FUCKS DISTRIBUTING PROPAGANDA AT OUR FACTORY GATES, NO WAY.
WE'RE NOT LETTING THOSE FASCISTS INVADE OUR WORKPLACE.
AND THEIR THREATS... IGNORE 'EM. A UNION MEMBER DOESN'T BOW TO THE BROWN PERIL.
WELL SAID, JOAKIM!
TOGETHER!
NO TO FASCISM!

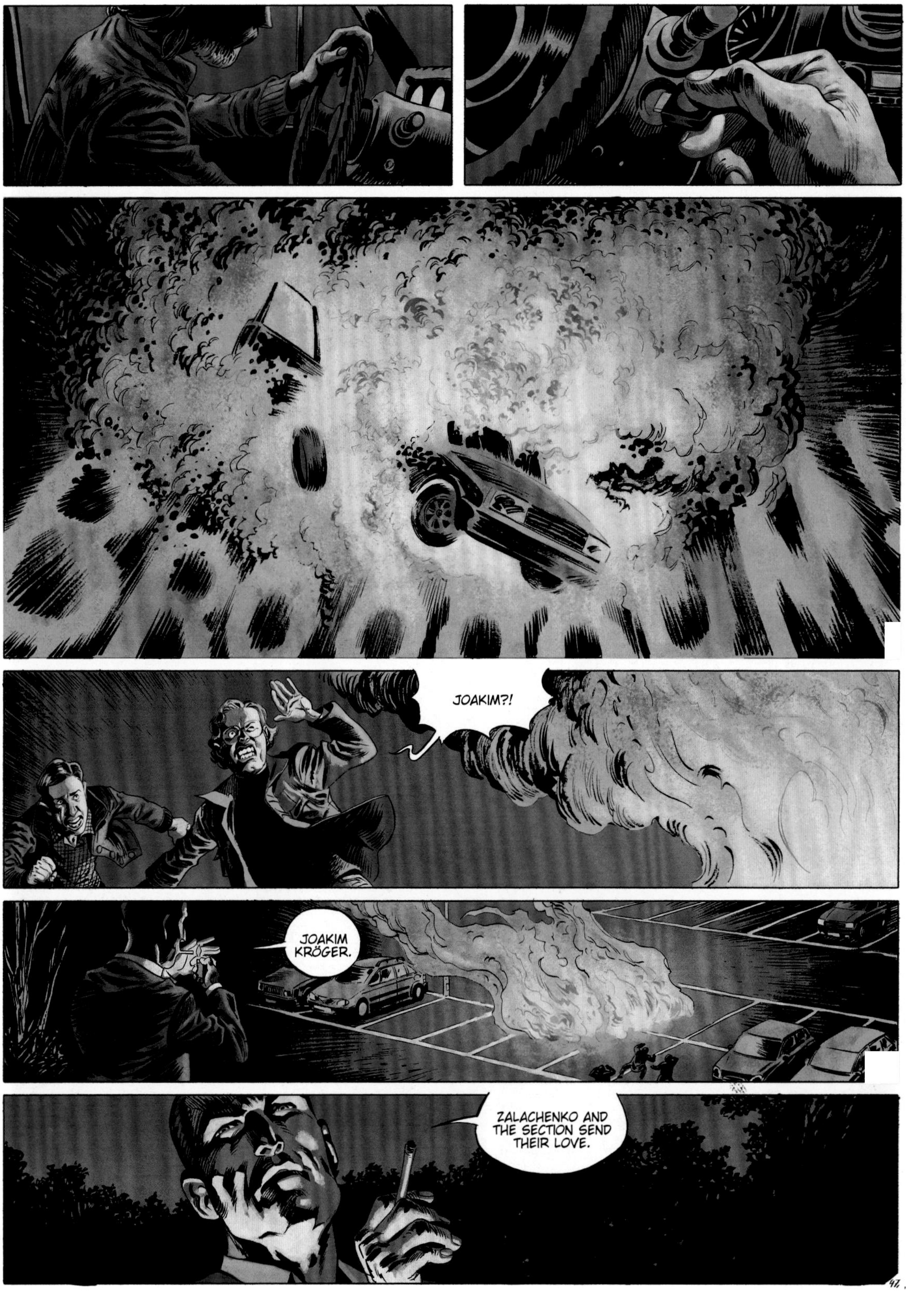
JOAKIM?!
JOAKIM KRÖGER.
ZALACHENKO AND THE SECTION SEND THEIR LOVE.

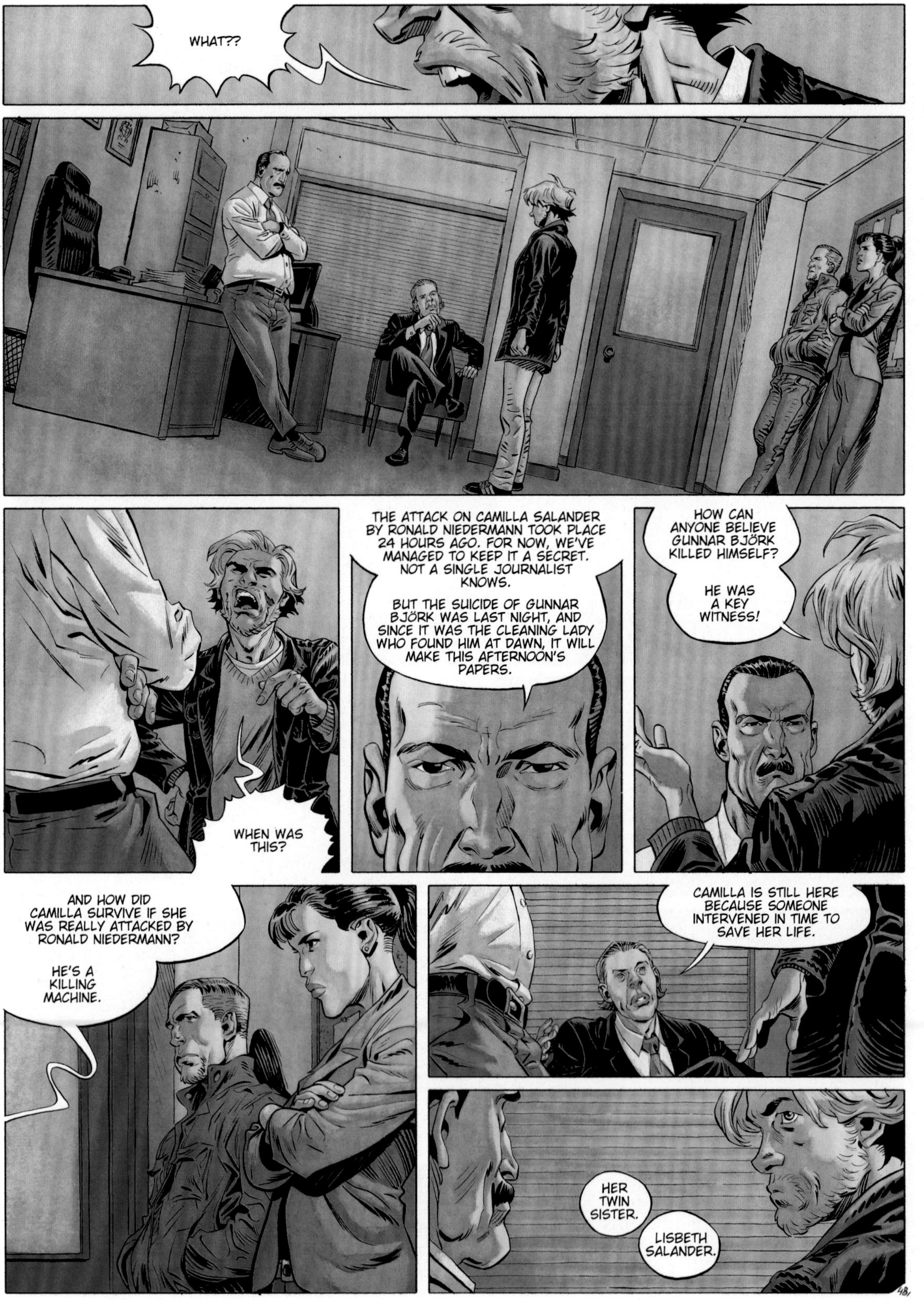
WHAT??
WHEN WAS THIS?
THE ATTACK ON CAMILLA SALANDER BY RONALD NIEDERMANN TOOK PLACE 24 HOURS AGO. FOR NOW, WE'VE MANAGED TO KEEP IT A SECRET. NOT A SINGLE JOURNALIST KNOWS.
BUT THE SUICIDE OF GUNNAR BJÖRK WAS LAST NIGHT, AND SINCE IT WAS THE CLEANING LADY WHO FOUND HIM AT DAWN, IT WILL MAKE THIS AFTERNOON'S PAPERS.
HOW CAN ANYONE BELIEVE GUNNAR BJÖRK KILLED HIMSELF?
HE WAS A KEY WITNESS!
AND HOW DID CAMILLA SURVIVE IF SHE WAS REALLY ATTACKED BY RONALD NIEDERMANN?
HE'S A KILLING MACHINE.
CAMILLA IS STILL HERE BECAUSE SOMEONE INTERVENED IN TIME TO SAVE HER LIFE.
HER TWIN SISTER.
LISBETH SALANDER.

CAMILLA DOESN'T KNOW WHAT LISBETH WAS DOING THERE, BUT SHE'S CATEGORICAL...

IT WAS LISBETH WHO MADE NIEDERMANN FLEE.

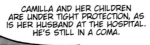

CAMILLA AND HER CHILDREN ARE UNDER TIGHT PROTECTION, AS IS HER HUSBAND AT THE HOSPITAL. HE'S STILL IN A COMA.

WE'RE STILL TRYING TO KEEP THIS UNDER WRAPS FOR NOW.

GIVEN WHAT JUST HAPPENED, I'LL START INVESTIGATING WITHIN THE SÄPO, ESPECIALLY ANY TIES AMONG NILS BJURMAN, GUNNAR BJÖRK, EVERT GULBERG AND ANY OTHER MEMBERS OF THE SECRET SERVICE.

LIVING ONES, IF POSSIBLE.

MIKAEL, I SUGGEST WE JOIN FORCES AND COLLABORATE.

LET'S POOL OUR INFORMATION SO JUSTICE CAN PREVAIL.

SWEDISH DEMOCRACY CERTAINLY OWES LISBETH SALANDER JUSTICE.

BUT LET'S BE CLEAR. I'M A JOURNALIST, NOT AN INFORMANT.

AS FOR SHARING SOME INFORMATION, WHY NOT? BUT WE EACH HAVE OUR PLACE.

I UNDERSTAND YOUR POSITION. AND I RESPECT IT, BELIEVE ME.

YOU'RE RIGHT MIKAEL, LISBETH SALANDER DESERVES JUSTICE.

AND FROM NOW ON...

YOU'RE NOT ALONE IN FIGHTING FOR IT.

POLISEN

47.

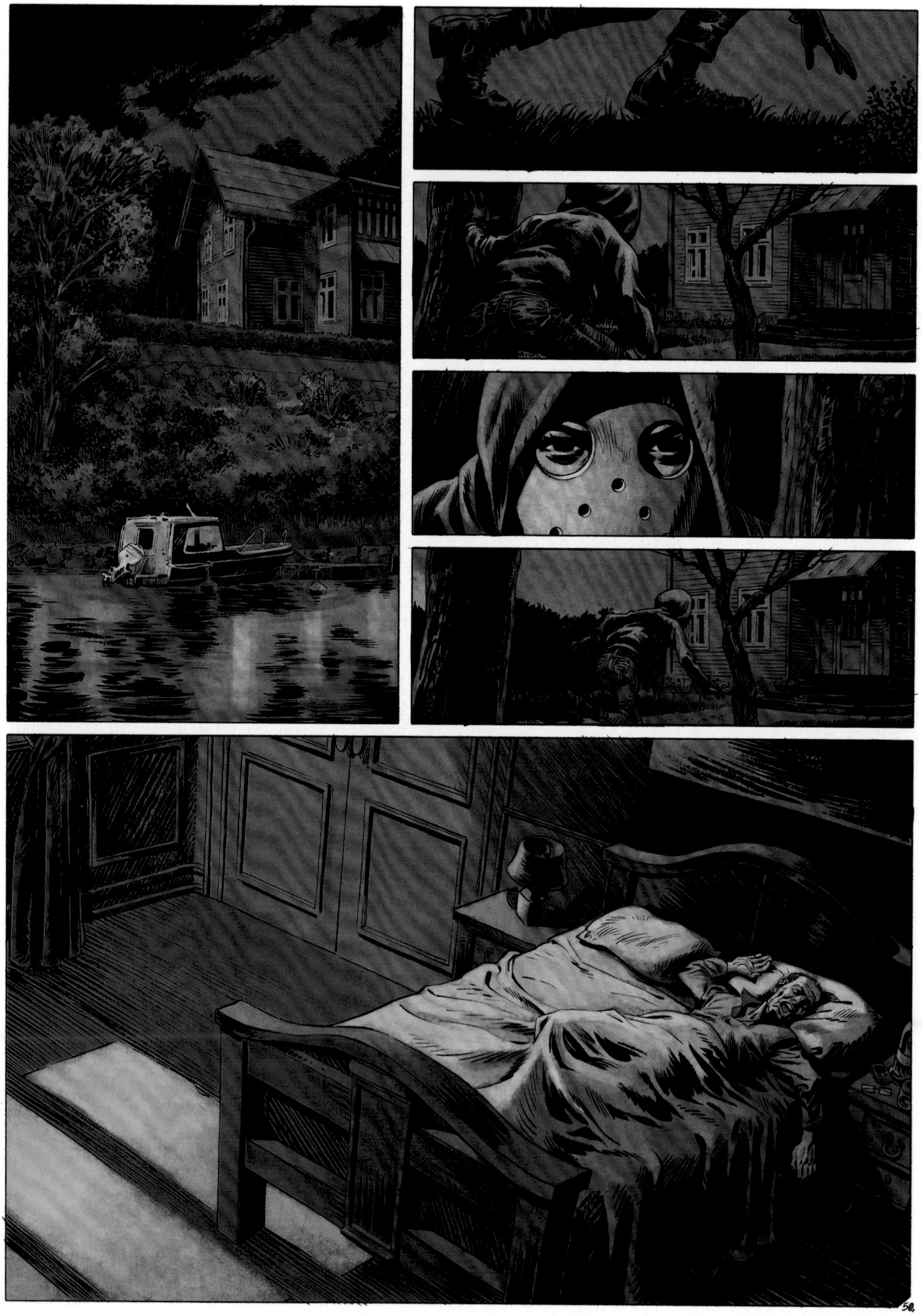

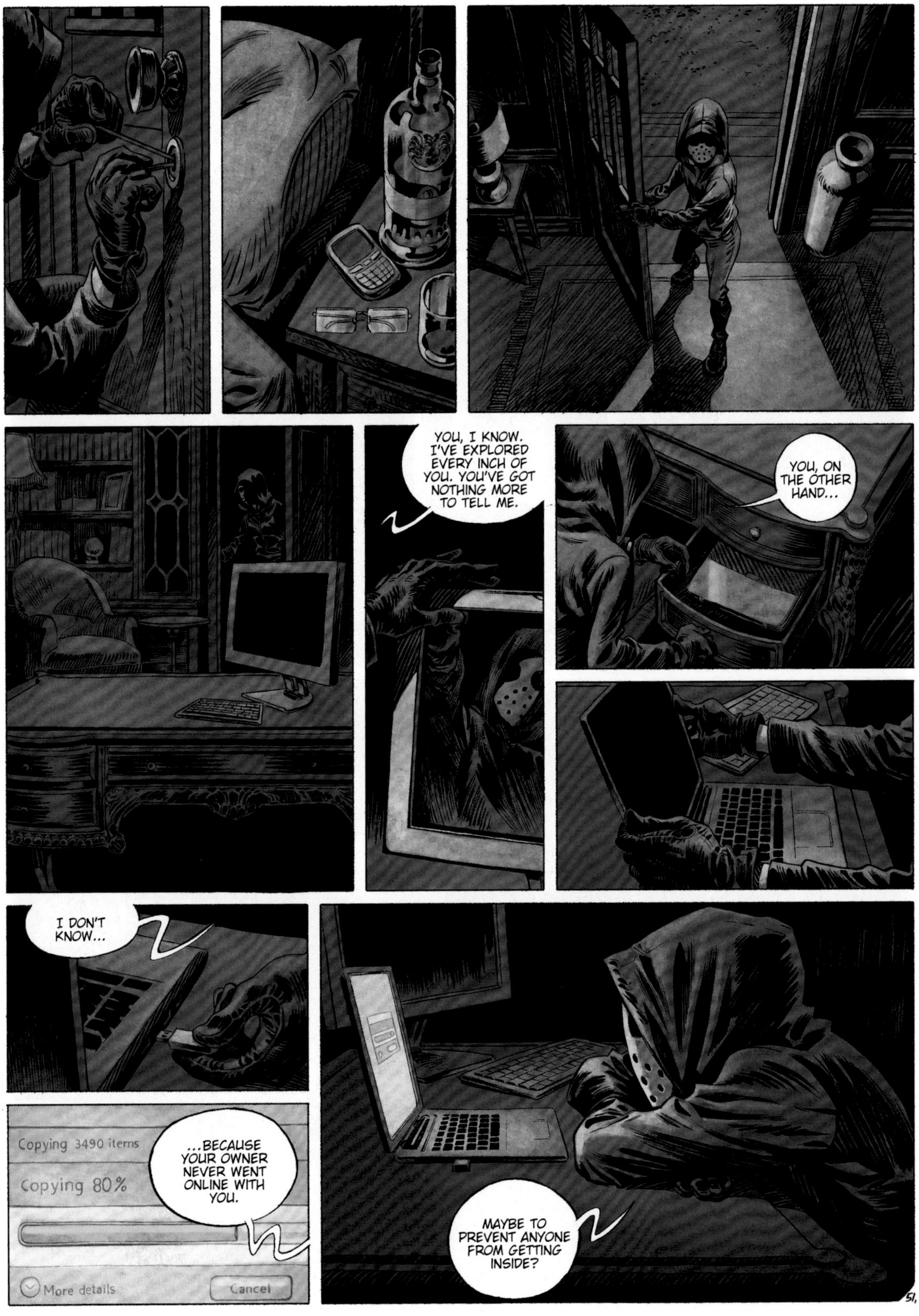
YOU, I KNOW. I'VE EXPLORED EVERY INCH OF YOU. YOU'VE GOT NOTHING MORE TO TELL ME.
YOU, ON THE OTHER HAND...
I DON'T KNOW...
Copying 3490 items
Copying 80%
More details
Cancel
...BECAUSE YOUR OWNER NEVER WENT ONLINE WITH YOU.
MAYBE TO PREVENT ANYONE FROM GETTING INSIDE?

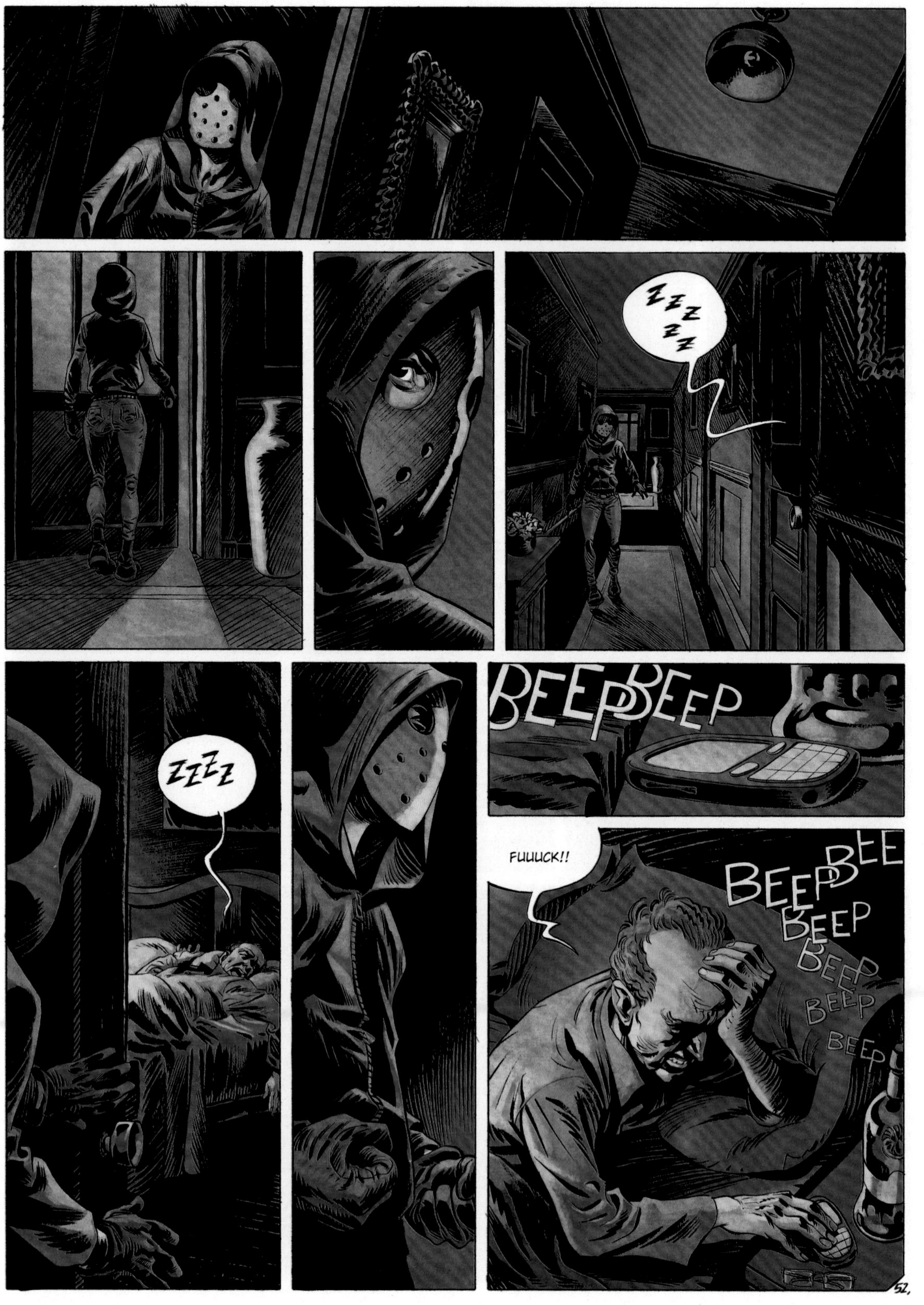
Z Z Z Z Z
Z Z Z Z
BEEP BEEP
FUUUCK!!
BEEP BEE
BEEP
BEEP
BEEP
BEEP

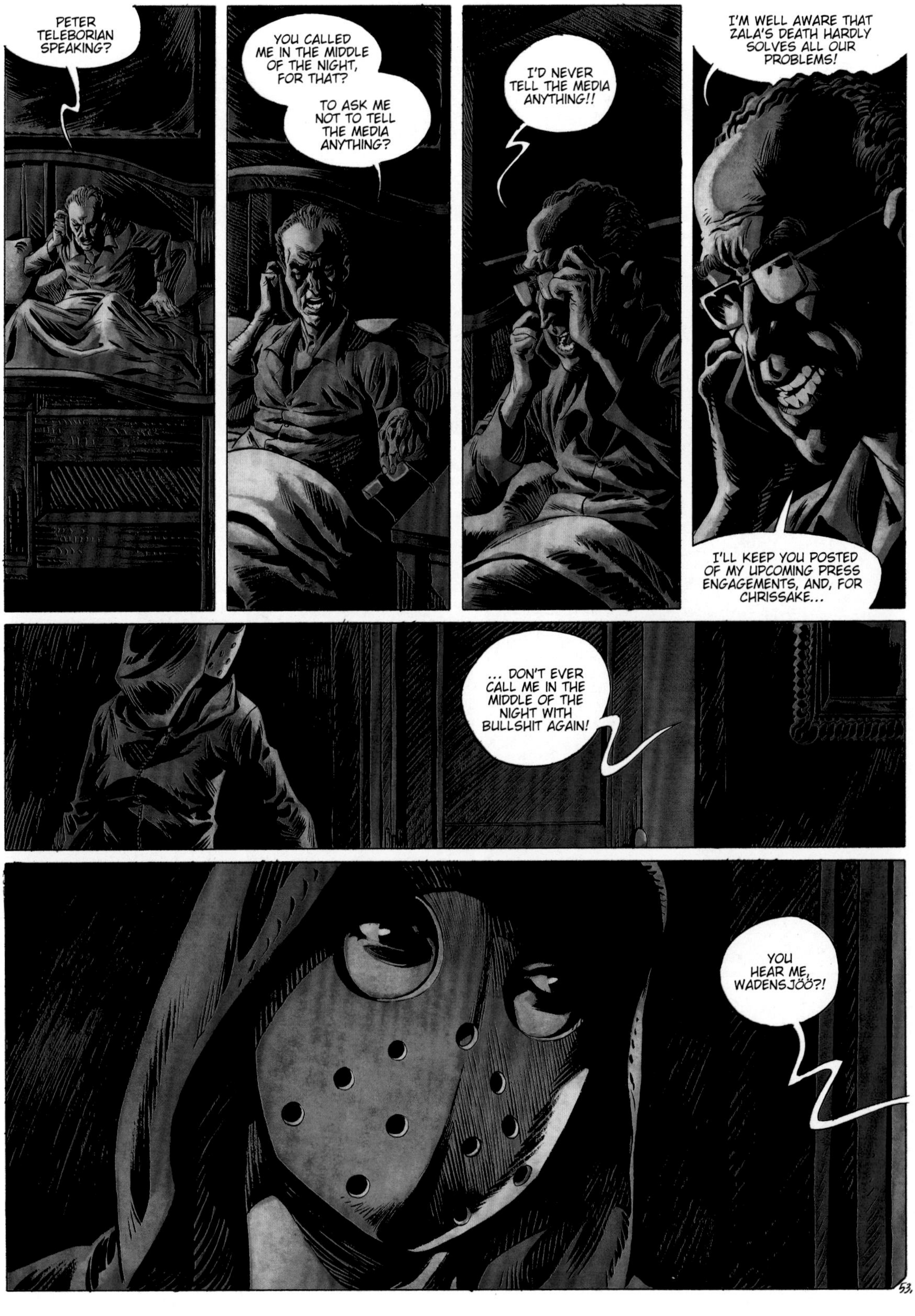
PETER TELEBORIAN SPEAKING?
YOU CALLED ME IN THE MIDDLE OF THE NIGHT, FOR THAT?
TO ASK ME NOT TO TELL THE MEDIA ANYTHING?
I'D NEVER TELL THE MEDIA ANYTHING!!
I'M WELL AWARE THAT ZALA'S DEATH HARDLY SOLVES ALL OUR PROBLEMS!
I'LL KEEP YOU POSTED OF MY UPCOMING PRESS ENGAGEMENTS, AND, FOR CHRISSAKE...
... DON'T EVER CALL ME IN THE MIDDLE OF THE NIGHT WITH BULLSHIT AGAIN!
YOU HEAR ME, WADENSJÖÖ?!
53.

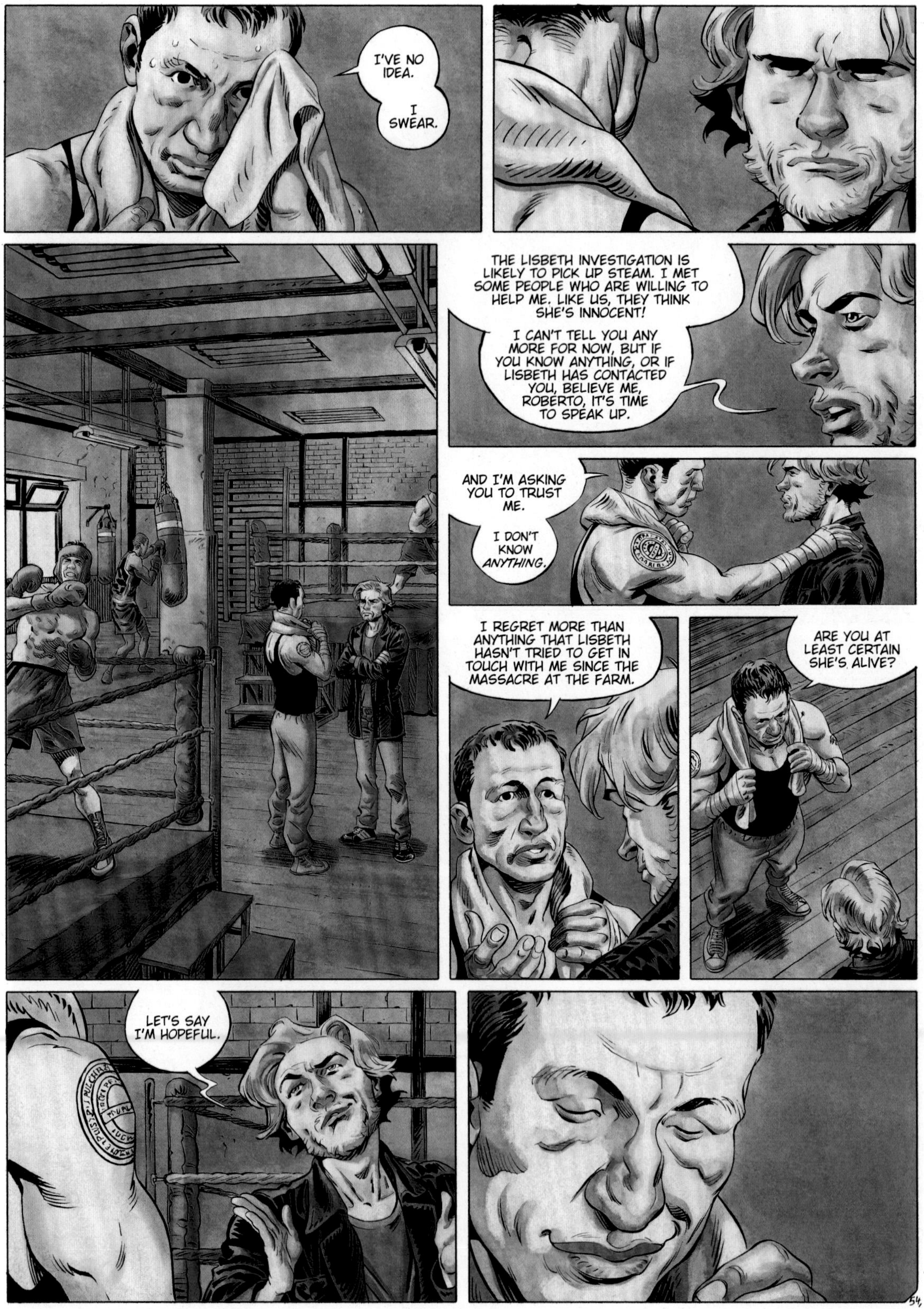
I'VE NO IDEA.
I SWEAR.
THE LISBETH INVESTIGATION IS LIKELY TO PICK UP STEAM. I MET SOME PEOPLE WHO ARE WILLING TO HELP ME. LIKE US, THEY THINK SHE'S INNOCENT!
I CAN'T TELL YOU ANY MORE FOR NOW, BUT IF YOU KNOW ANYTHING, OR IF LISBETH HAS CONTACTED YOU, BELIEVE ME, ROBERTO, IT'S TIME TO SPEAK UP.
AND I'M ASKING YOU TO TRUST ME.
I DON'T KNOW *ANYTHING*.
I REGRET MORE THAN ANYTHING THAT LISBETH HASN'T TRIED TO GET IN TOUCH WITH ME SINCE THE MASSACRE AT THE FARM.
ARE YOU AT LEAST CERTAIN SHE'S ALIVE?
LET'S SAY I'M HOPEFUL.

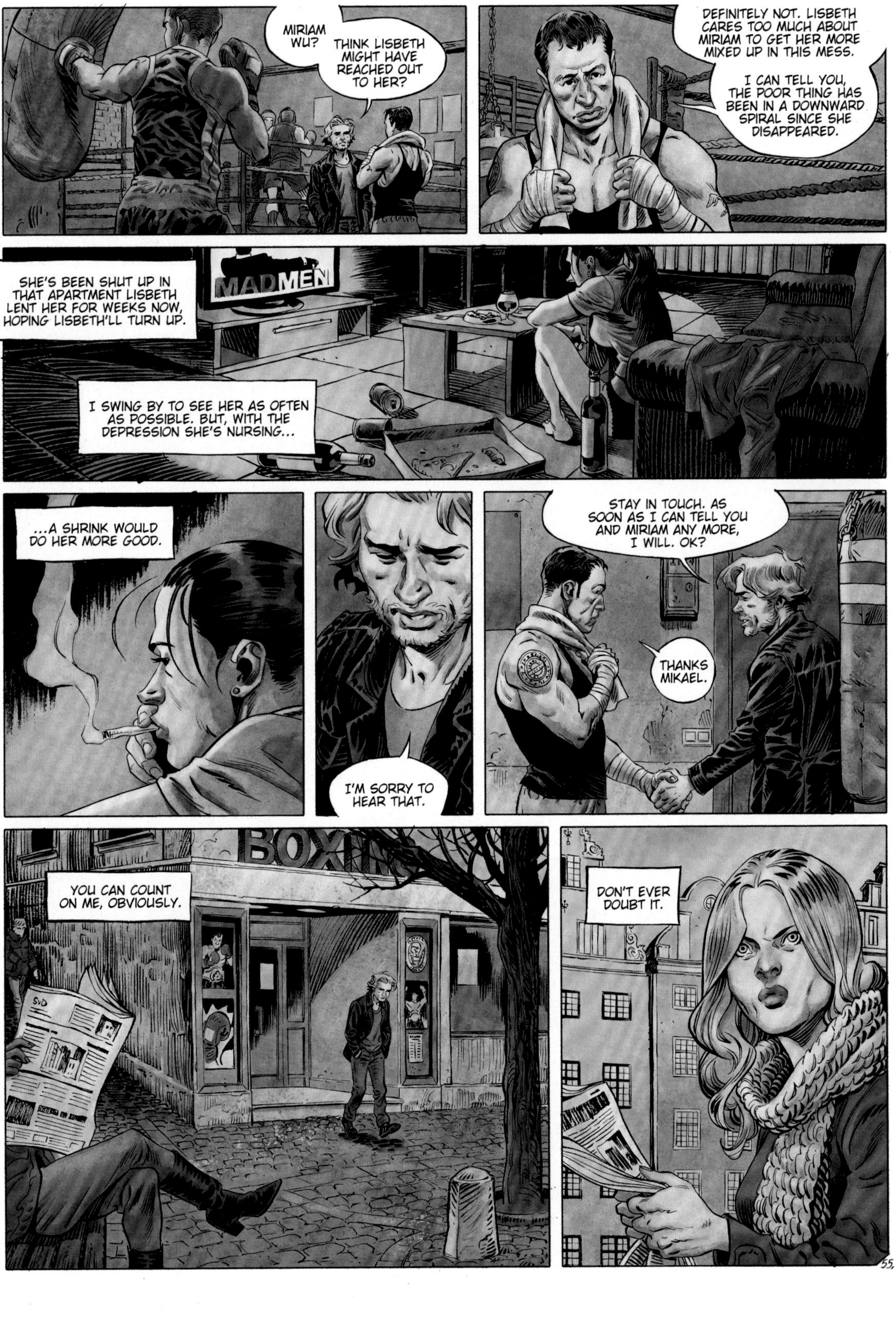
MIRIAM WU?
THINK LISBETH MIGHT HAVE REACHED OUT TO HER?
DEFINITELY NOT. LISBETH CARES TOO MUCH ABOUT MIRIAM TO GET HER MORE MIXED UP IN THIS MESS.
I CAN TELL YOU, THE POOR THING HAS BEEN IN A DOWNWARD SPIRAL SINCE SHE DISAPPEARED.
MADMEN
SHE'S BEEN SHUT UP IN THAT APARTMENT LISBETH LENT HER FOR WEEKS NOW, HOPING LISBETH'LL TURN UP.
I SWING BY TO SEE HER AS OFTEN AS POSSIBLE. BUT, WITH THE DEPRESSION SHE'S NURSING...
...A SHRINK WOULD DO HER MORE GOOD.
I'M SORRY TO HEAR THAT.
STAY IN TOUCH. AS SOON AS I CAN TELL YOU AND MIRIAM ANY MORE, I WILL. OK?
THANKS MIKAEL.
BOXIN
YOU CAN COUNT ON ME, OBVIOUSLY.
SvD
DON'T EVER DOUBT IT.

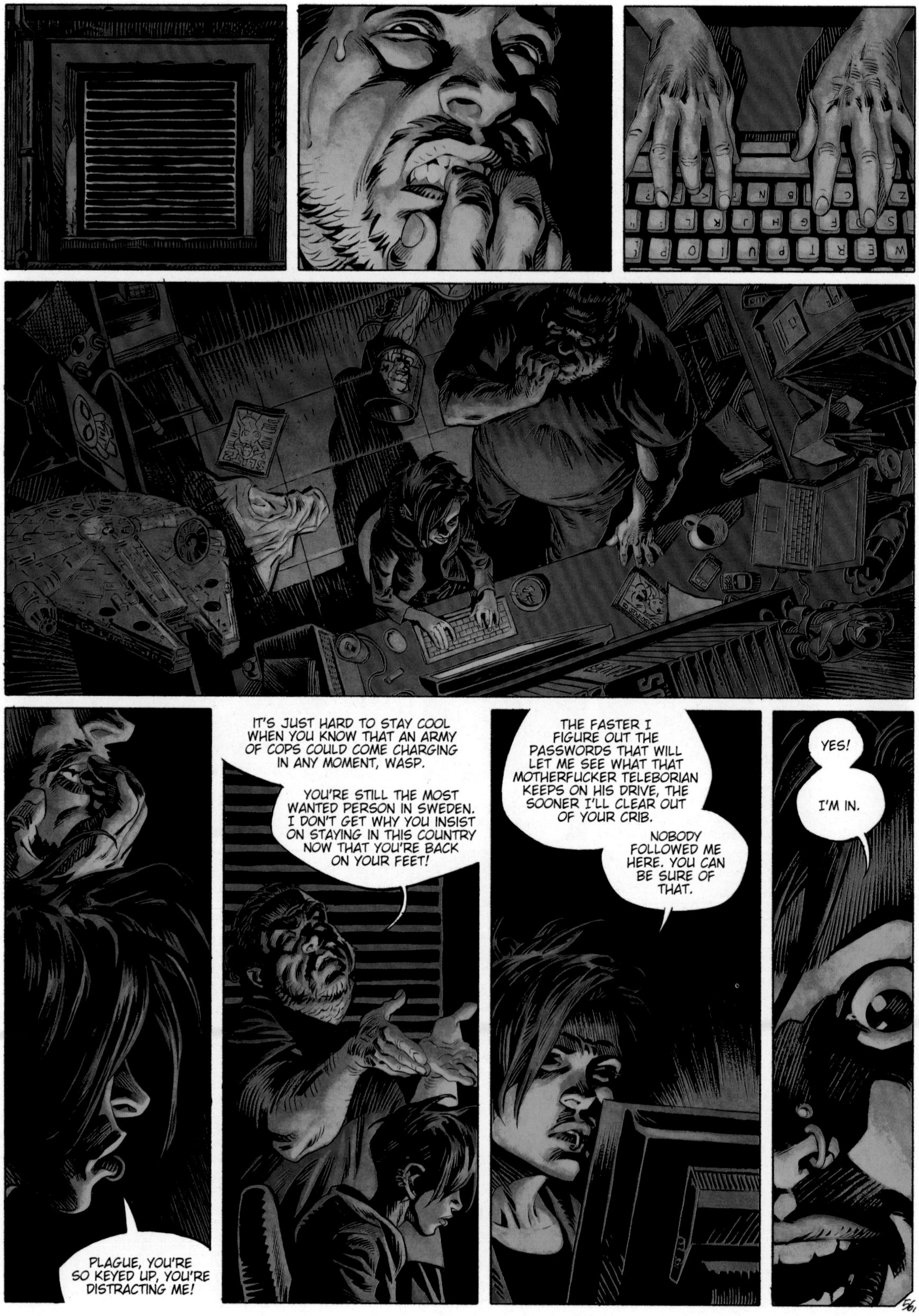
PLAGUE, YOU'RE SO KEYED UP, YOU'RE DISTRACTING ME!
IT'S JUST HARD TO STAY COOL WHEN YOU KNOW THAT AN ARMY OF COPS COULD COME CHARGING IN ANY MOMENT, WASP.
YOU'RE STILL THE MOST WANTED PERSON IN SWEDEN. I DON'T GET WHY YOU INSIST ON STAYING IN THIS COUNTRY NOW THAT YOU'RE BACK ON YOUR FEET!
THE FASTER I FIGURE OUT THE PASSWORDS THAT WILL LET ME SEE WHAT THAT MOTHERFUCKER TELEBORIAN KEEPS ON HIS DRIVE, THE SOONER I'LL CLEAR OUT OF YOUR CRIB.
NOBODY FOLLOWED ME HERE. YOU CAN BE SURE OF THAT.
YES!
I'M IN.

YOU'RE THE BEST, WASP!

AND YOU'VE GOT THE BEST GEAR THERE IS, PLAGUE! TOGETHER, WE'RE UNBEATABLE.

SO, ANYTHING INTERESTING?

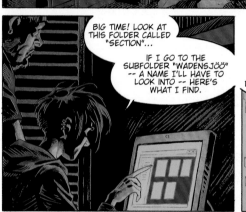

BIG TIME! LOOK AT THIS FOLDER CALLED "SECTION"...

IF I GO TO THE SUBFOLDER "WADENSJÖÖ" -- A NAME I'LL HAVE TO LOOK INTO -- HERE'S WHAT I FIND.

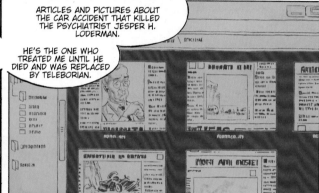

ARTICLES AND PICTURES ABOUT THE CAR ACCIDENT THAT KILLED THE PSYCHIATRIST JESPER H. LODERMAN.

HE'S THE ONE WHO TREATED ME UNTIL HE DIED AND WAS REPLACED BY TELEBORIAN.

AND LOOK, WHAT'S THIS FOLDER LABELLED...

"CANDYLAND"?

Candyland

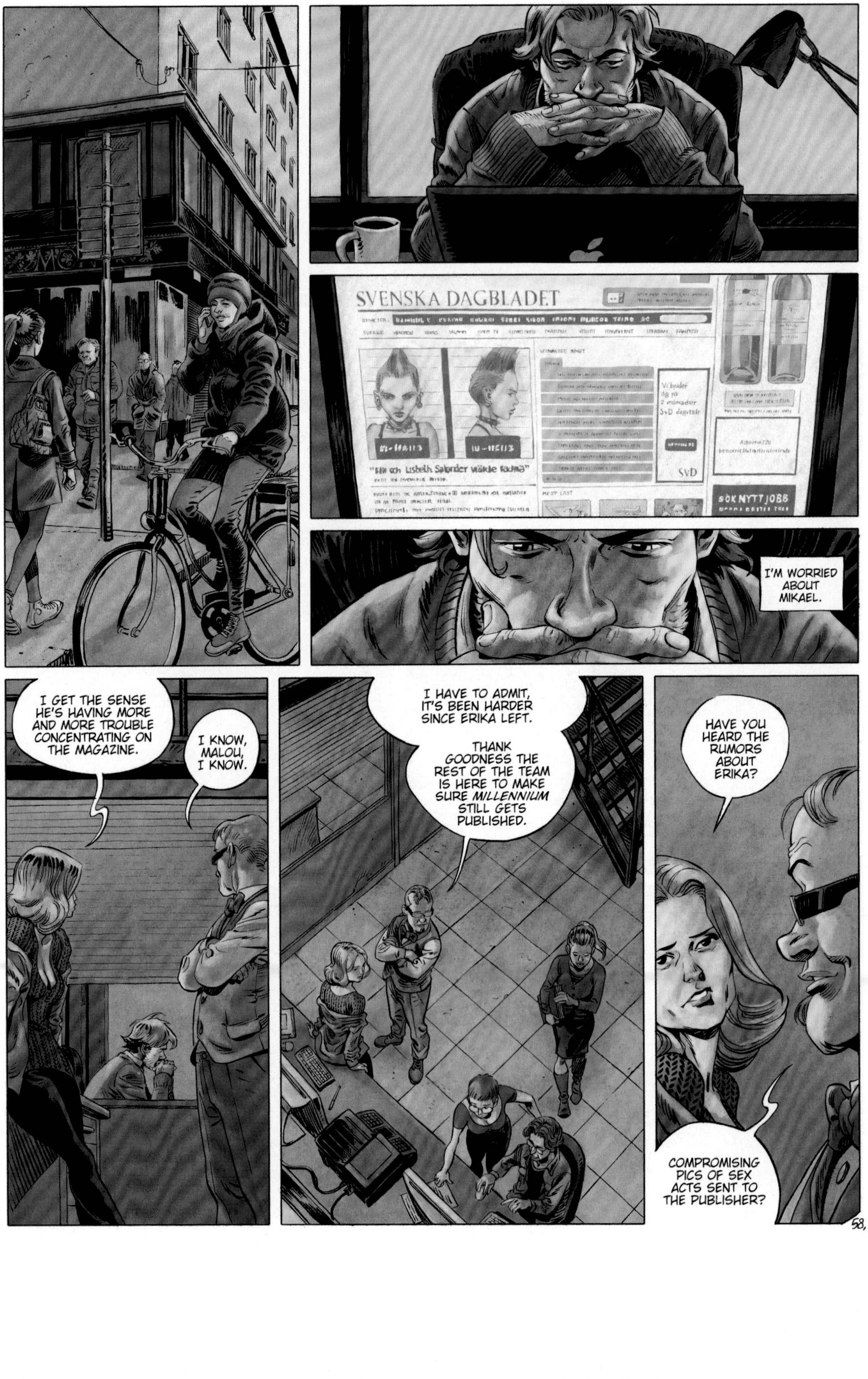
SVENSKA DAGBLADET
Vi bjuder dig på 2 månader SvD digitalt
SvD
SÖK NYTT JOBB
I'M WORRIED ABOUT MIKAEL.
I GET THE SENSE HE'S HAVING MORE AND MORE TROUBLE CONCENTRATING ON THE MAGAZINE.
I KNOW, MALOU, I KNOW.
I HAVE TO ADMIT, IT'S BEEN HARDER SINCE ERIKA LEFT.
THANK GOODNESS THE REST OF THE TEAM IS HERE TO MAKE SURE *MILLENNIUM* STILL GETS PUBLISHED.
HAVE YOU HEARD THE RUMORS ABOUT ERIKA?
COMPROMISING PICS OF SEX ACTS SENT TO THE PUBLISHER?

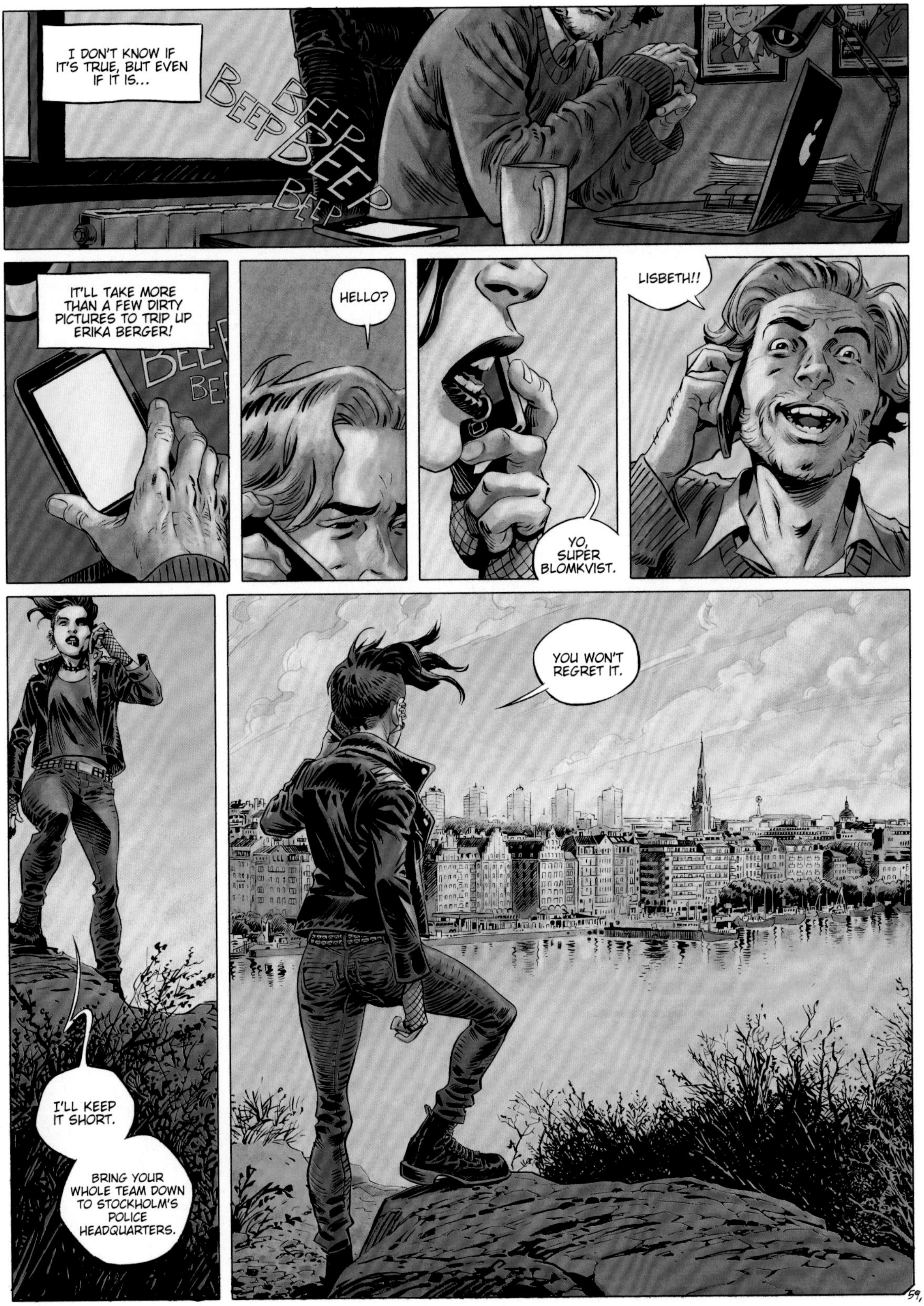
I DON'T KNOW IF IT'S TRUE, BUT EVEN IF IT IS...
BEEP BEEP BEEP BEEP
IT'LL TAKE MORE THAN A FEW DIRTY PICTURES TO TRIP UP ERIKA BERGER!
HELLO?
YO, SUPER BLOMKVIST.
LISBETH!!
I'LL KEEP IT SHORT.
BRING YOUR WHOLE TEAM DOWN TO STOCKHOLM'S POLICE HEADQUARTERS.
YOU WON'T REGRET IT.

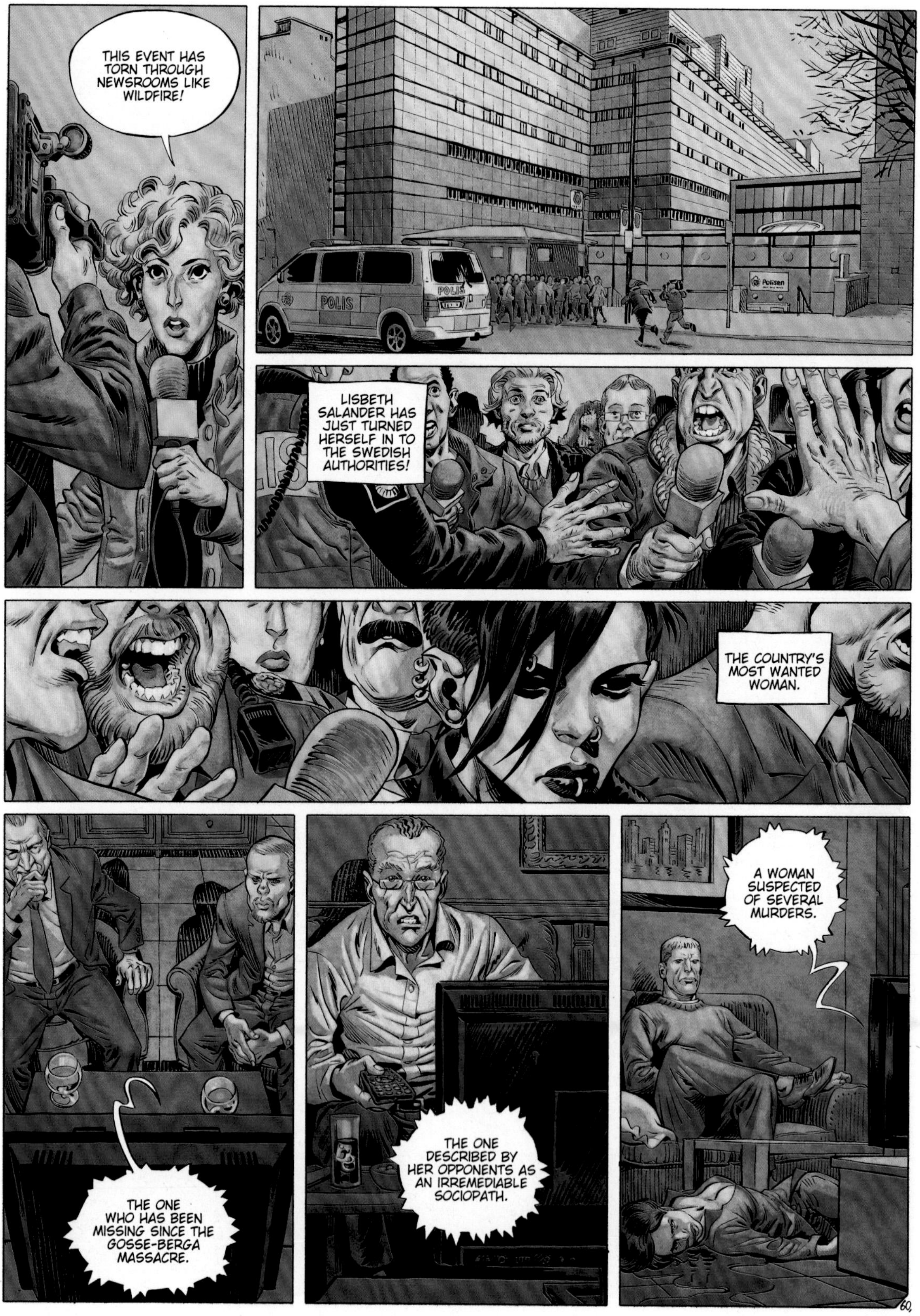
THIS EVENT HAS TORN THROUGH NEWSROOMS LIKE WILDFIRE!
POLIS
POLIS
Polisen
LISBETH SALANDER HAS JUST TURNED HERSELF IN TO THE SWEDISH AUTHORITIES!
THE COUNTRY'S MOST WANTED WOMAN.
THE ONE WHO HAS BEEN MISSING SINCE THE GOSSE-BERGA MASSACRE.
THE ONE DESCRIBED BY HER OPPONENTS AS AN IRREMEDIABLE SOCIOPATH.
A WOMAN SUSPECTED OF SEVERAL MURDERS.

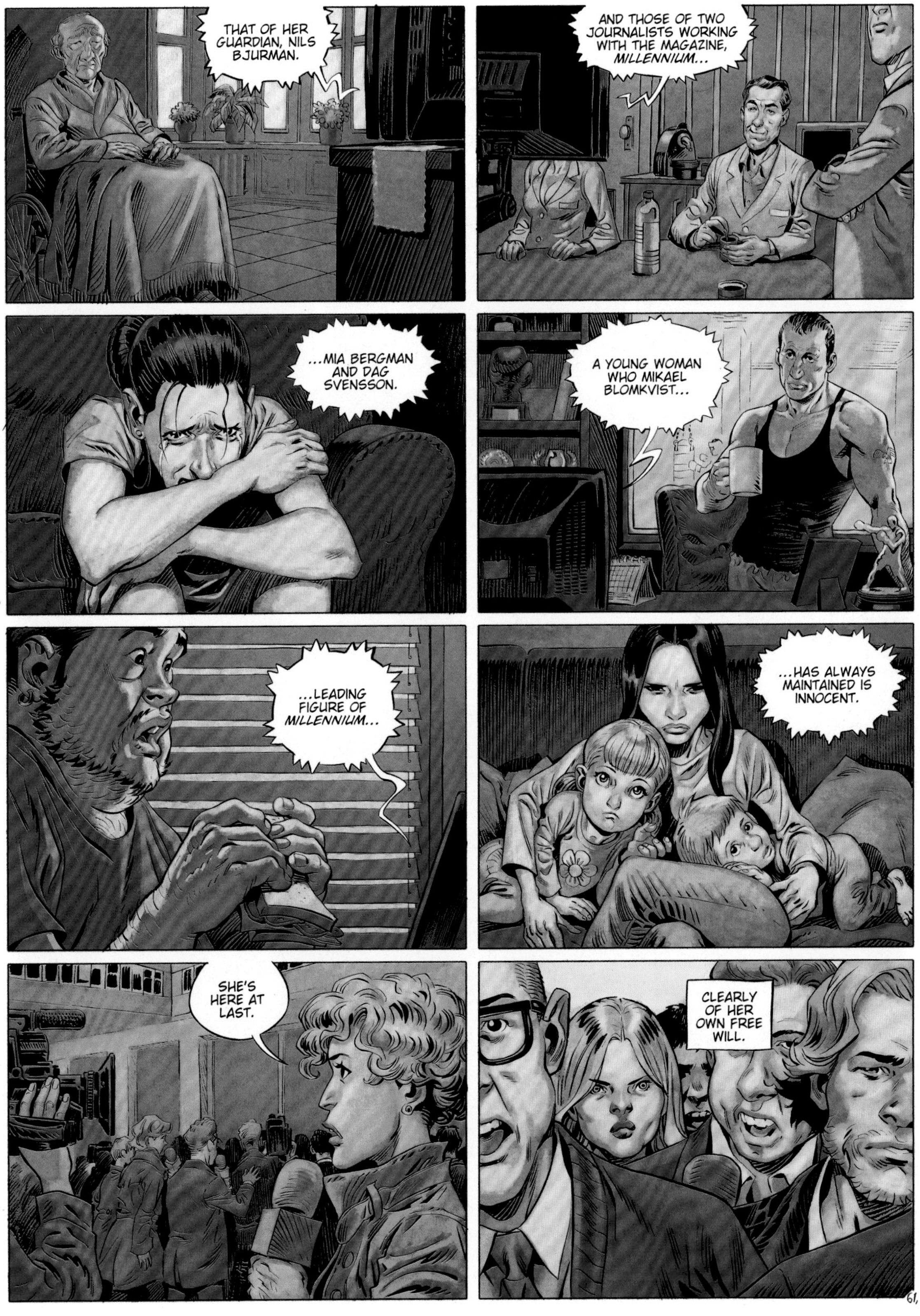
THAT OF HER GUARDIAN, NILS BJURMAN.
AND THOSE OF TWO JOURNALISTS WORKING WITH THE MAGAZINE, *MILLENNIUM*...
...MIA BERGMAN AND DAG SVENSSON.
A YOUNG WOMAN WHO MIKAEL BLOMKVIST...
...LEADING FIGURE OF *MILLENNIUM*...
...HAS ALWAYS MAINTAINED IS INNOCENT.
SHE'S HERE AT LAST.
CLEARLY OF HER OWN FREE WILL.

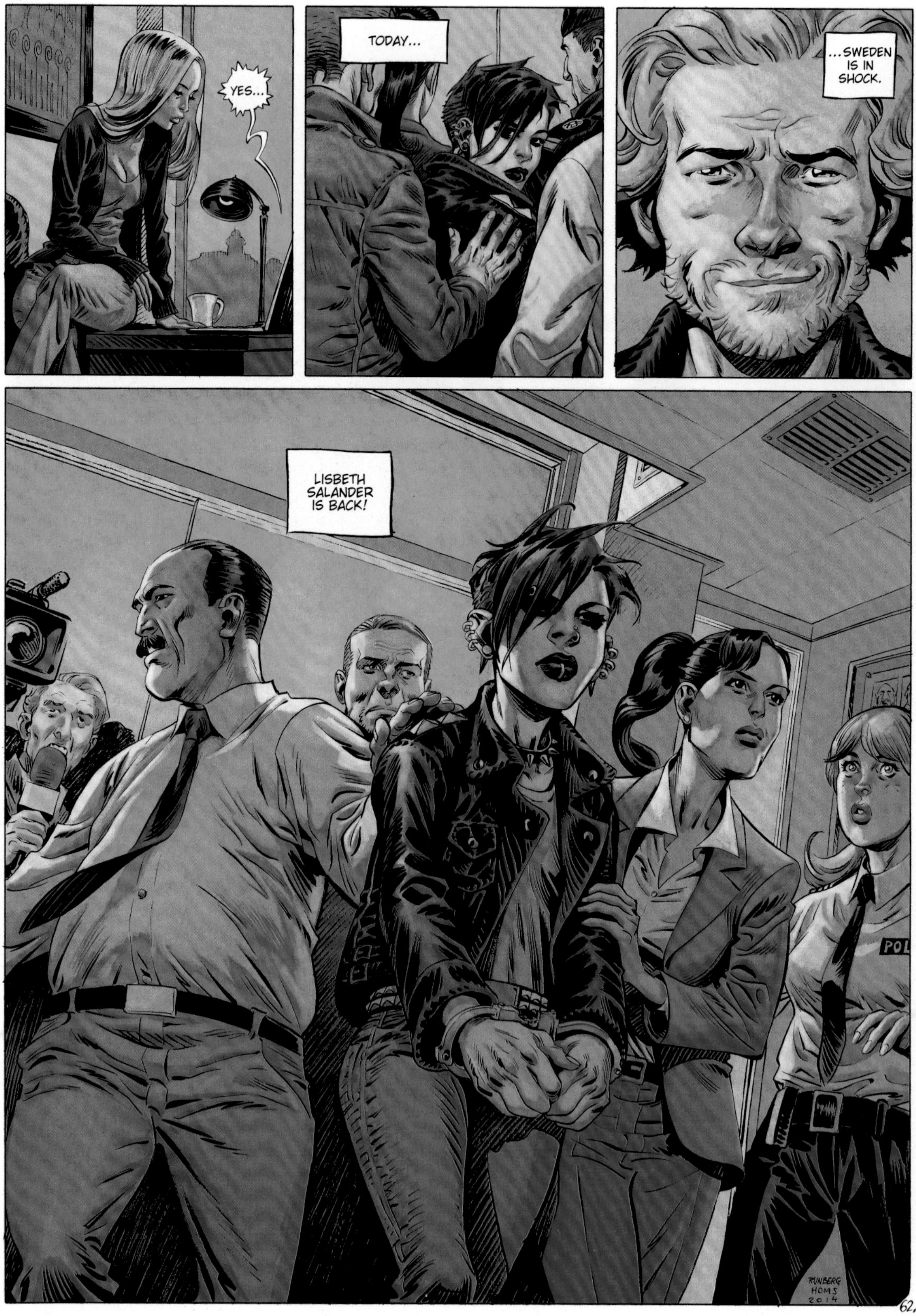
YES...
TODAY...
...SWEDEN IS IN SHOCK.
LISBETH SALANDER IS BACK!
POL
RUNBERG HOMS 2014

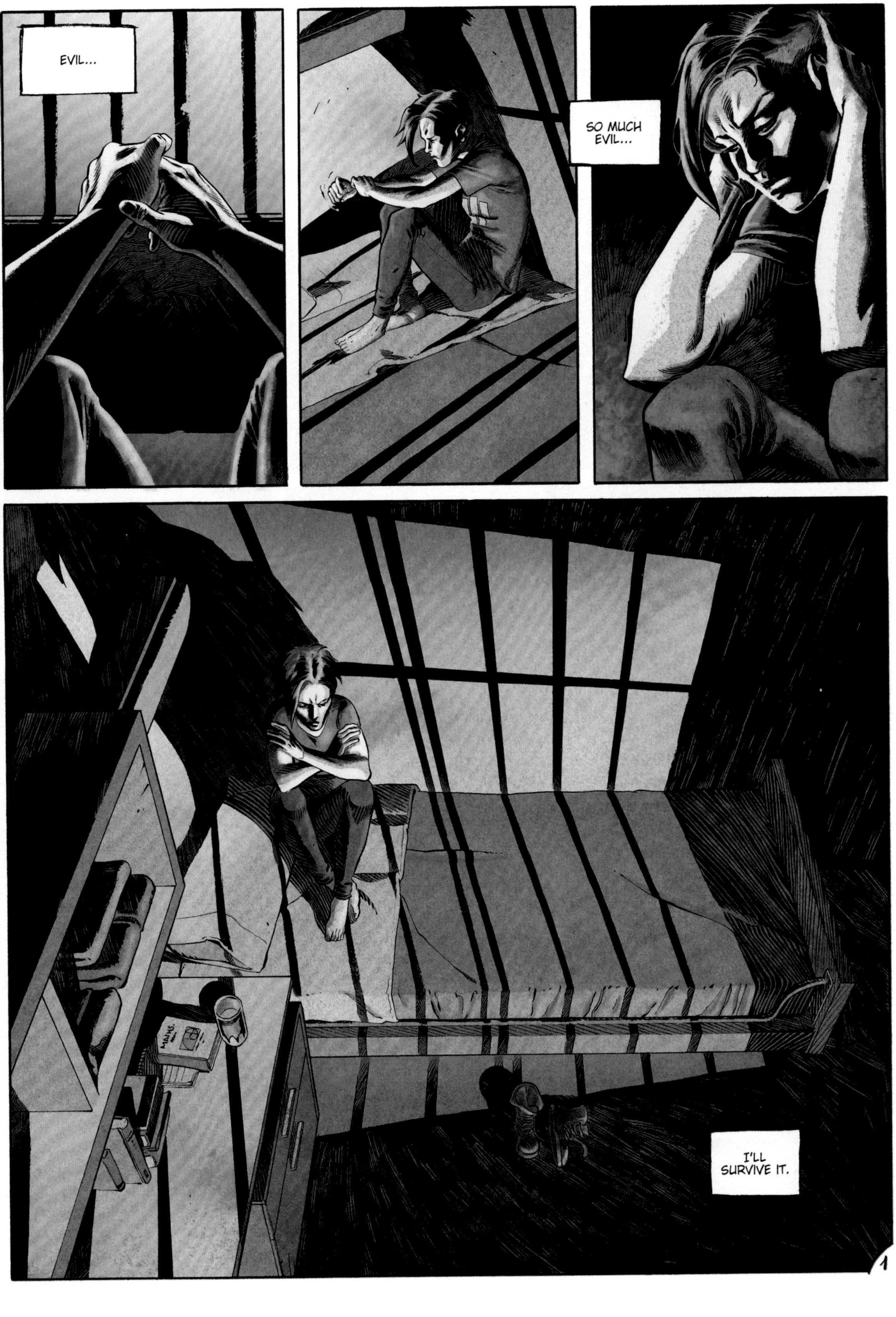
EVIL...
SO MUCH EVIL...
I'LL SURVIVE IT.

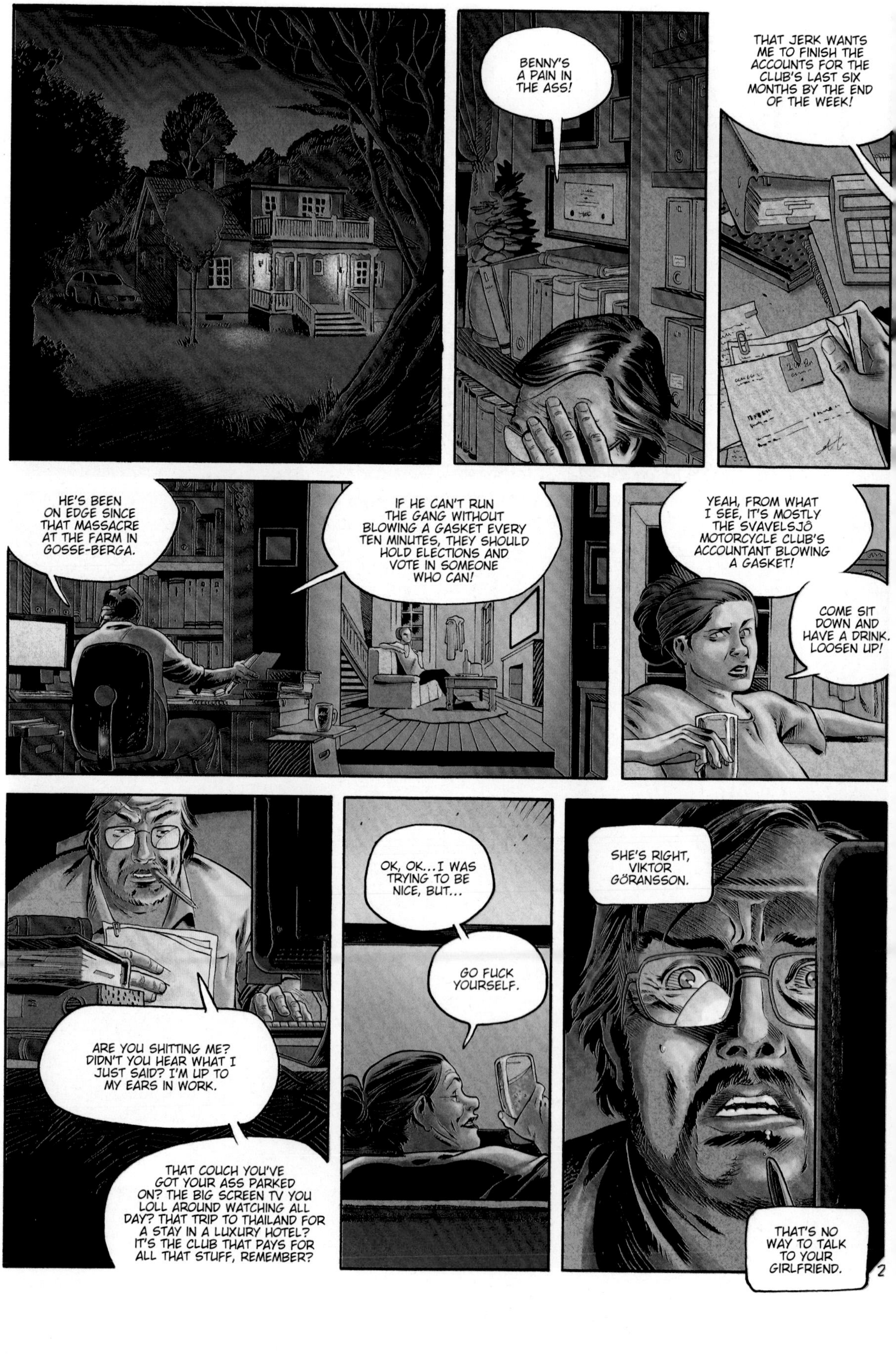
BENNY'S A PAIN IN THE ASS!
THAT JERK WANTS ME TO FINISH THE ACCOUNTS FOR THE CLUB'S LAST SIX MONTHS BY THE END OF THE WEEK!
HE'S BEEN ON EDGE SINCE THAT MASSACRE AT THE FARM IN GOSSE-BERGA.
IF HE CAN'T RUN THE GANG WITHOUT BLOWING A GASKET EVERY TEN MINUTES, THEY SHOULD HOLD ELECTIONS AND VOTE IN SOMEONE WHO CAN!
YEAH, FROM WHAT I SEE, IT'S MOSTLY THE SVAVELSJÖ MOTORCYCLE CLUB'S ACCOUNTANT BLOWING A GASKET!
COME SIT DOWN AND HAVE A DRINK. LOOSEN UP!
ARE YOU SHITTING ME? DIDN'T YOU HEAR WHAT I JUST SAID? I'M UP TO MY EARS IN WORK.
THAT COUCH YOU'VE GOT YOUR ASS PARKED ON? THE BIG SCREEN TV YOU LOLL AROUND WATCHING ALL DAY? THAT TRIP TO THAILAND FOR A STAY IN A LUXURY HOTEL? IT'S THE CLUB THAT PAYS FOR ALL THAT STUFF, REMEMBER?
OK, OK... I WAS TRYING TO BE NICE, BUT...
GO FUCK YOURSELF.
SHE'S RIGHT, VIKTOR GÖRANSSON.
THAT'S NO WAY TO TALK TO YOUR GIRLFRIEND.

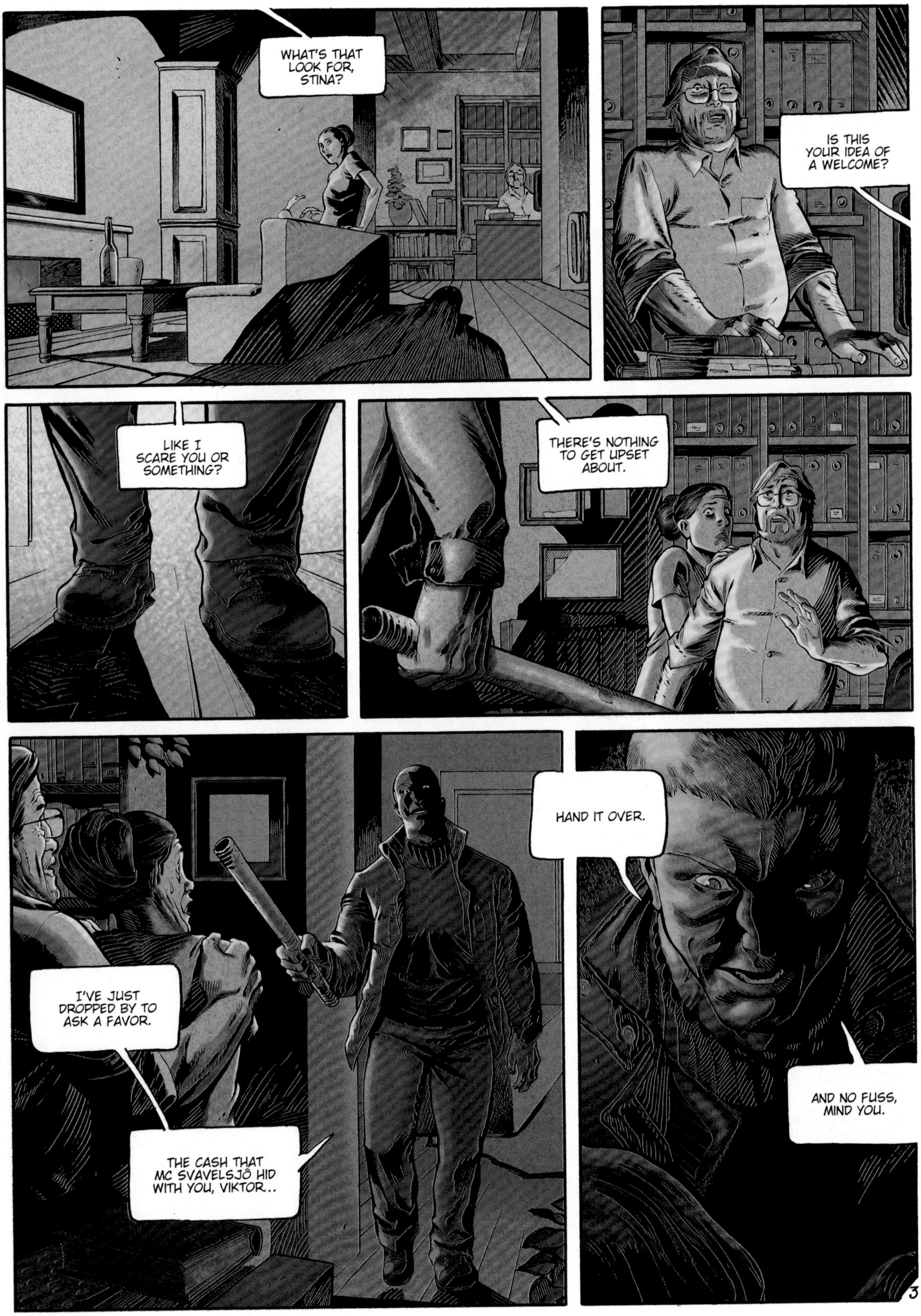
WHAT'S THAT LOOK FOR, STINA?
IS THIS YOUR IDEA OF A WELCOME?
LIKE I SCARE YOU OR SOMETHING?
THERE'S NOTHING TO GET UPSET ABOUT.
I'VE JUST DROPPED BY TO ASK A FAVOR.
THE CASH THAT MC SVAVELSJÖ HID WITH YOU, VIKTOR..
HAND IT OVER.
AND NO FUSS, MIND YOU.

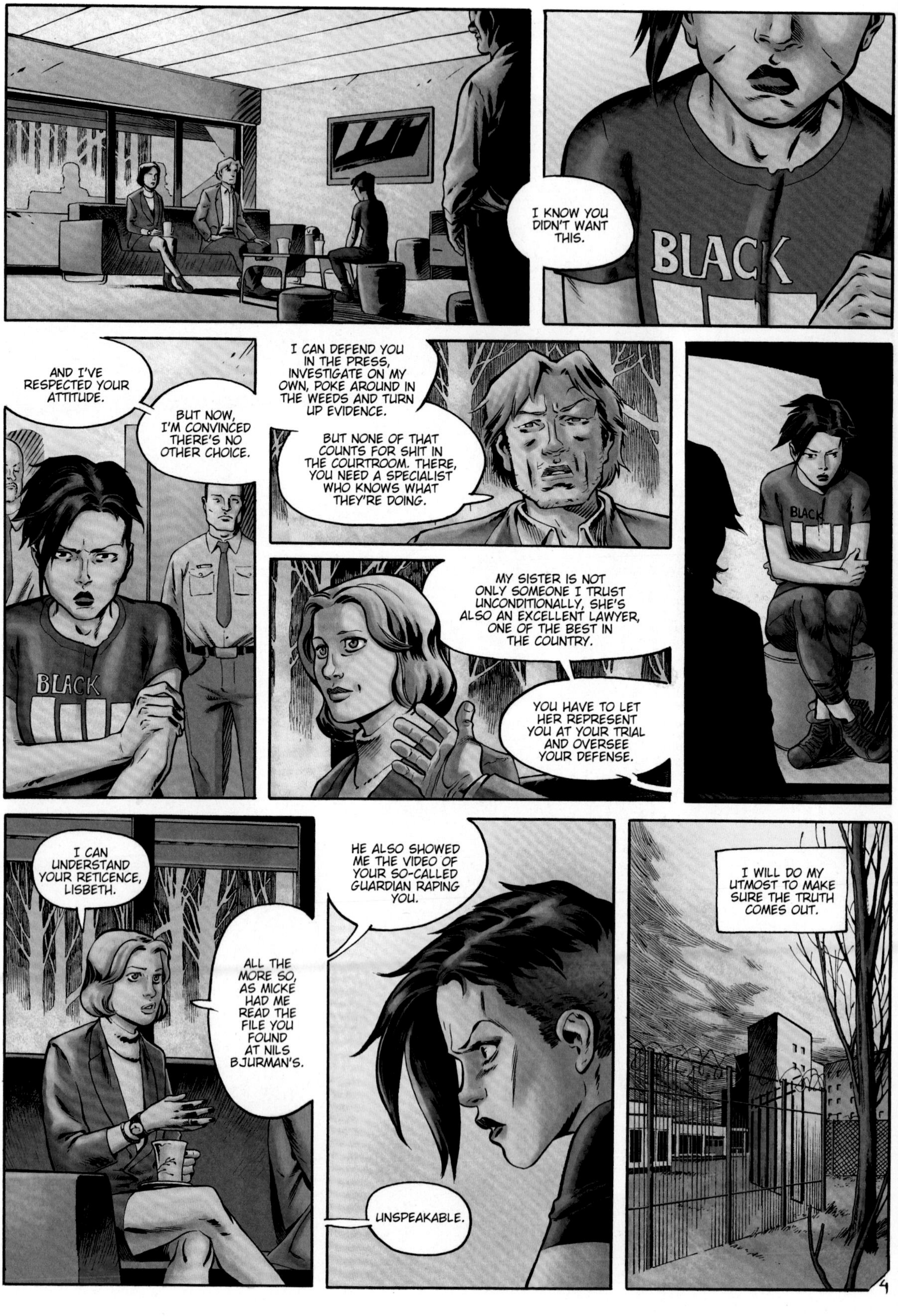
I KNOW YOU DIDN'T WANT THIS.
BLACK
AND I'VE RESPECTED YOUR ATTITUDE.
BUT NOW, I'M CONVINCED THERE'S NO OTHER CHOICE.
BLACK
I CAN DEFEND YOU IN THE PRESS, INVESTIGATE ON MY OWN, POKE AROUND IN THE WEEDS AND TURN UP EVIDENCE.
BUT NONE OF THAT COUNTS FOR SHIT IN THE COURTROOM. THERE, YOU NEED A SPECIALIST WHO KNOWS WHAT THEY'RE DOING.
MY SISTER IS NOT ONLY SOMEONE I TRUST UNCONDITIONALLY, SHE'S ALSO AN EXCELLENT LAWYER, ONE OF THE BEST IN THE COUNTRY.
YOU HAVE TO LET HER REPRESENT YOU AT YOUR TRIAL AND OVERSEE YOUR DEFENSE.
BLACK
I CAN UNDERSTAND YOUR RETICENCE, LISBETH.
ALL THE MORE SO, AS MICKE HAD ME READ THE FILE YOU FOUND AT NILS BJURMAN'S.
HE ALSO SHOWED ME THE VIDEO OF YOUR SO-CALLED GUARDIAN RAPING YOU.
UNSPEAKABLE.
I WILL DO MY UTMOST TO MAKE SURE THE TRUTH COMES OUT.

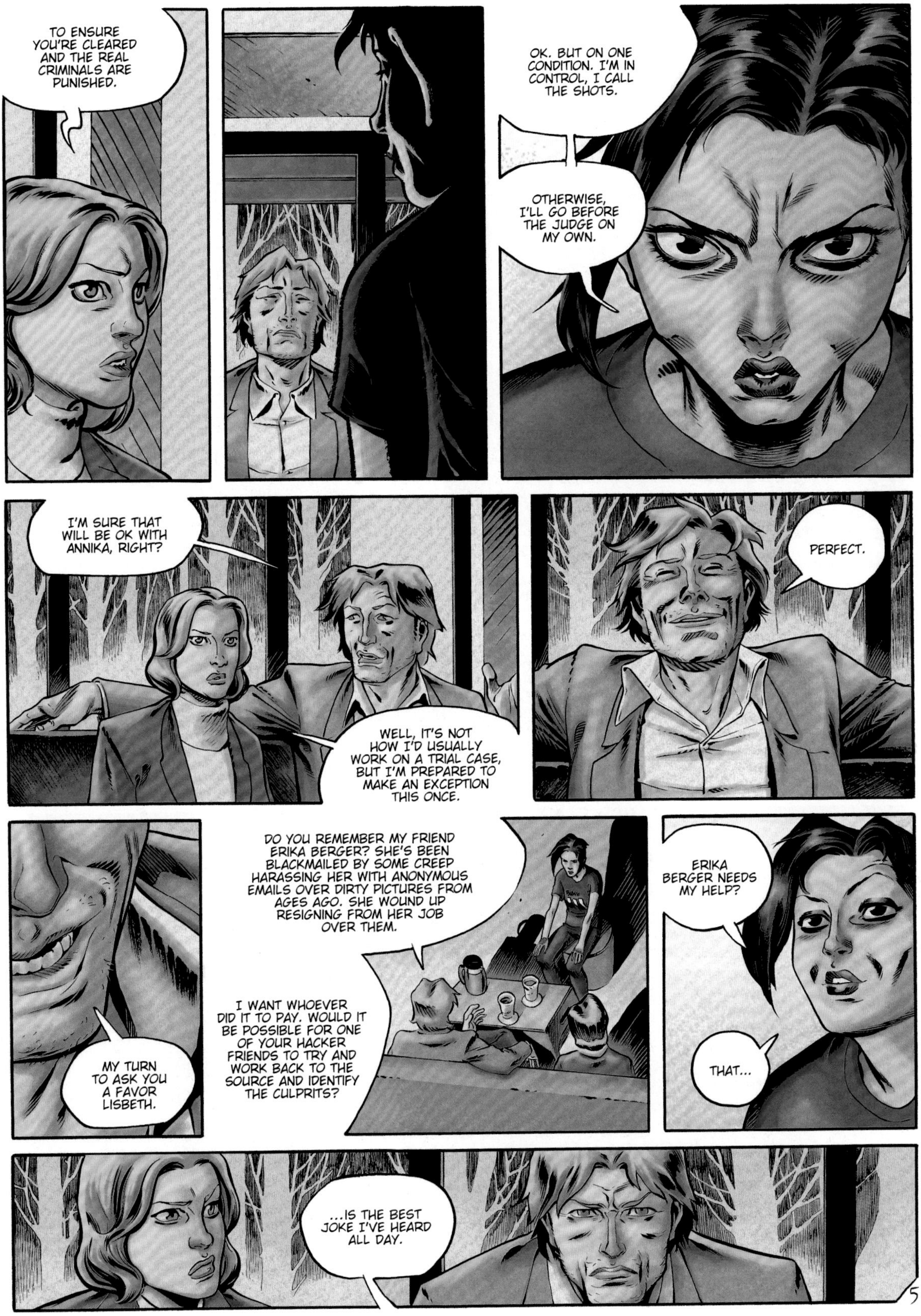
TO ENSURE YOU'RE CLEARED AND THE REAL CRIMINALS ARE PUNISHED.
OK. BUT ON ONE CONDITION. I'M IN CONTROL, I CALL THE SHOTS.
OTHERWISE, I'LL GO BEFORE THE JUDGE ON MY OWN.
I'M SURE THAT WILL BE OK WITH ANNIKA, RIGHT?
WELL, IT'S NOT HOW I'D USUALLY WORK ON A TRIAL CASE, BUT I'M PREPARED TO MAKE AN EXCEPTION THIS ONCE.
PERFECT.
MY TURN TO ASK YOU A FAVOR LISBETH.
DO YOU REMEMBER MY FRIEND ERIKA BERGER? SHE'S BEEN BLACKMAILED BY SOME CREEP HARASSING HER WITH ANONYMOUS EMAILS OVER DIRTY PICTURES FROM AGES AGO. SHE WOUND UP RESIGNING FROM HER JOB OVER THEM.
I WANT WHOEVER DID IT TO PAY. WOULD IT BE POSSIBLE FOR ONE OF YOUR HACKER FRIENDS TO TRY AND WORK BACK TO THE SOURCE AND IDENTIFY THE CULPRITS?
ERIKA BERGER NEEDS MY HELP?
THAT...
...IS THE BEST JOKE I'VE HEARD ALL DAY.

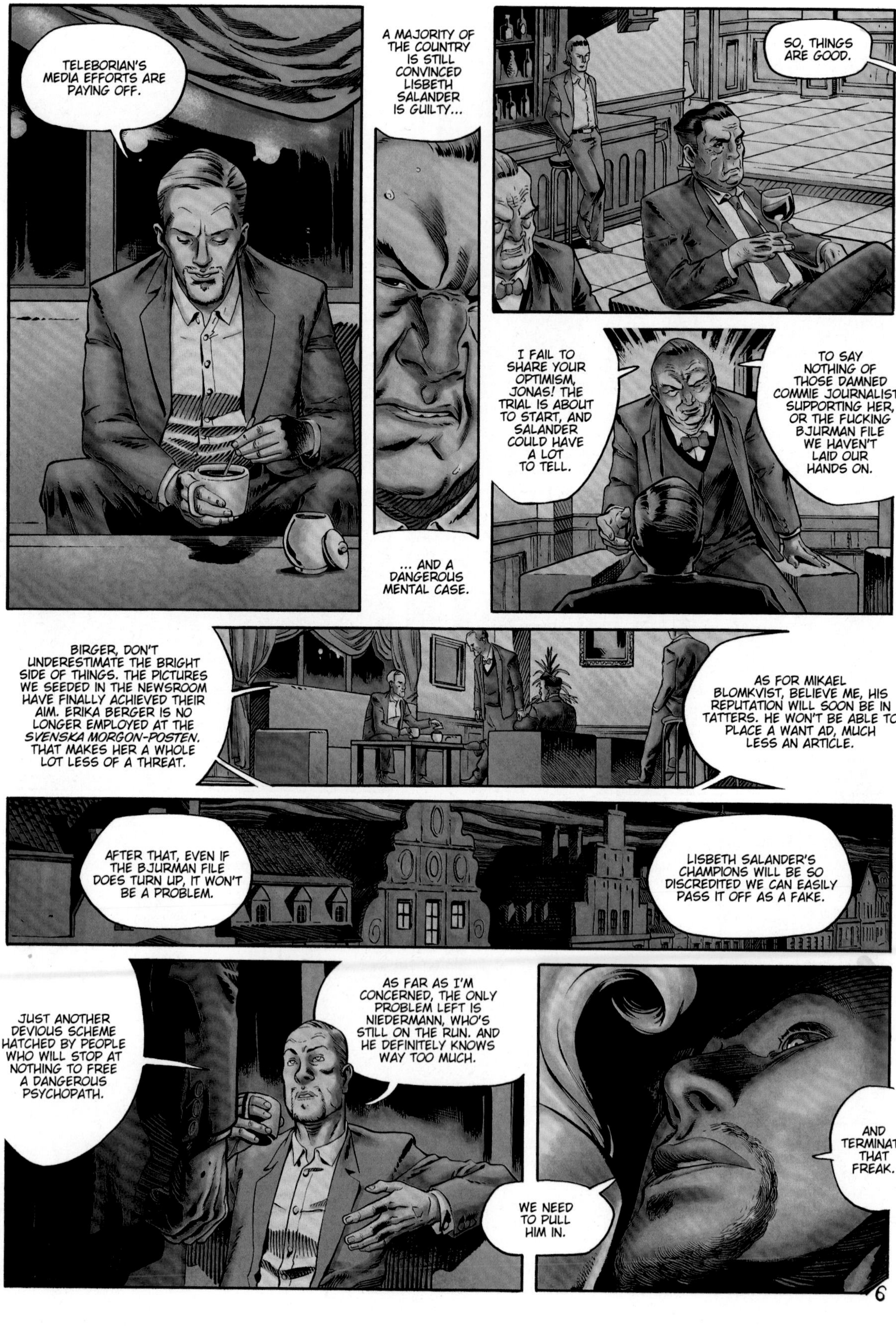
TELEBORIAN'S MEDIA EFFORTS ARE PAYING OFF.
A MAJORITY OF THE COUNTRY IS STILL CONVINCED LISBETH SALANDER IS GUILTY...
... AND A DANGEROUS MENTAL CASE.
SO, THINGS ARE GOOD.
I FAIL TO SHARE YOUR OPTIMISM, JONAS! THE TRIAL IS ABOUT TO START, AND SALANDER COULD HAVE A LOT TO TELL.
TO SAY NOTHING OF THOSE DAMNED COMMIE JOURNALISTS SUPPORTING HER, OR THE FUCKING BJURMAN FILE WE HAVEN'T LAID OUR HANDS ON.
BIRGER, DON'T UNDERESTIMATE THE BRIGHT SIDE OF THINGS. THE PICTURES WE SEEDED IN THE NEWSROOM HAVE FINALLY ACHIEVED THEIR AIM. ERIKA BERGER IS NO LONGER EMPLOYED AT THE *SVENSKA MORGON-POSTEN*. THAT MAKES HER A WHOLE LOT LESS OF A THREAT.
AS FOR MIKAEL BLOMKVIST, BELIEVE ME, HIS REPUTATION WILL SOON BE IN TATTERS. HE WON'T BE ABLE TO PLACE A WANT AD, MUCH LESS AN ARTICLE.
AFTER THAT, EVEN IF THE BJURMAN FILE DOES TURN UP, IT WON'T BE A PROBLEM.
LISBETH SALANDER'S CHAMPIONS WILL BE SO DISCREDITED WE CAN EASILY PASS IT OFF AS A FAKE.
JUST ANOTHER DEVIOUS SCHEME HATCHED BY PEOPLE WHO WILL STOP AT NOTHING TO FREE A DANGEROUS PSYCHOPATH.
AS FAR AS I'M CONCERNED, THE ONLY PROBLEM LEFT IS NIEDERMANN, WHO'S STILL ON THE RUN. AND HE DEFINITELY KNOWS WAY TOO MUCH.
WE NEED TO PULL HIM IN.
AND TERMINATE THAT FREAK.

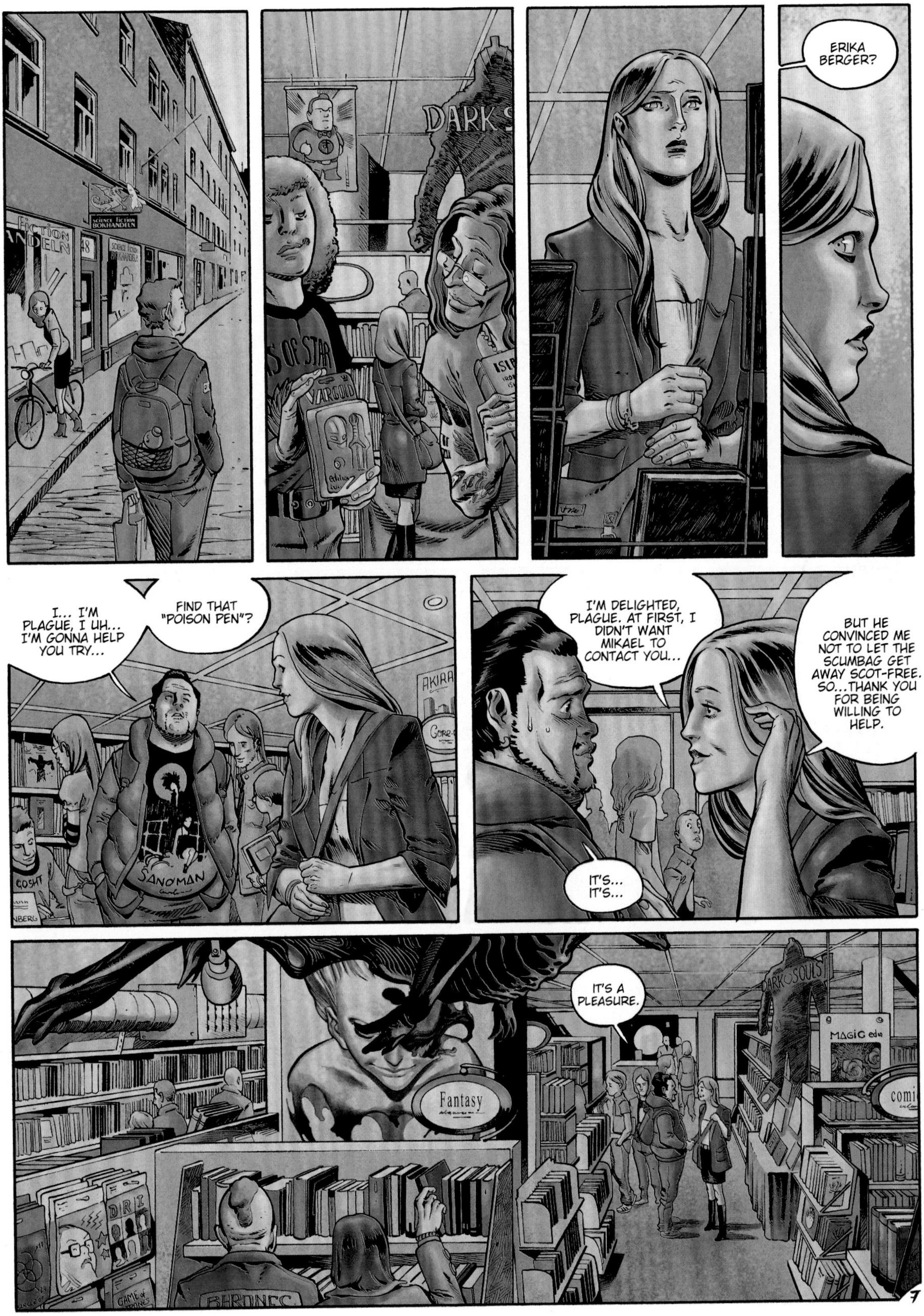
science fiction BOKHANDELN
ERIKA BERGER?
I... I'M PLAGUE, I UH... I'M GONNA HELP YOU TRY...
FIND THAT "POISON PEN"?
SANDMAN
AKIRA
I'M DELIGHTED, PLAGUE. AT FIRST, I DIDN'T WANT MIKAEL TO CONTACT YOU...
BUT HE CONVINCED ME NOT TO LET THE SCUMBAG GET AWAY SCOT-FREE. SO...THANK YOU FOR BEING WILLING TO HELP.
IT'S... IT'S...
IT'S A PLEASURE.
Fantasy
DARKSOULS
MAGIC
GAME of THRONES

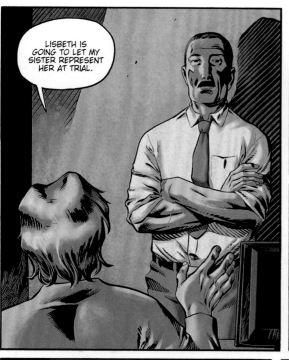

LISBETH IS GOING TO LET MY SISTER REPRESENT HER AT TRIAL.

BUT, MORE IMPORTANTLY, SHE'S GIVEN US NEW INFORMATION.

I'VE GOT A LEAD... A NAME.

SOMEONE WHO MIGHT BE INVOLVED IN WHAT'S HAPPENED TO HER SINCE SHE WAS INTERNED AS A CHILD, SOMEONE WHO'S IN TOUCH WITH TELEBORIAN...

HE'S FORMER SÄPO, NOW RETIRED.

BIRGER WADENSJÖÖ.

DOES THE NAME RING A BELL FOR ANYONE?

BIRGER WADENSJÖÖ? I'VE HEARD OF HIM. HE HASN'T BEEN ON ACTIVE DUTY FOR A DECADE OR SO, IT'S TRUE...

BUT HE'S HIGHLY RESPECTED WITHIN THE SECRET SERVICE, AND HIS RECORD IS IMMACULATE.

IT'S ALWAYS LIKE THAT ON THE SURFACE, BUT WHEN YOU DIG DOWN A BIT...

HOW DOES HE LEAN, POLITICALLY?

HE'S NOT EXACTLY LEADING A REVOLUTION, IF THAT'S WHAT YOU'RE ASKING.

FROM WHAT I KNOW, WADENSJÖÖ IS A HARD-LINE CONSERVATIVE, SOME MIGHT EVEN CALL HIM... REACTIONARY.

BUT HE'S NEVER, TO MY KNOWLEDGE, SUPPORTED THE FAR RIGHT.

8

UNLESS, OF COURSE, HE BELONGED TO A SECRET SOCIETY.

MAY I REMIND YOU THAT, AMONG THE MANY CASES HOVERING AROUND THIS ONE, THERE'S THAT REPORTER WHO DROWNED, ANDERS ROLLEN?

I'D FORGOTTEN ABOUT THAT. I HADN'T STARTED YET, BUT...

YOU'RE RIGHT, WADENSJÖÖ'S NAME DID COME UP BEFORE THE WHOLE THING WAS SHELVED FOR LACK OF EVIDENCE.

ROLLEN HAD MENTIONED THE POSSIBILITY THAT DATA WAS ILLEGALLY COLLECTED ON LEFT-LEANING PERSONS BY MEMBERS OF THE SÄPO BELONGING TO A SECRET SOCIETY, BUT AFTER HE DIED, NO ONE FOLLOWED UP.

WADENSJÖÖ WAS STILL WORKING BACK THEN, RIGHT?

BUT, HOW DO YOU KNOW ALL THAT? I'M SURE WADENSJÖÖ'S NAME NEVER MADE THE PAPERS AT THE TIME.

I DIDN'T KNOW. I TRY AND FIT THINGS TOGETHER, LIKE A PUZZLE...

WHICH IS, AFTER ALL, MY JOB.

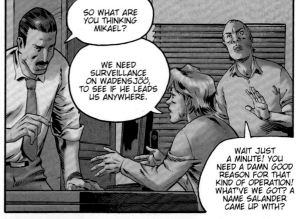

SO WHAT ARE YOU THINKING MIKAEL?

WE NEED SURVEILLANCE ON WADENSJÖÖ, TO SEE IF HE LEADS US ANYWHERE.

WAIT JUST A MINUTE! YOU NEED A DAMN GOOD REASON FOR THAT KIND OF OPERATION! WHAT'VE WE GOT? A NAME SALANDER CAME UP WITH?

THE FOREMOST REASON IS TO REPAIR THE TREMENDOUS HARM THAT SWEDEN'S INSTITUTIONS HAVE DONE TO LISBETH SALANDER!

AND, FOR THE FIRST TIME ...

...TO TRUST HER.

9

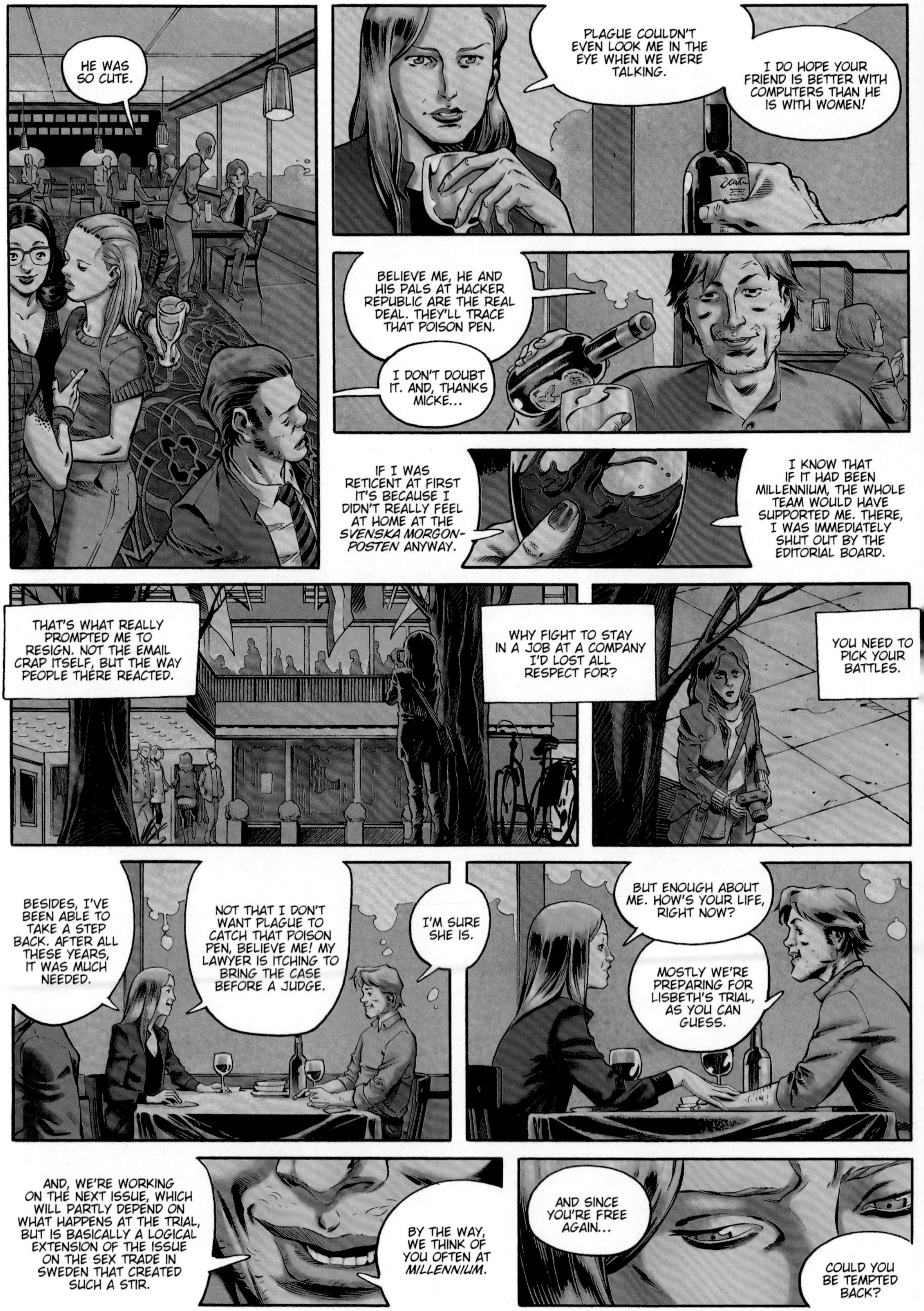
HE WAS SO CUTE.
PLAGUE COULDN'T EVEN LOOK ME IN THE EYE WHEN WE WERE TALKING.
I DO HOPE YOUR FRIEND IS BETTER WITH COMPUTERS THAN HE IS WITH WOMEN!
BELIEVE ME, HE AND HIS PALS AT HACKER REPUBLIC ARE THE REAL DEAL. THEY'LL TRACE THAT POISON PEN.
I DON'T DOUBT IT. AND, THANKS MICKE...
IF I WAS RETICENT AT FIRST IT'S BECAUSE I DIDN'T REALLY FEEL AT HOME AT THE *SVENSKA MORGON-POSTEN* ANYWAY.
I KNOW THAT IF IT HAD BEEN MILLENNIUM, THE WHOLE TEAM WOULD HAVE SUPPORTED ME. THERE, I WAS IMMEDIATELY SHUT OUT BY THE EDITORIAL BOARD.
THAT'S WHAT REALLY PROMPTED ME TO RESIGN. NOT THE EMAIL CRAP ITSELF, BUT THE WAY PEOPLE THERE REACTED.
WHY FIGHT TO STAY IN A JOB AT A COMPANY I'D LOST ALL RESPECT FOR?
YOU NEED TO PICK YOUR BATTLES.
BESIDES, I'VE BEEN ABLE TO TAKE A STEP BACK. AFTER ALL THESE YEARS, IT WAS MUCH NEEDED.
NOT THAT I DON'T WANT PLAGUE TO CATCH THAT POISON PEN, BELIEVE ME! MY LAWYER IS ITCHING TO BRING THE CASE BEFORE A JUDGE.
I'M SURE SHE IS.
BUT ENOUGH ABOUT ME. HOW'S YOUR LIFE, RIGHT NOW?
MOSTLY WE'RE PREPARING FOR LISBETH'S TRIAL, AS YOU CAN GUESS.
AND, WE'RE WORKING ON THE NEXT ISSUE, WHICH WILL PARTLY DEPEND ON WHAT HAPPENS AT THE TRIAL, BUT IS BASICALLY A LOGICAL EXTENSION OF THE ISSUE ON THE SEX TRADE IN SWEDEN THAT CREATED SUCH A STIR.
BY THE WAY, WE THINK OF YOU OFTEN AT *MILLENNIUM*.
AND SINCE YOU'RE FREE AGAIN...
COULD YOU BE TEMPTED BACK?

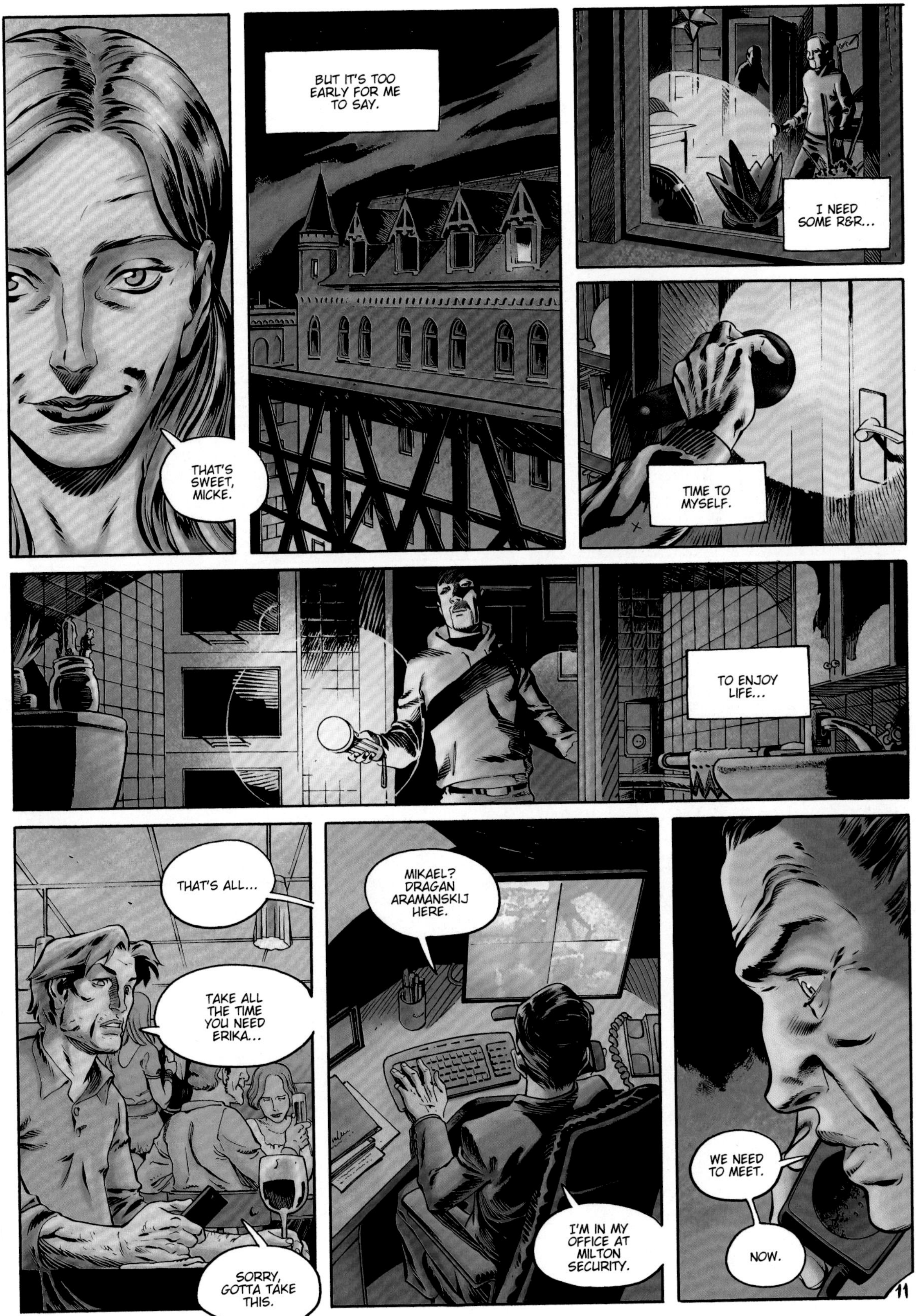
THAT'S SWEET, MICKE.
BUT IT'S TOO EARLY FOR ME TO SAY.
I NEED SOME R&R...
TIME TO MYSELF.
TO ENJOY LIFE...
THAT'S ALL...
TAKE ALL THE TIME YOU NEED ERIKA...
SORRY, GOTTA TAKE THIS.
MIKAEL? DRAGAN ARAMANSKIJ HERE.
I'M IN MY OFFICE AT MILTON SECURITY.
WE NEED TO MEET.
NOW.

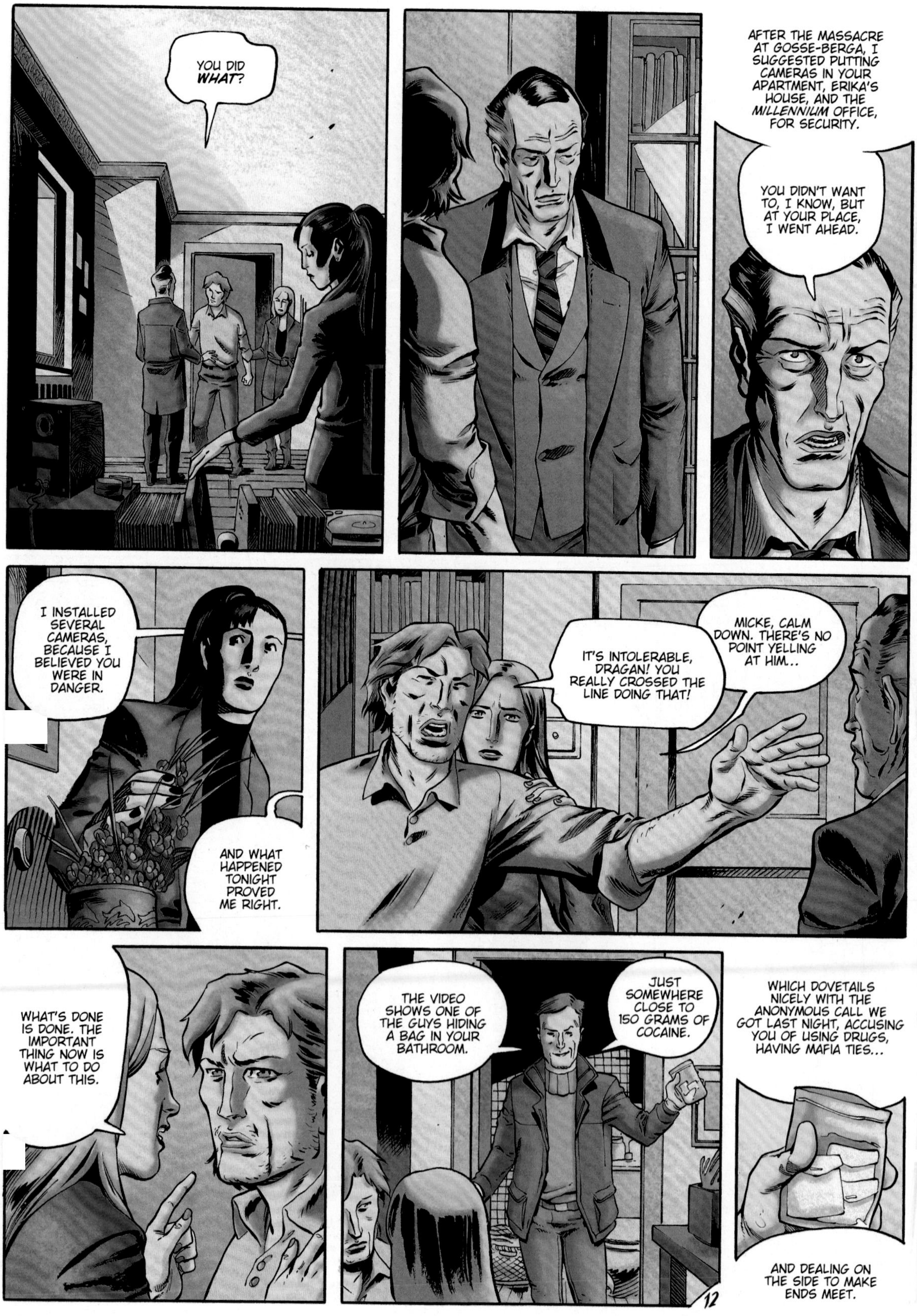

YOU DID *WHAT*?
AFTER THE MASSACRE AT GOSSE-BERGA, I SUGGESTED PUTTING CAMERAS IN YOUR APARTMENT, ERIKA'S HOUSE, AND THE *MILLENNIUM* OFFICE, FOR SECURITY.
YOU DIDN'T WANT TO, I KNOW, BUT AT YOUR PLACE, I WENT AHEAD.
I INSTALLED SEVERAL CAMERAS, BECAUSE I BELIEVED YOU WERE IN DANGER.
AND WHAT HAPPENED TONIGHT PROVED ME RIGHT.
IT'S INTOLERABLE, DRAGAN! YOU REALLY CROSSED THE LINE DOING THAT!
MICKE, CALM DOWN. THERE'S NO POINT YELLING AT HIM...
WHAT'S DONE IS DONE. THE IMPORTANT THING NOW IS WHAT TO DO ABOUT THIS.
THE VIDEO SHOWS ONE OF THE GUYS HIDING A BAG IN YOUR BATHROOM.
JUST SOMEWHERE CLOSE TO 150 GRAMS OF COCAINE.
WHICH DOVETAILS NICELY WITH THE ANONYMOUS CALL WE GOT LAST NIGHT, ACCUSING YOU OF USING DRUGS, HAVING MAFIA TIES...
AND DEALING ON THE SIDE TO MAKE ENDS MEET.

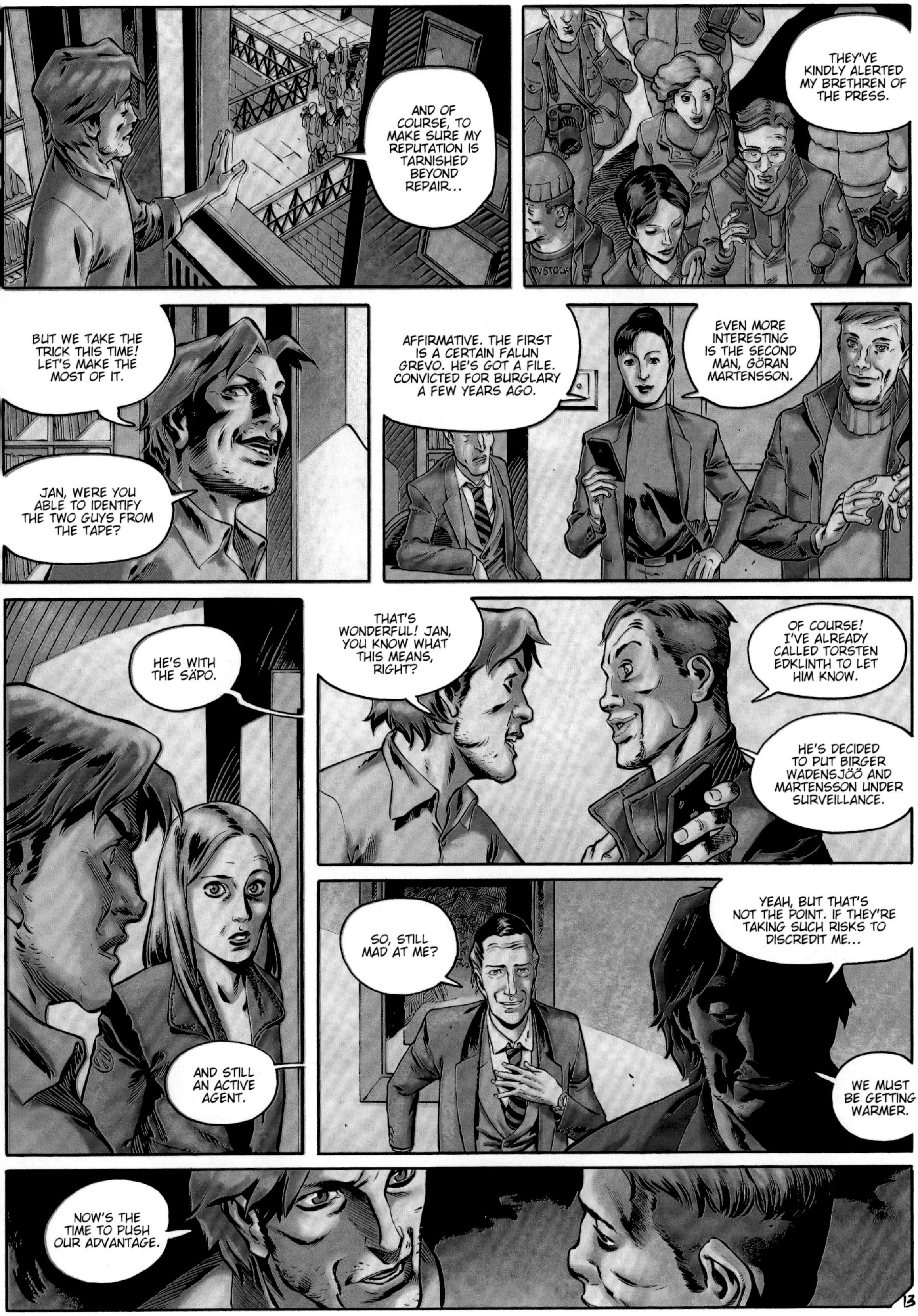
AND OF COURSE, TO MAKE SURE MY REPUTATION IS TARNISHED BEYOND REPAIR...
THEY'VE KINDLY ALERTED MY BRETHREN OF THE PRESS.
TV STOCK
BUT WE TAKE THE TRICK THIS TIME! LET'S MAKE THE MOST OF IT.
JAN, WERE YOU ABLE TO IDENTIFY THE TWO GUYS FROM THE TAPE?
AFFIRMATIVE. THE FIRST IS A CERTAIN FALUN GREVO. HE'S GOT A FILE. CONVICTED FOR BURGLARY A FEW YEARS AGO.
EVEN MORE INTERESTING IS THE SECOND MAN, GÖRAN MARTENSSON.
HE'S WITH THE SÄPO.
AND STILL AN ACTIVE AGENT.
THAT'S WONDERFUL! JAN, YOU KNOW WHAT THIS MEANS, RIGHT?
OF COURSE! I'VE ALREADY CALLED TORSTEN EDKLINTH TO LET HIM KNOW.
HE'S DECIDED TO PUT BIRGER WADENSJÖÖ AND MARTENSSON UNDER SURVEILLANCE.
SO, STILL MAD AT ME?
YEAH, BUT THAT'S NOT THE POINT. IF THEY'RE TAKING SUCH RISKS TO DISCREDIT ME...
WE MUST BE GETTING WARMER.
NOW'S THE TIME TO PUSH OUR ADVANTAGE.

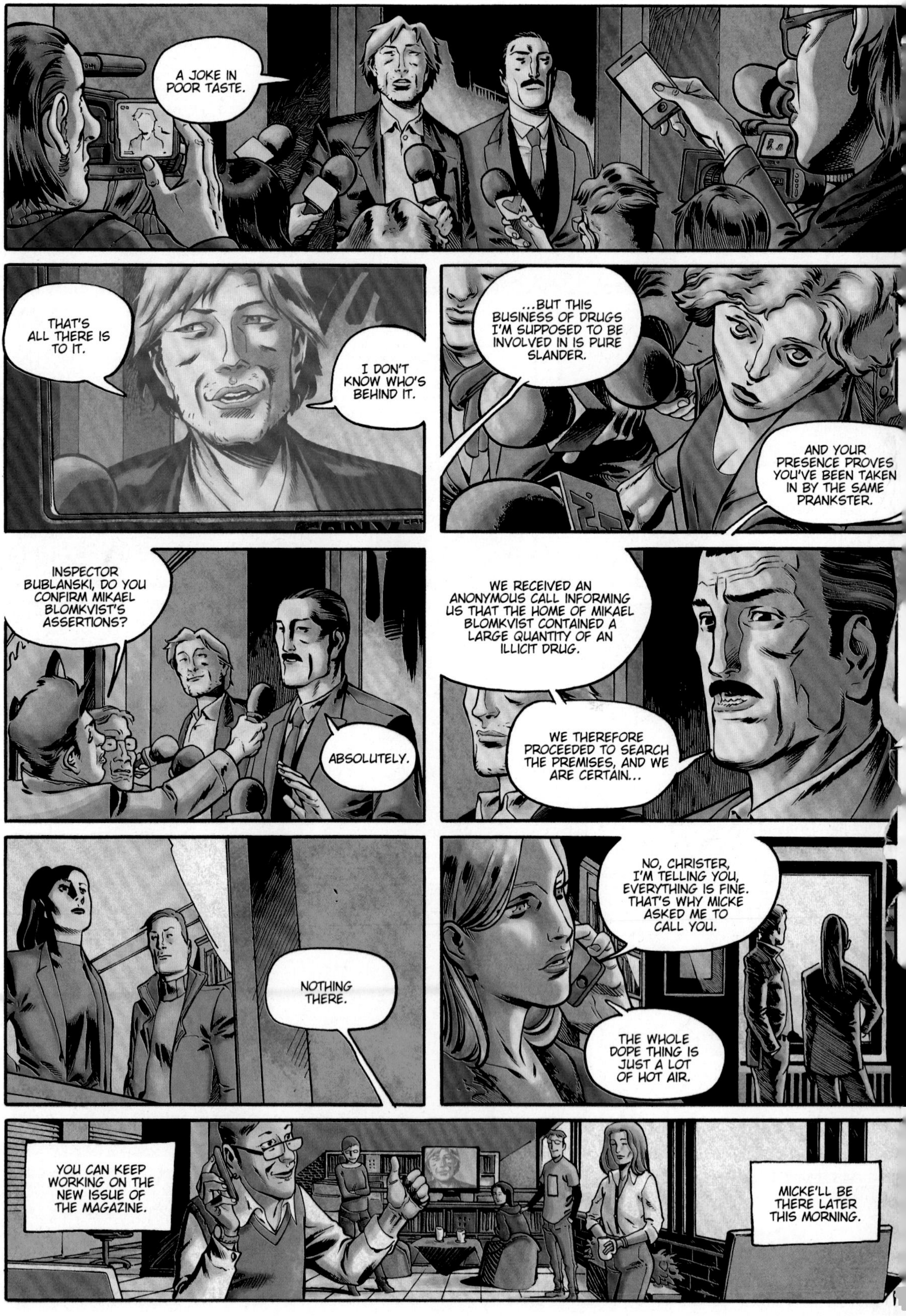
A JOKE IN POOR TASTE.
THAT'S ALL THERE IS TO IT.
I DON'T KNOW WHO'S BEHIND IT.
...BUT THIS BUSINESS OF DRUGS I'M SUPPOSED TO BE INVOLVED IN IS PURE SLANDER.
AND YOUR PRESENCE PROVES YOU'VE BEEN TAKEN IN BY THE SAME PRANKSTER.
INSPECTOR BUBLANSKI, DO YOU CONFIRM MIKAEL BLOMKVIST'S ASSERTIONS?
ABSOLUTELY.
WE RECEIVED AN ANONYMOUS CALL INFORMING US THAT THE HOME OF MIKAEL BLOMKVIST CONTAINED A LARGE QUANTITY OF AN ILLICIT DRUG.
WE THEREFORE PROCEEDED TO SEARCH THE PREMISES, AND WE ARE CERTAIN...
NOTHING THERE.
NO, CHRISTER, I'M TELLING YOU, EVERYTHING IS FINE. THAT'S WHY MICKE ASKED ME TO CALL YOU.
THE WHOLE DOPE THING IS JUST A LOT OF HOT AIR.
YOU CAN KEEP WORKING ON THE NEW ISSUE OF THE MAGAZINE.
MICKE'LL BE THERE LATER THIS MORNING.

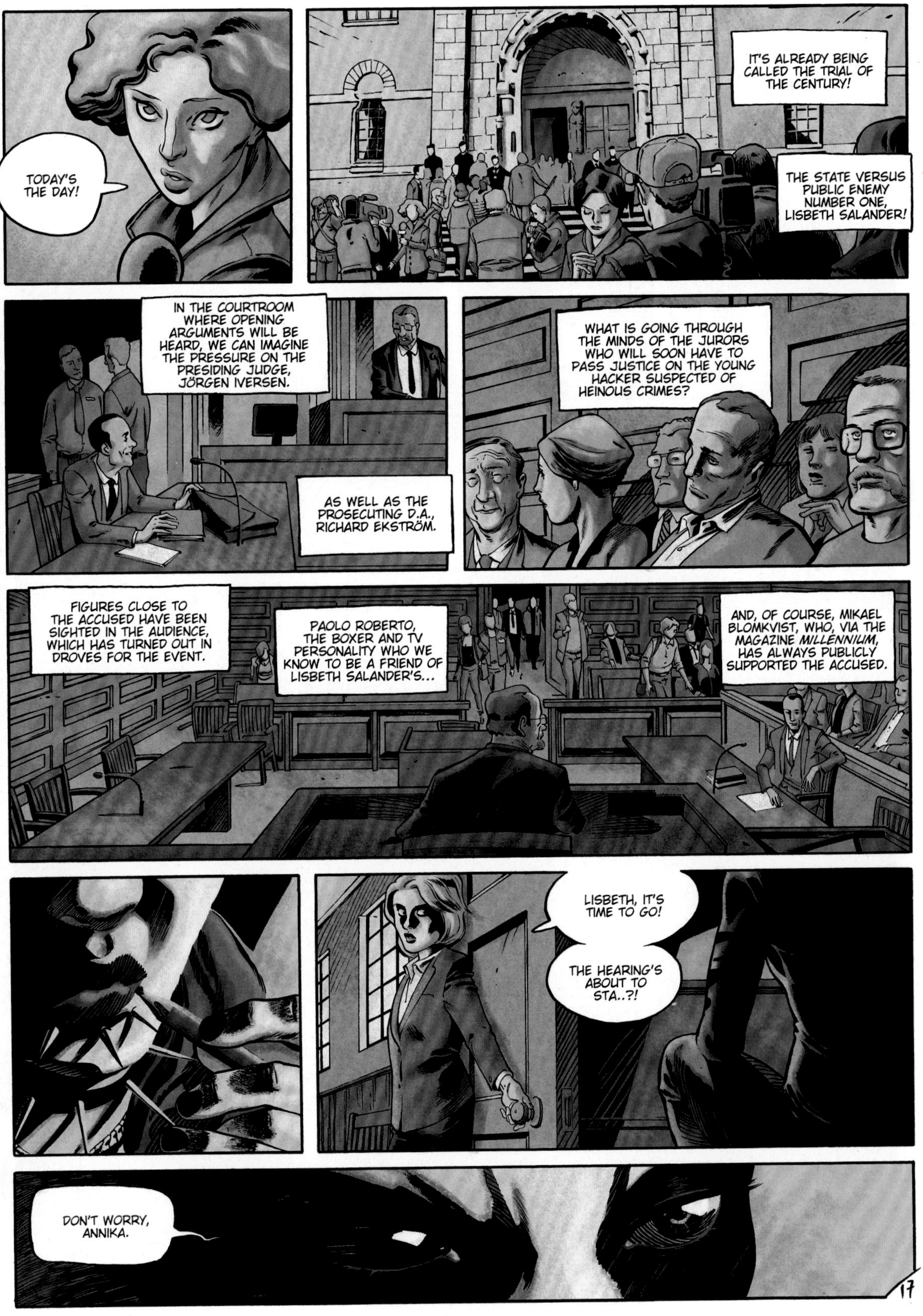
TODAY'S THE DAY!
IT'S ALREADY BEING CALLED THE TRIAL OF THE CENTURY!
THE STATE VERSUS PUBLIC ENEMY NUMBER ONE, LISBETH SALANDER!
IN THE COURTROOM WHERE OPENING ARGUMENTS WILL BE HEARD, WE CAN IMAGINE THE PRESSURE ON THE PRESIDING JUDGE, JÖRGEN IVERSEN.
AS WELL AS THE PROSECUTING D.A., RICHARD EKSTRÖM.
WHAT IS GOING THROUGH THE MINDS OF THE JURORS WHO WILL SOON HAVE TO PASS JUSTICE ON THE YOUNG HACKER SUSPECTED OF HEINOUS CRIMES?
FIGURES CLOSE TO THE ACCUSED HAVE BEEN SIGHTED IN THE AUDIENCE, WHICH HAS TURNED OUT IN DROVES FOR THE EVENT.
PAOLO ROBERTO, THE BOXER AND TV PERSONALITY WHO WE KNOW TO BE A FRIEND OF LISBETH SALANDER'S...
AND, OF COURSE, MIKAEL BLOMKVIST, WHO, VIA THE MAGAZINE *MILLENNIUM*, HAS ALWAYS PUBLICLY SUPPORTED THE ACCUSED.
LISBETH, IT'S TIME TO GO!
THE HEARING'S ABOUT TO STA..?!
DON'T WORRY, ANNIKA.

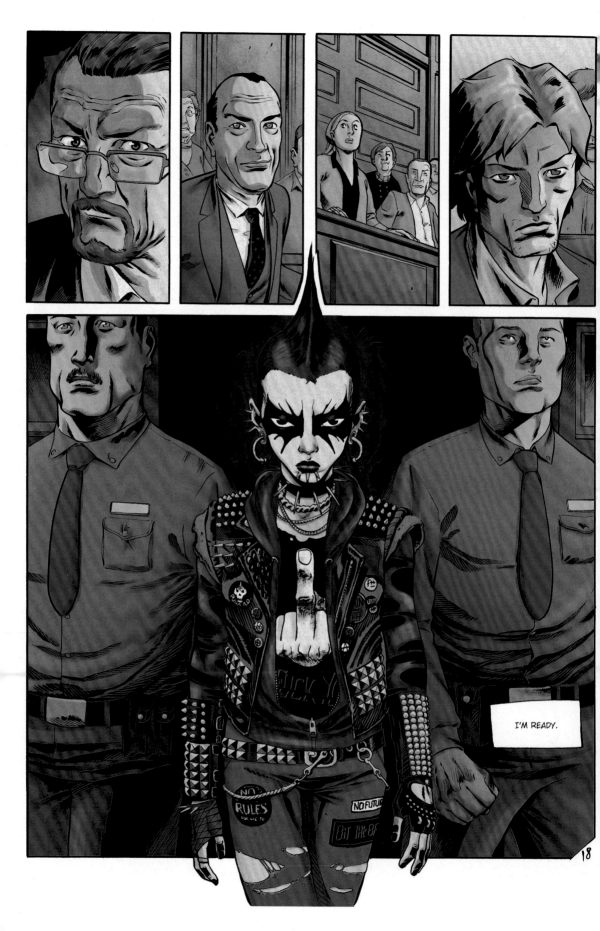

I'M READY.

18

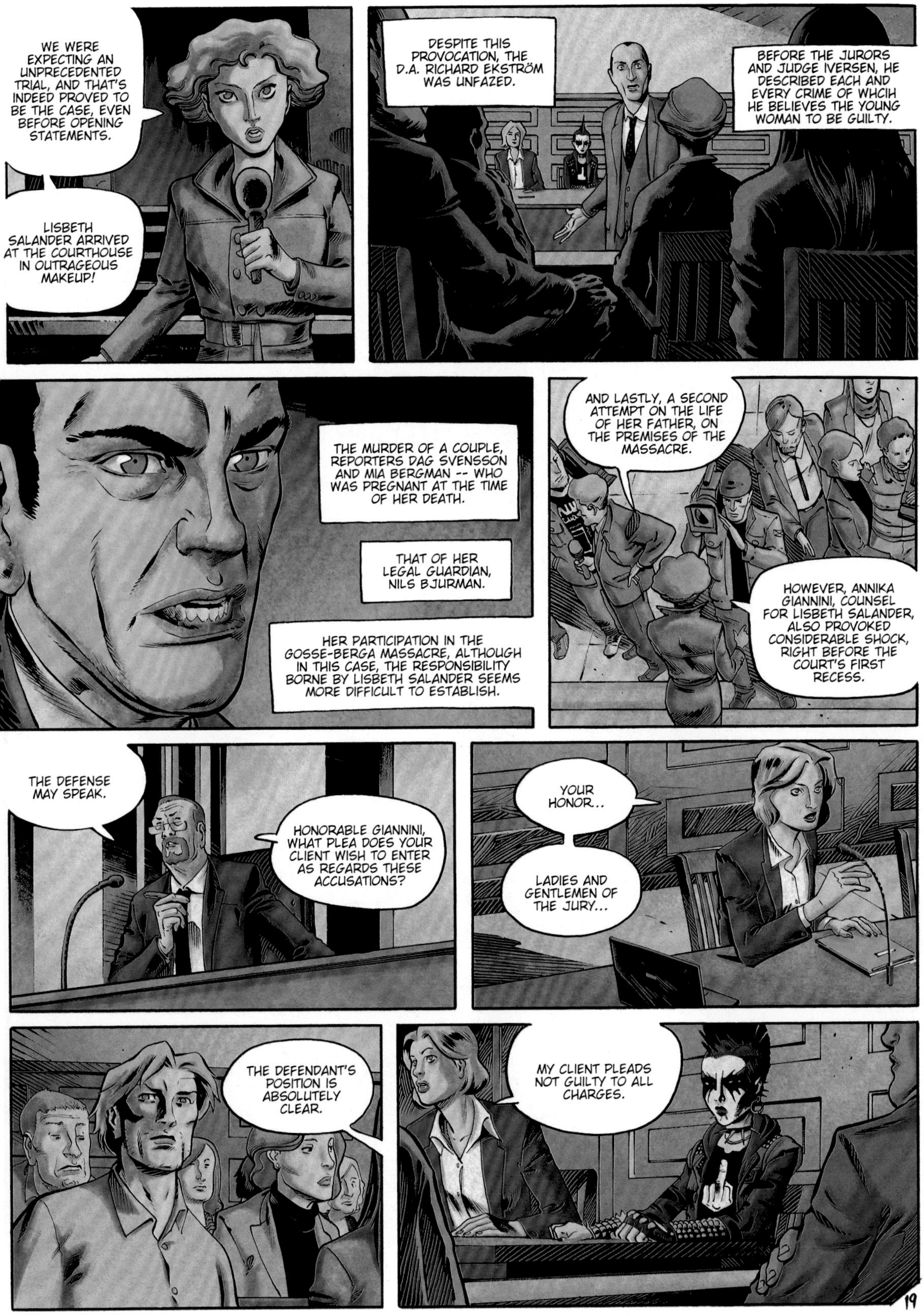
WE WERE EXPECTING AN UNPRECEDENTED TRIAL, AND THAT'S INDEED PROVED TO BE THE CASE, EVEN BEFORE OPENING STATEMENTS.
LISBETH SALANDER ARRIVED AT THE COURTHOUSE IN OUTRAGEOUS MAKEUP!
DESPITE THIS PROVOCATION, THE D.A. RICHARD EKSTRÖM WAS UNFAZED.
BEFORE THE JURORS AND JUDGE IVERSEN, HE DESCRIBED EACH AND EVERY CRIME OF WHCIH HE BELIEVES THE YOUNG WOMAN TO BE GUILTY.
THE MURDER OF A COUPLE, REPORTERS DAG SVENSSON AND MIA BERGMAN -- WHO WAS PREGNANT AT THE TIME OF HER DEATH.
THAT OF HER LEGAL GUARDIAN, NILS BJURMAN.
HER PARTICIPATION IN THE GOSSE-BERGA MASSACRE, ALTHOUGH IN THIS CASE, THE RESPONSIBILITY BORNE BY LISBETH SALANDER SEEMS MORE DIFFICULT TO ESTABLISH.
AND LASTLY, A SECOND ATTEMPT ON THE LIFE OF HER FATHER, ON THE PREMISES OF THE MASSACRE.
HOWEVER, ANNIKA GIANNINI, COUNSEL FOR LISBETH SALANDER, ALSO PROVOKED CONSIDERABLE SHOCK, RIGHT BEFORE THE COURT'S FIRST RECESS.
THE DEFENSE MAY SPEAK.
HONORABLE GIANNINI, WHAT PLEA DOES YOUR CLIENT WISH TO ENTER AS REGARDS THESE ACCUSATIONS?
YOUR HONOR...
LADIES AND GENTLEMEN OF THE JURY...
THE DEFENDANT'S POSITION IS ABSOLUTELY CLEAR.
MY CLIENT PLEADS NOT GUILTY TO ALL CHARGES.

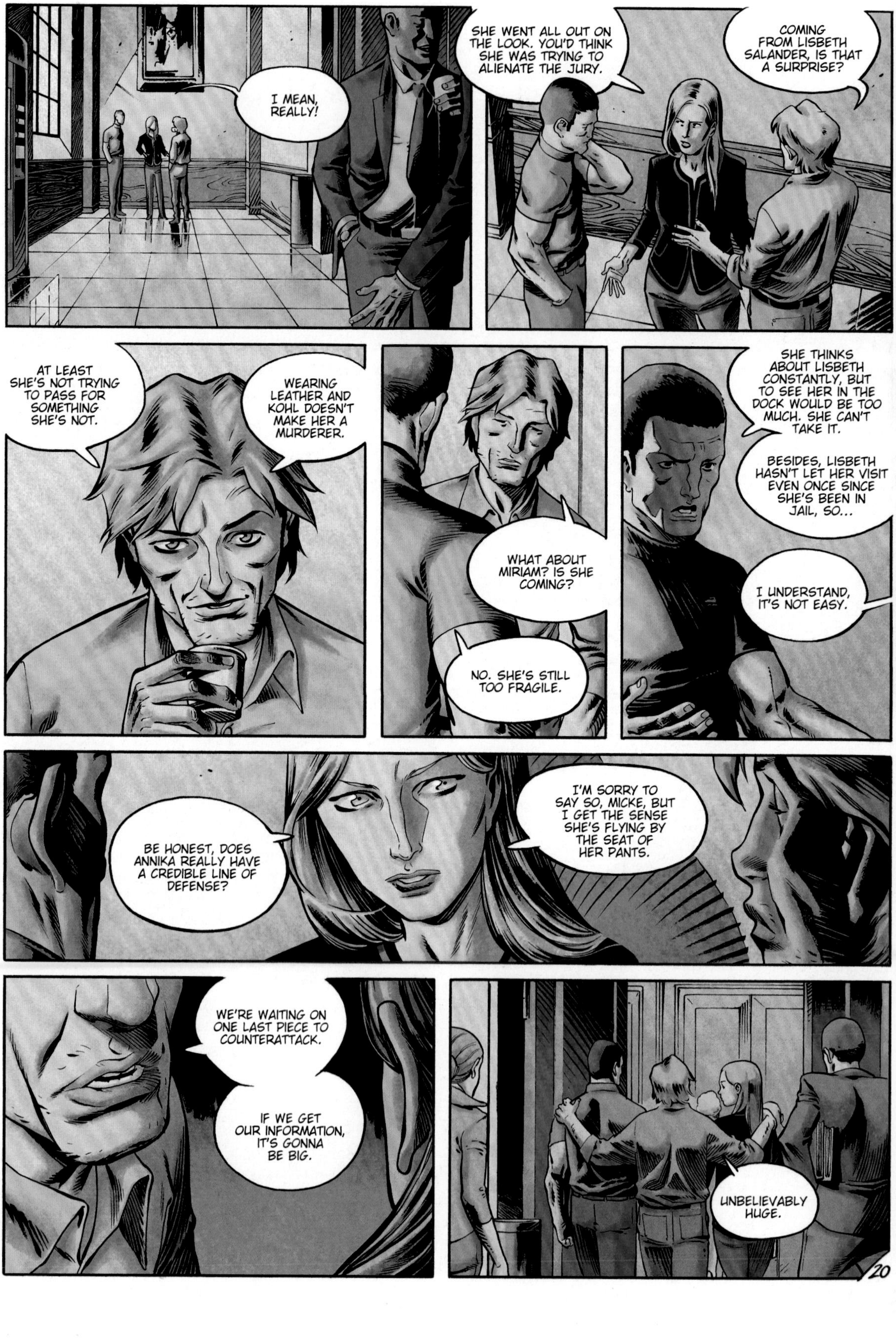
I MEAN, REALLY!
SHE WENT ALL OUT ON THE LOOK. YOU'D THINK SHE WAS TRYING TO ALIENATE THE JURY.
COMING FROM LISBETH SALANDER, IS THAT A SURPRISE?
AT LEAST SHE'S NOT TRYING TO PASS FOR SOMETHING SHE'S NOT.
WEARING LEATHER AND KOHL DOESN'T MAKE HER A MURDERER.
WHAT ABOUT MIRIAM? IS SHE COMING?
NO. SHE'S STILL TOO FRAGILE.
SHE THINKS ABOUT LISBETH CONSTANTLY, BUT TO SEE HER IN THE DOCK WOULD BE TOO MUCH. SHE CAN'T TAKE IT.
BESIDES, LISBETH HASN'T LET HER VISIT EVEN ONCE SINCE SHE'S BEEN IN JAIL, SO...
I UNDERSTAND, IT'S NOT EASY.
BE HONEST, DOES ANNIKA REALLY HAVE A CREDIBLE LINE OF DEFENSE?
I'M SORRY TO SAY SO, MICKE, BUT I GET THE SENSE SHE'S FLYING BY THE SEAT OF HER PANTS.
WE'RE WAITING ON ONE LAST PIECE TO COUNTERATTACK.
IF WE GET OUR INFORMATION, IT'S GONNA BE BIG.
UNBELIEVABLY HUGE.

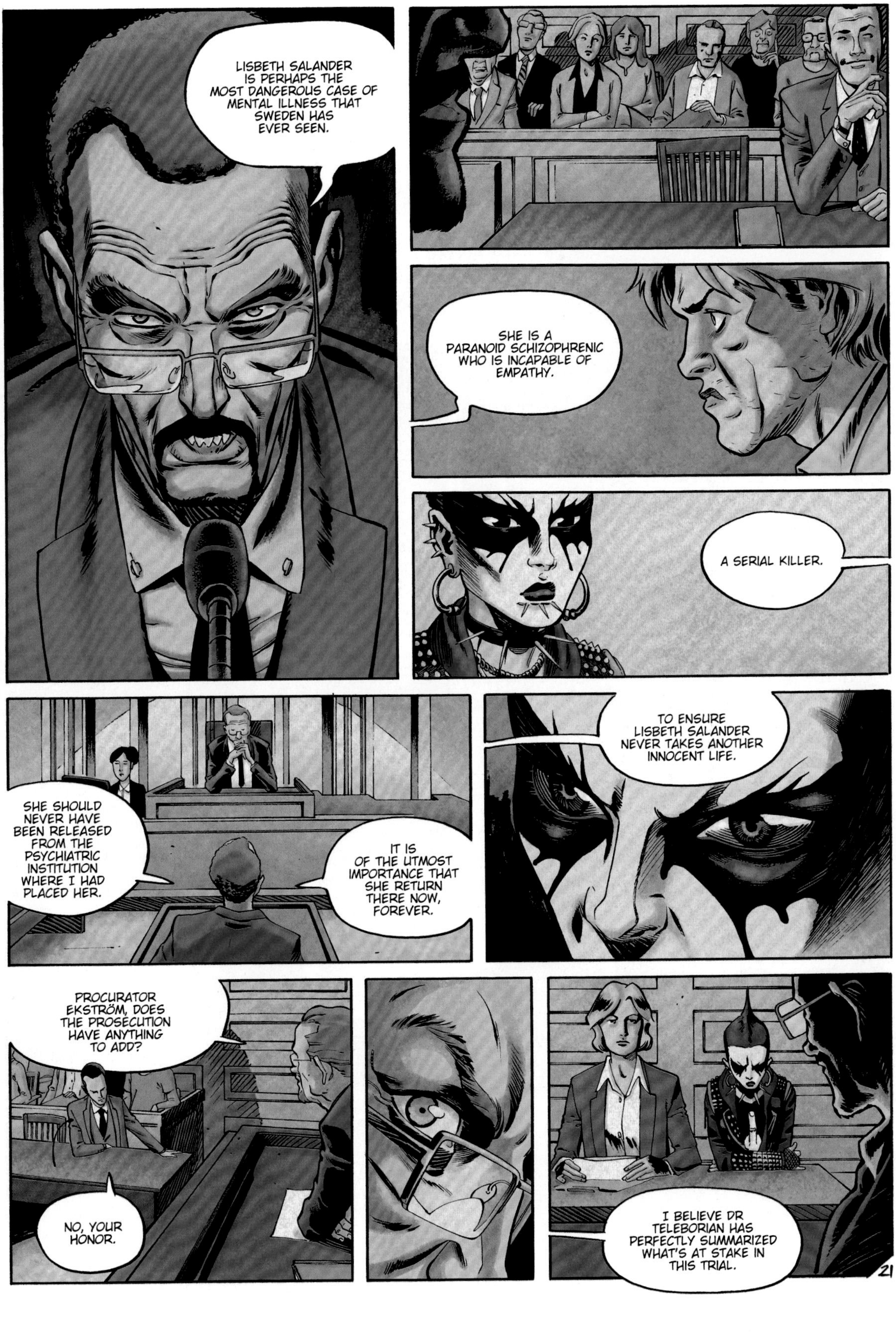
LISBETH SALANDER IS PERHAPS THE MOST DANGEROUS CASE OF MENTAL ILLNESS THAT SWEDEN HAS EVER SEEN.
SHE IS A PARANOID SCHIZOPHRENIC WHO IS INCAPABLE OF EMPATHY.
A SERIAL KILLER.
SHE SHOULD NEVER HAVE BEEN RELEASED FROM THE PSYCHIATRIC INSTITUTION WHERE I HAD PLACED HER.
IT IS OF THE UTMOST IMPORTANCE THAT SHE RETURN THERE NOW, FOREVER.
TO ENSURE LISBETH SALANDER NEVER TAKES ANOTHER INNOCENT LIFE.
PROCURATOR EKSTRÖM, DOES THE PROSECUTION HAVE ANYTHING TO ADD?
NO, YOUR HONOR.
I BELIEVE DR TELEBORIAN HAS PERFECTLY SUMMARIZED WHAT'S AT STAKE IN THIS TRIAL.

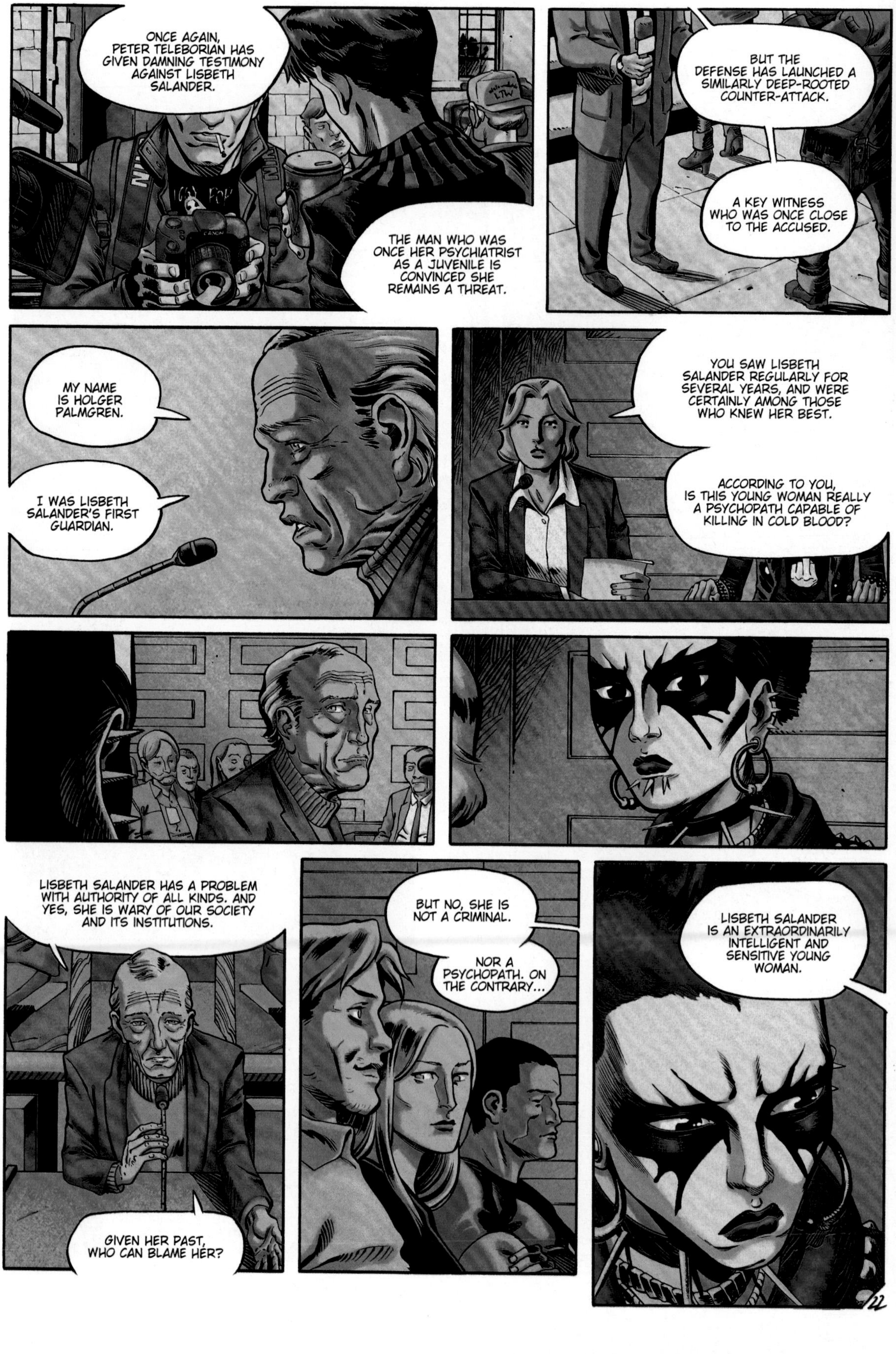
ONCE AGAIN, PETER TELEBORIAN HAS GIVEN DAMNING TESTIMONY AGAINST LISBETH SALANDER.
THE MAN WHO WAS ONCE HER PSYCHIATRIST AS A JUVENILE IS CONVINCED SHE REMAINS A THREAT.
BUT THE DEFENSE HAS LAUNCHED A SIMILARLY DEEP-ROOTED COUNTER-ATTACK.
A KEY WITNESS WHO WAS ONCE CLOSE TO THE ACCUSED.
MY NAME IS HOLGER PALMGREN.
I WAS LISBETH SALANDER'S FIRST GUARDIAN.
YOU SAW LISBETH SALANDER REGULARLY FOR SEVERAL YEARS, AND WERE CERTAINLY AMONG THOSE WHO KNEW HER BEST.
ACCORDING TO YOU, IS THIS YOUNG WOMAN REALLY A PSYCHOPATH CAPABLE OF KILLING IN COLD BLOOD?
LISBETH SALANDER HAS A PROBLEM WITH AUTHORITY OF ALL KINDS. AND YES, SHE IS WARY OF OUR SOCIETY AND ITS INSTITUTIONS.
GIVEN HER PAST, WHO CAN BLAME HER?
BUT NO, SHE IS NOT A CRIMINAL.
NOR A PSYCHOPATH. ON THE CONTRARY...
LISBETH SALANDER IS AN EXTRAORDINARILY INTELLIGENT AND SENSITIVE YOUNG WOMAN.

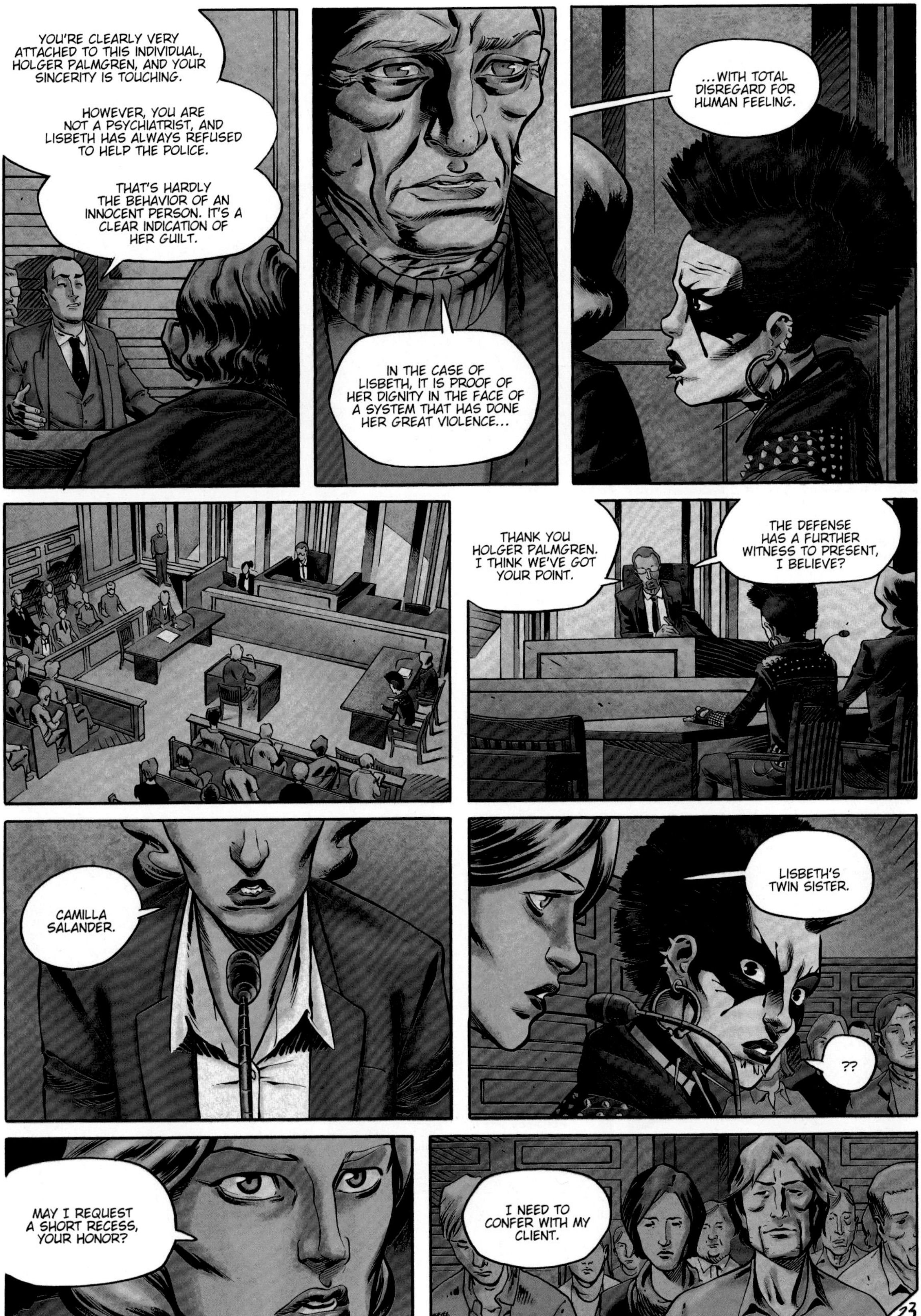
YOU'RE CLEARLY VERY ATTACHED TO THIS INDIVIDUAL, HOLGER PALMGREN, AND YOUR SINCERITY IS TOUCHING.
HOWEVER, YOU ARE NOT A PSYCHIATRIST, AND LISBETH HAS ALWAYS REFUSED TO HELP THE POLICE.
THAT'S HARDLY THE BEHAVIOR OF AN INNOCENT PERSON. IT'S A CLEAR INDICATION OF HER GUILT.
IN THE CASE OF LISBETH, IT IS PROOF OF HER DIGNITY IN THE FACE OF A SYSTEM THAT HAS DONE HER GREAT VIOLENCE...
...WITH TOTAL DISREGARD FOR HUMAN FEELING.
THANK YOU HOLGER PALMGREN. I THINK WE'VE GOT YOUR POINT.
THE DEFENSE HAS A FURTHER WITNESS TO PRESENT, I BELIEVE?
CAMILLA SALANDER.
LISBETH'S TWIN SISTER.
??
MAY I REQUEST A SHORT RECESS, YOUR HONOR?
I NEED TO CONFER WITH MY CLIENT.
23

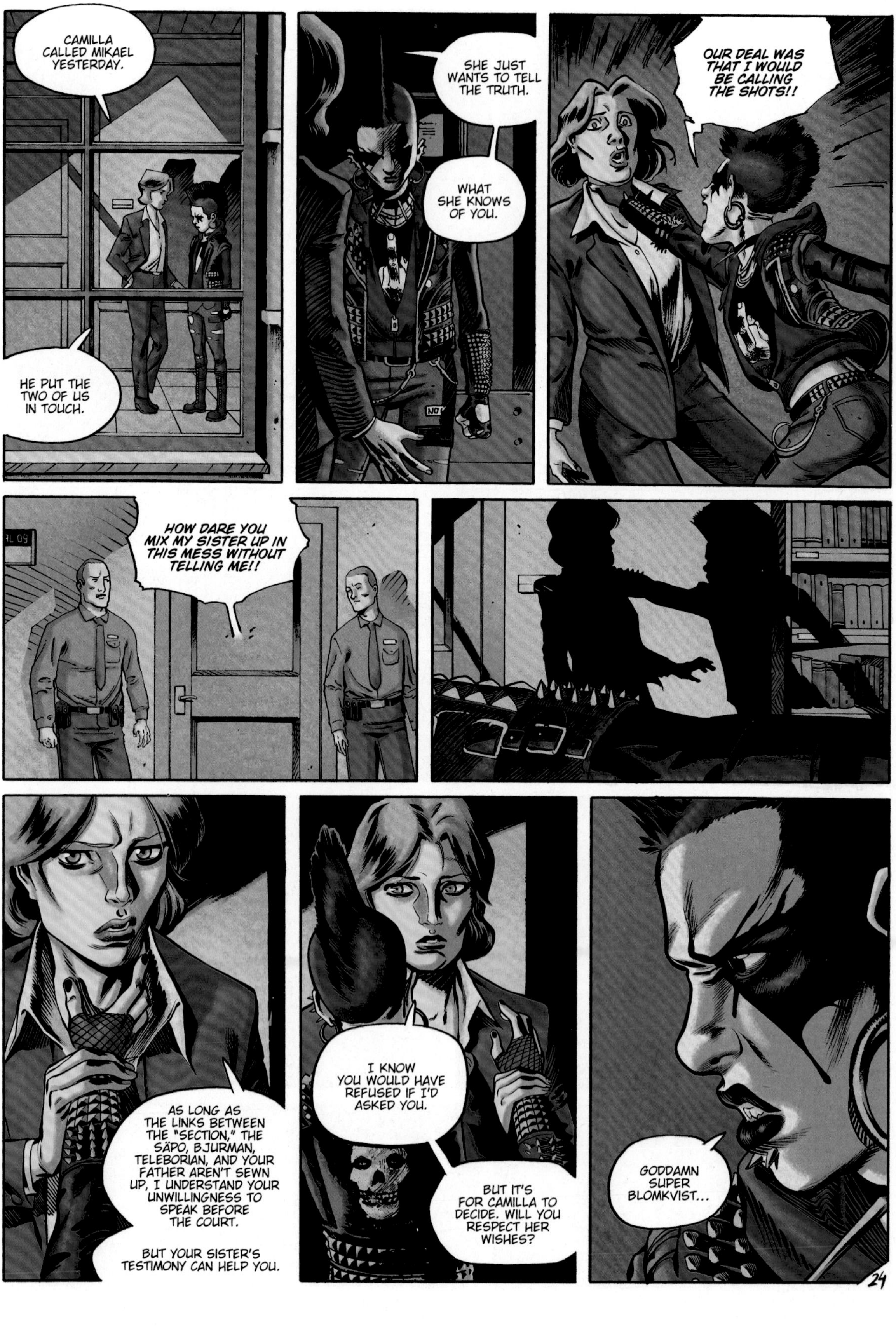
CAMILLA CALLED MIKAEL YESTERDAY.
HE PUT THE TWO OF US IN TOUCH.
SHE JUST WANTS TO TELL THE TRUTH.
WHAT SHE KNOWS OF YOU.
OUR DEAL WAS THAT I WOULD BE CALLING THE SHOTS!!
HOW DARE YOU MIX MY SISTER UP IN THIS MESS WITHOUT TELLING ME!!
AS LONG AS THE LINKS BETWEEN THE "SECTION," THE SÄPO, BJURMAN, TELEBORIAN, AND YOUR FATHER AREN'T SEWN UP, I UNDERSTAND YOUR UNWILLINGNESS TO SPEAK BEFORE THE COURT.
BUT YOUR SISTER'S TESTIMONY CAN HELP YOU.
I KNOW YOU WOULD HAVE REFUSED IF I'D ASKED YOU.
BUT IT'S FOR CAMILLA TO DECIDE. WILL YOU RESPECT HER WISHES?
GODDAMN SUPER BLOMKVIST...
24

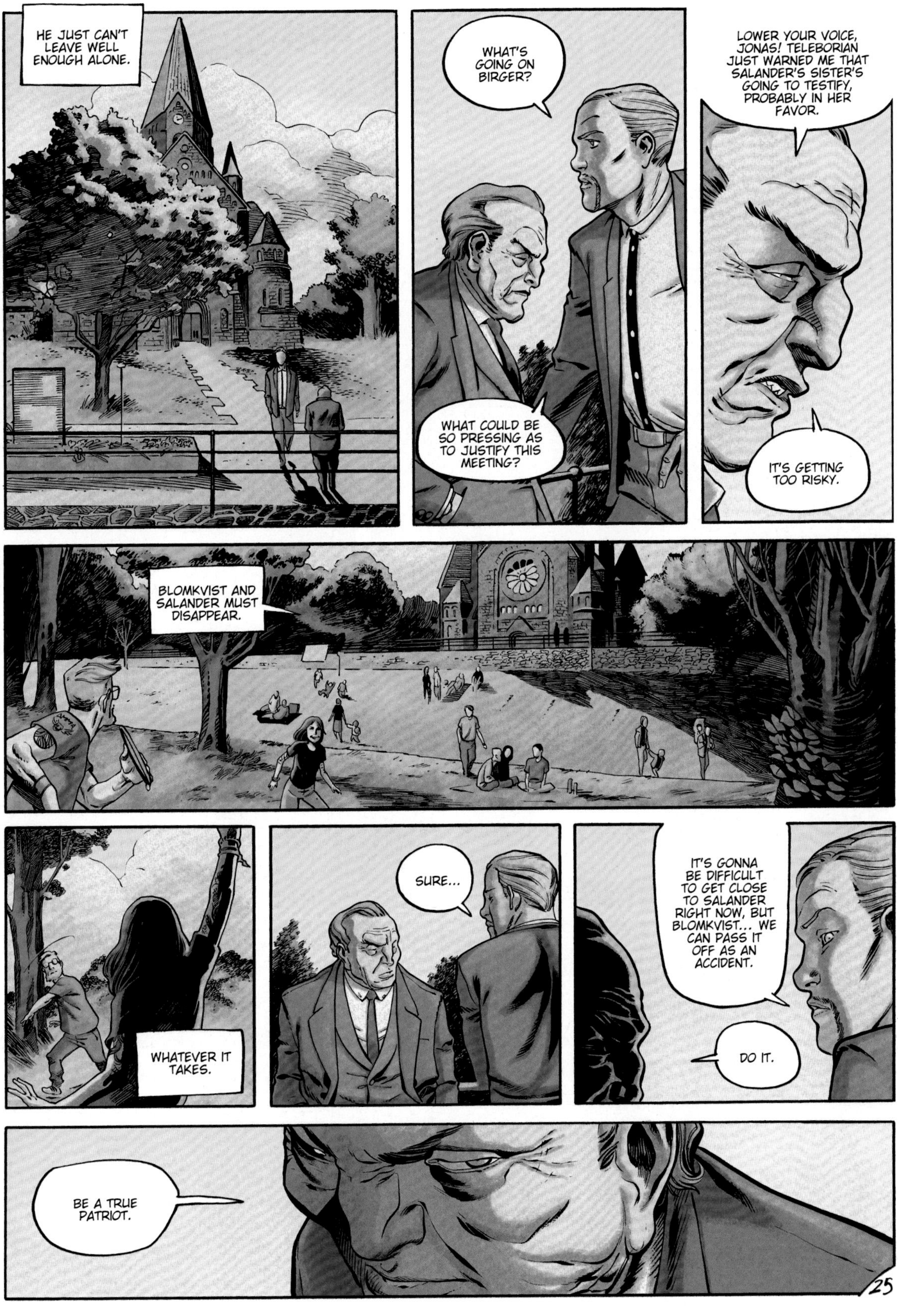
HE JUST CAN'T LEAVE WELL ENOUGH ALONE.
WHAT'S GOING ON BIRGER?
WHAT COULD BE SO PRESSING AS TO JUSTIFY THIS MEETING?
LOWER YOUR VOICE, JONAS! TELEBORIAN JUST WARNED ME THAT SALANDER'S SISTER'S GOING TO TESTIFY, PROBABLY IN HER FAVOR.
IT'S GETTING TOO RISKY.
BLOMKVIST AND SALANDER MUST DISAPPEAR.
WHATEVER IT TAKES.
SURE...
IT'S GONNA BE DIFFICULT TO GET CLOSE TO SALANDER RIGHT NOW, BUT BLOMKVIST... WE CAN PASS IT OFF AS AN ACCIDENT.
DO IT.
BE A TRUE PATRIOT.

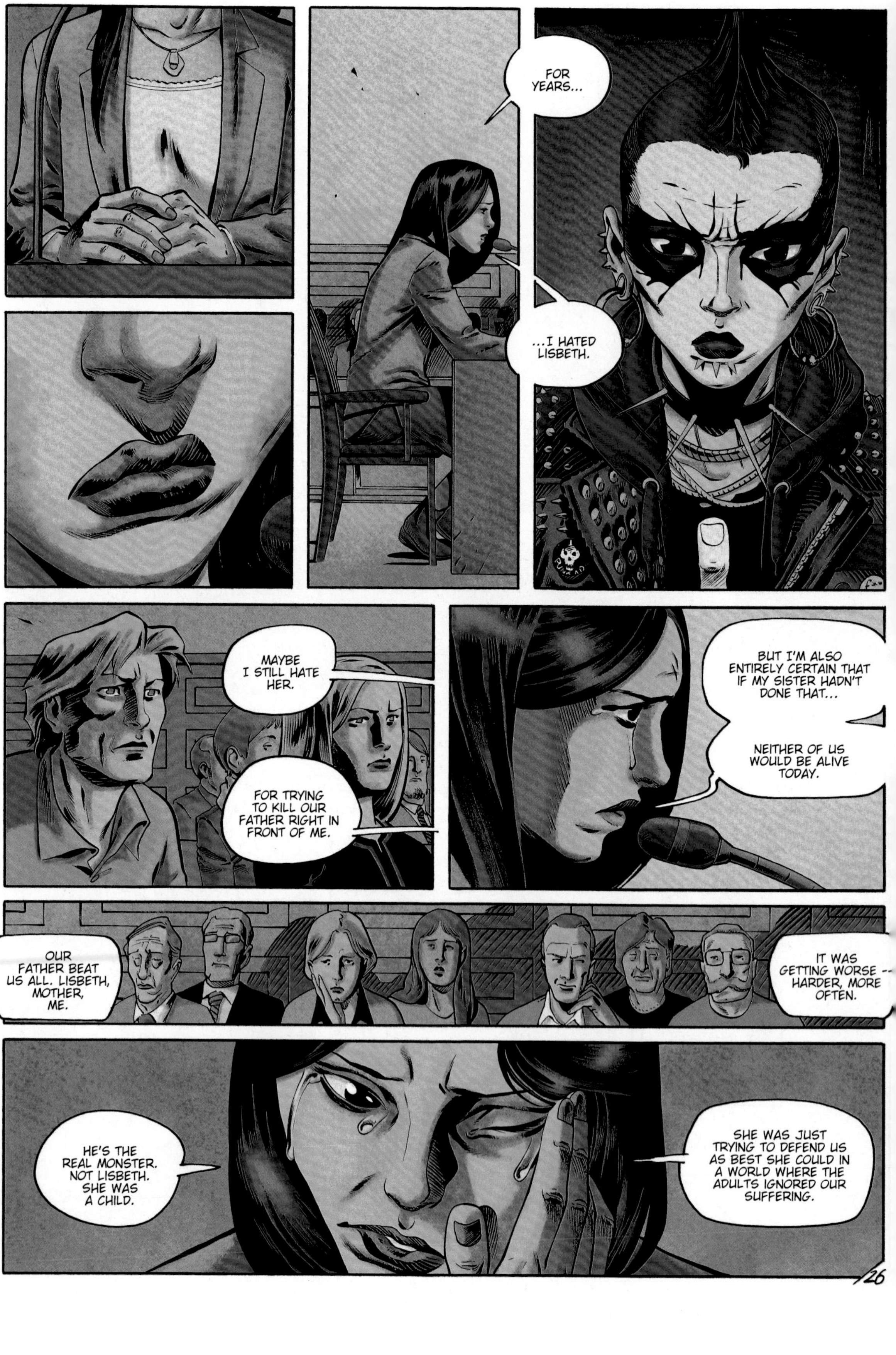
FOR YEARS...
...I HATED LISBETH.
MAYBE I STILL HATE HER.
FOR TRYING TO KILL OUR FATHER RIGHT IN FRONT OF ME.
BUT I'M ALSO ENTIRELY CERTAIN THAT IF MY SISTER HADN'T DONE THAT...
NEITHER OF US WOULD BE ALIVE TODAY.
OUR FATHER BEAT US ALL. LISBETH, MOTHER, ME.
IT WAS GETTING WORSE -- HARDER, MORE OFTEN.
HE'S THE REAL MONSTER. NOT LISBETH. SHE WAS A CHILD.
SHE WAS JUST TRYING TO DEFEND US AS BEST SHE COULD IN A WORLD WHERE THE ADULTS IGNORED OUR SUFFERING.

CAMILLA, YOU REFUSED ALL CONTACT WITH YOUR SISTER FOR YEARS.

YOU CONCEALED HER EXISTENCE FROM YOUR HUSBAND AND CHILDREN.

WHAT MADE YOU DECIDE TO COME FORTH AT HER TRIAL?

I HAVEN'T CHANGED MY MIND.

THERE'S STILL NO PLACE FOR LISBETH IN MY LIFE.

BUT WHEN WE WERE ASSAULTED BY THAT MONSTER; SHE WAS THE ONE WHO PREVENTED HIM FROM SLAUGHTERING US.

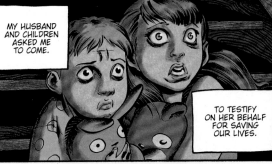

MY HUSBAND AND CHILDREN ASKED ME TO COME.

TO TESTIFY ON HER BEHALF FOR SAVING OUR LIVES.

THEY WERE RIGHT.

MY SISTER DESERVES JUSTICE.

AS FOR ME...

...I WISH HER WELL.

27.

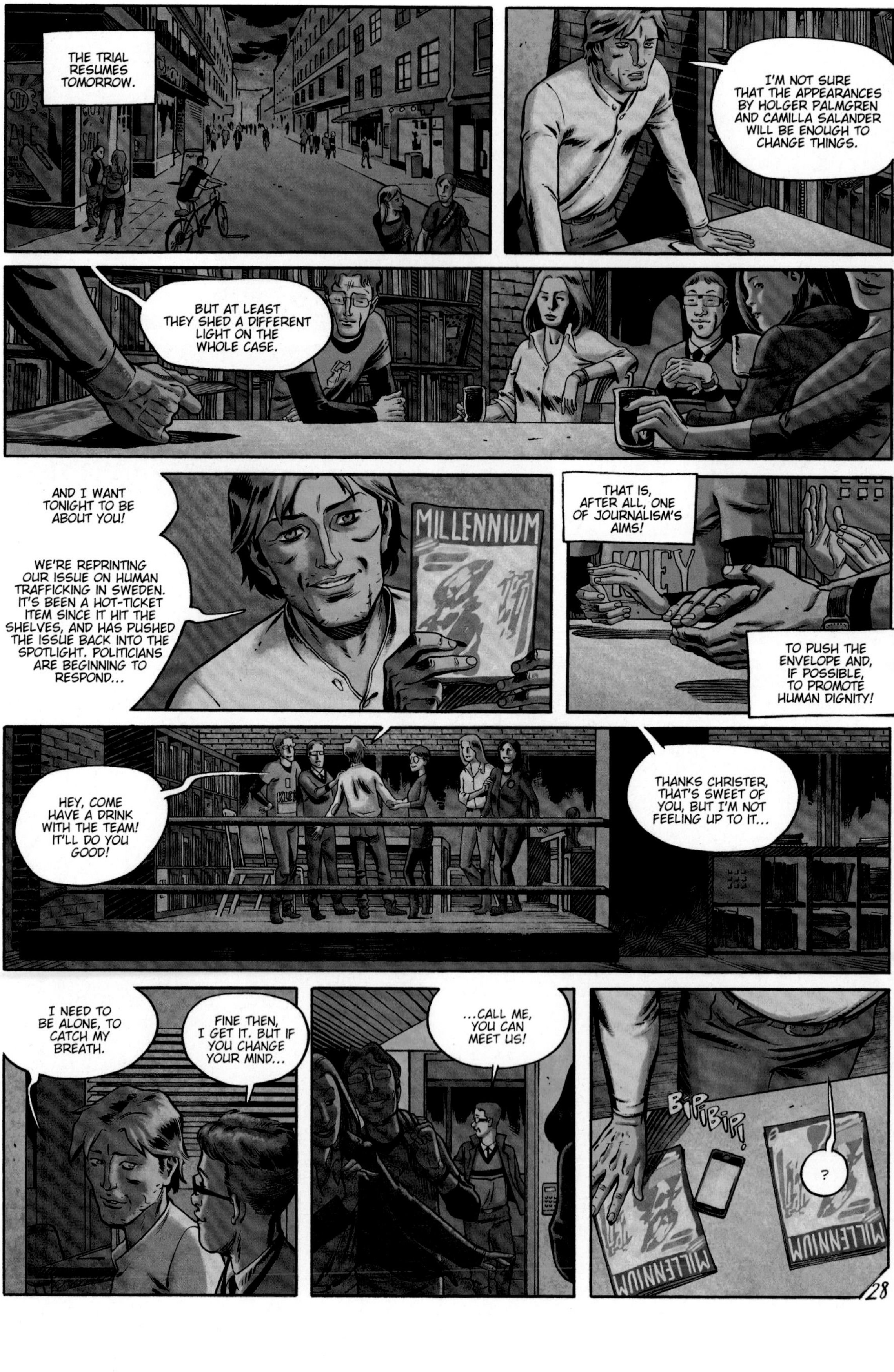
THE TRIAL RESUMES TOMORROW.
I'M NOT SURE THAT THE APPEARANCES BY HOLGER PALMGREN AND CAMILLA SALANDER WILL BE ENOUGH TO CHANGE THINGS.
BUT AT LEAST THEY SHED A DIFFERENT LIGHT ON THE WHOLE CASE.
AND I WANT TONIGHT TO BE ABOUT YOU!
WE'RE REPRINTING OUR ISSUE ON HUMAN TRAFFICKING IN SWEDEN. IT'S BEEN A HOT-TICKET ITEM SINCE IT HIT THE SHELVES, AND HAS PUSHED THE ISSUE BACK INTO THE SPOTLIGHT. POLITICIANS ARE BEGINNING TO RESPOND...
MILLENNIUM
THAT IS, AFTER ALL, ONE OF JOURNALISM'S AIMS!
TO PUSH THE ENVELOPE AND, IF POSSIBLE, TO PROMOTE HUMAN DIGNITY!
HEY, COME HAVE A DRINK WITH THE TEAM! IT'LL DO YOU GOOD!
THANKS CHRISTER, THAT'S SWEET OF YOU, BUT I'M NOT FEELING UP TO IT...
I NEED TO BE ALONE, TO CATCH MY BREATH.
FINE THEN, I GET IT. BUT IF YOU CHANGE YOUR MIND...
...CALL ME, YOU CAN MEET US!
BIPIBIP!
?
MILLENNIUM
MILLENNIUM

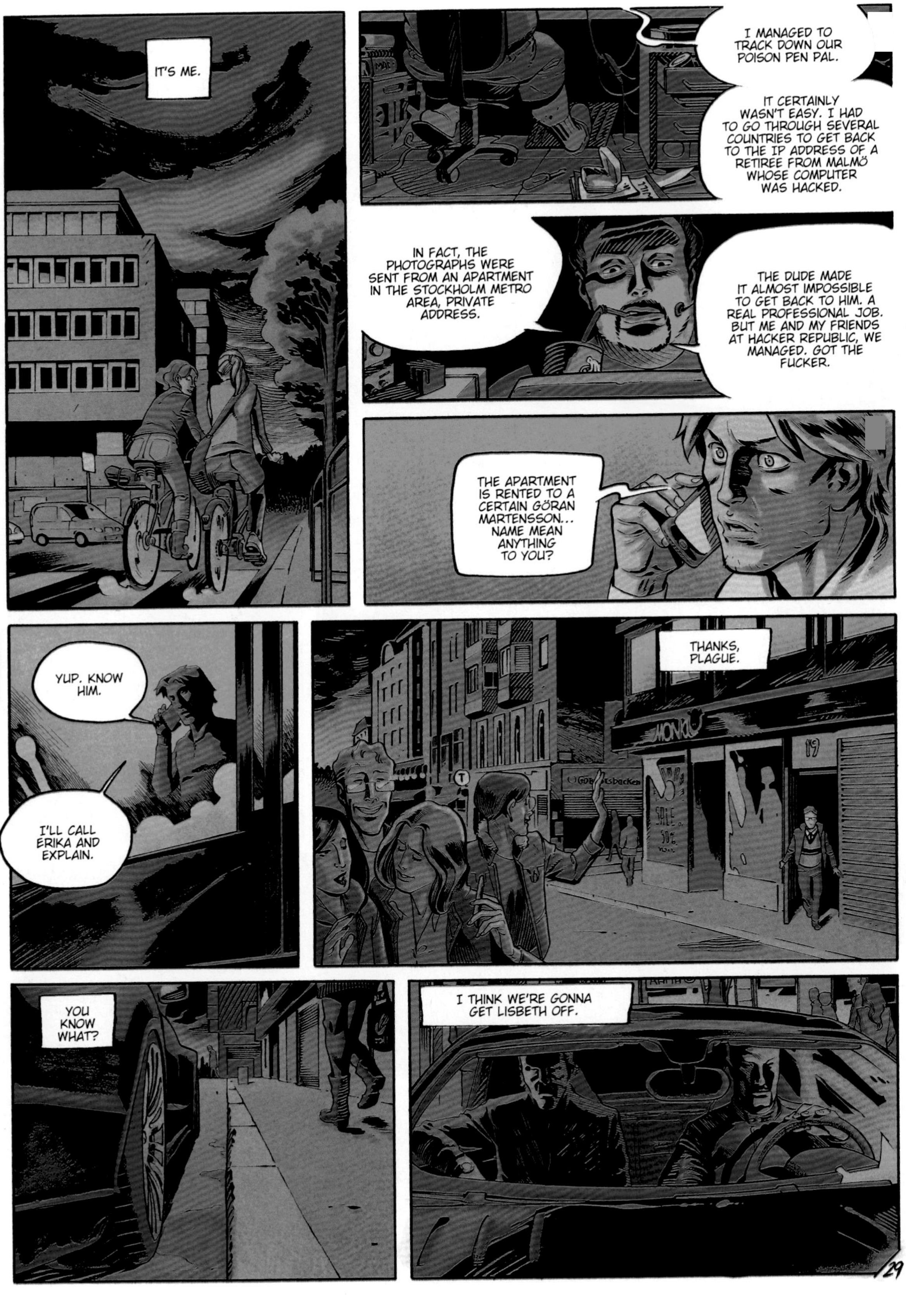
IT'S ME.
I MANAGED TO TRACK DOWN OUR POISON PEN PAL.
IT CERTAINLY WASN'T EASY. I HAD TO GO THROUGH SEVERAL COUNTRIES TO GET BACK TO THE IP ADDRESS OF A RETIREE FROM MALMÖ WHOSE COMPUTER WAS HACKED.
IN FACT, THE PHOTOGRAPHS WERE SENT FROM AN APARTMENT IN THE STOCKHOLM METRO AREA, PRIVATE ADDRESS.
THE DUDE MADE IT ALMOST IMPOSSIBLE TO GET BACK TO HIM. A REAL PROFESSIONAL JOB. BUT ME AND MY FRIENDS AT HACKER REPUBLIC, WE MANAGED. GOT THE FUCKER.
THE APARTMENT IS RENTED TO A CERTAIN GÖRAN MARTENSSON... NAME MEAN ANYTHING TO YOU?
YUP. KNOW HIM.
I'LL CALL ERIKA AND EXPLAIN.
THANKS, PLAGUE.
YOU KNOW WHAT?
I THINK WE'RE GONNA GET LISBETH OFF.

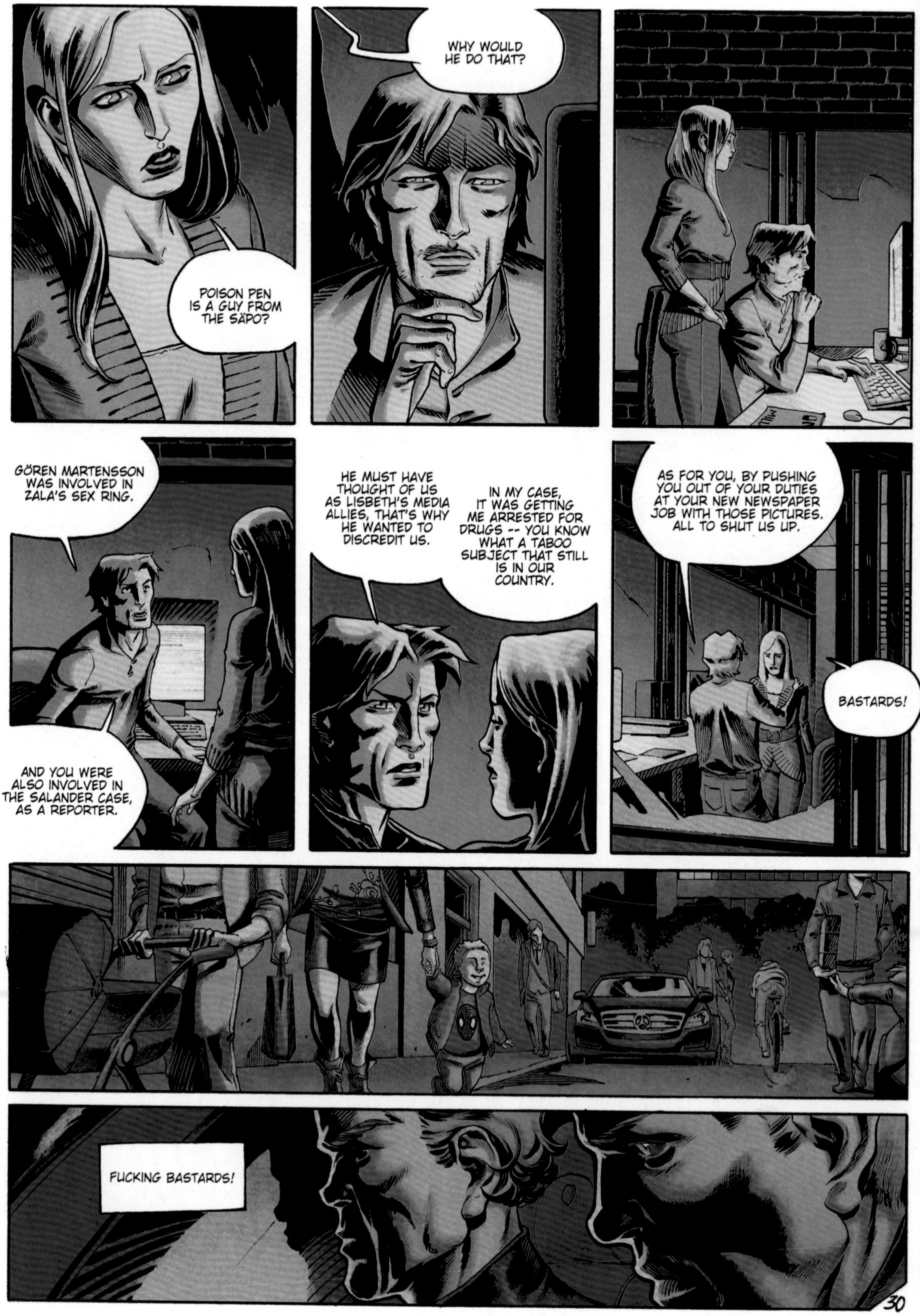
POISON PEN IS A GUY FROM THE SÄPO?
WHY WOULD HE DO THAT?
GÖREN MARTENSSON WAS INVOLVED IN ZALA'S SEX RING.
AND YOU WERE ALSO INVOLVED IN THE SALANDER CASE, AS A REPORTER.
HE MUST HAVE THOUGHT OF US AS LISBETH'S MEDIA ALLIES, THAT'S WHY HE WANTED TO DISCREDIT US.
IN MY CASE, IT WAS GETTING ME ARRESTED FOR DRUGS -- YOU KNOW WHAT A TABOO SUBJECT THAT STILL IS IN OUR COUNTRY.
AS FOR YOU, BY PUSHING YOU OUT OF YOUR DUTIES AT YOUR NEW NEWSPAPER JOB WITH THOSE PICTURES. ALL TO SHUT US UP.
BASTARDS!
FUCKING BASTARDS!

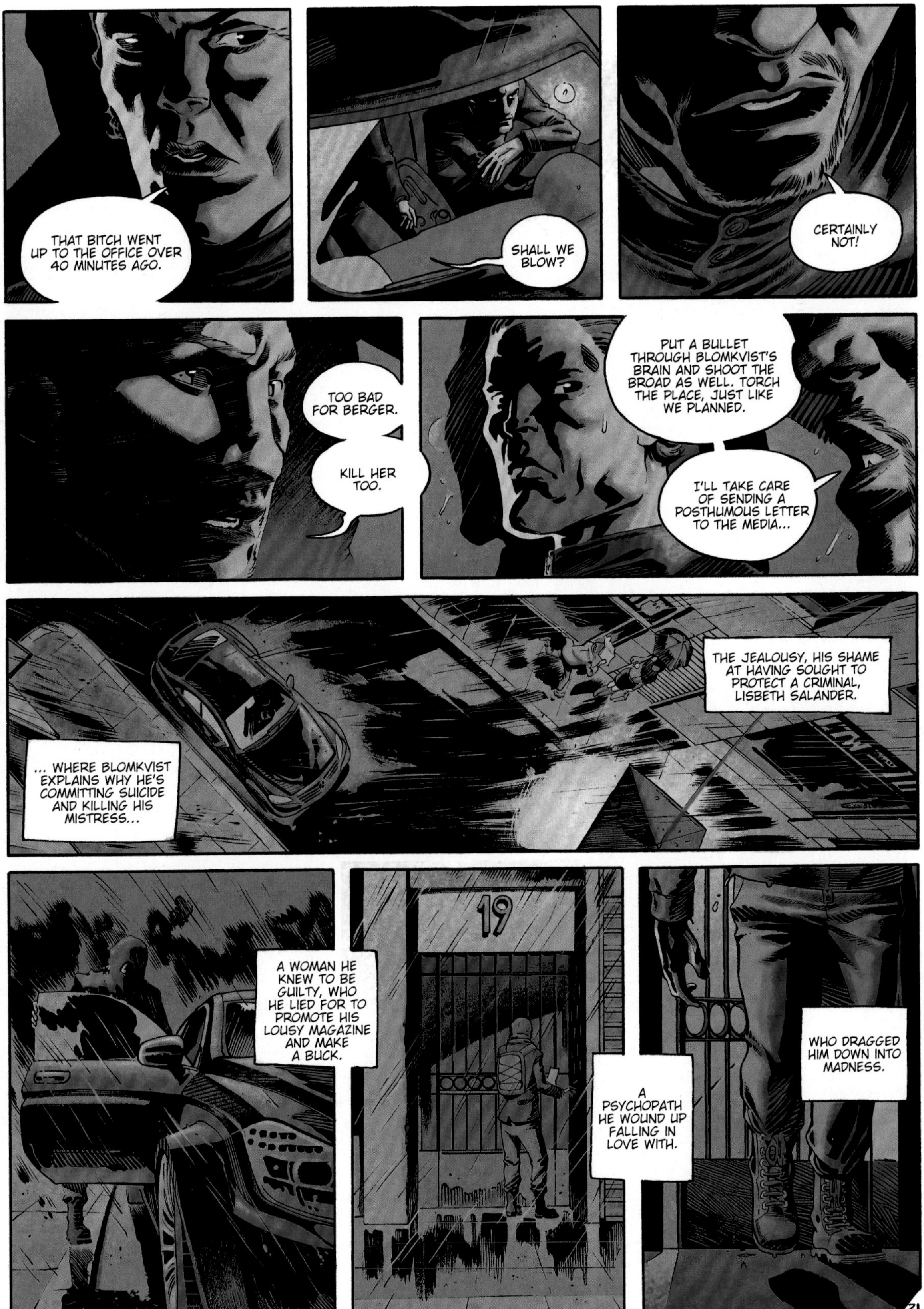
THAT BITCH WENT UP TO THE OFFICE OVER 40 MINUTES AGO.
SHALL WE BLOW?
CERTAINLY NOT!
TOO BAD FOR BERGER.
KILL HER TOO.
PUT A BULLET THROUGH BLOMKVIST'S BRAIN AND SHOOT THE BROAD AS WELL. TORCH THE PLACE, JUST LIKE WE PLANNED.
I'LL TAKE CARE OF SENDING A POSTHUMOUS LETTER TO THE MEDIA...
... WHERE BLOMKVIST EXPLAINS WHY HE'S COMMITTING SUICIDE AND KILLING HIS MISTRESS...
THE JEALOUSY, HIS SHAME AT HAVING SOUGHT TO PROTECT A CRIMINAL, LISBETH SALANDER.
A WOMAN HE KNEW TO BE GUILTY, WHO HE LIED FOR TO PROMOTE HIS LOUSY MAGAZINE AND MAKE A BUCK.
19
A PSYCHOPATH HE WOUND UP FALLING IN LOVE WITH.
WHO DRAGGED HIM DOWN INTO MADNESS.

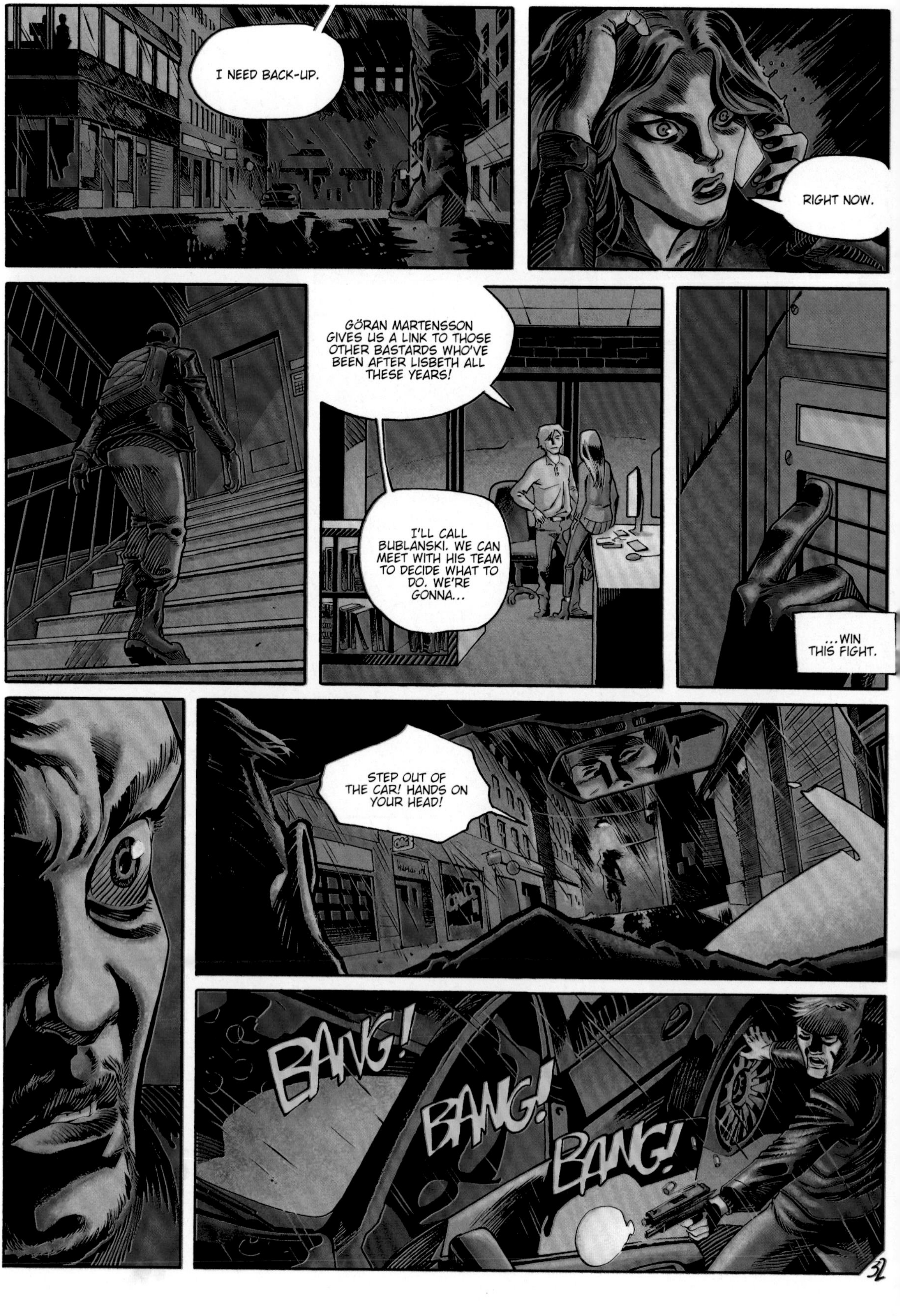
I NEED BACK-UP.
RIGHT NOW.
GÖRAN MARTENSSON GIVES US A LINK TO THOSE OTHER BASTARDS WHO'VE BEEN AFTER LISBETH ALL THESE YEARS!
I'LL CALL BUBLANSKI. WE CAN MEET WITH HIS TEAM TO DECIDE WHAT TO DO. WE'RE GONNA...
...WIN THIS FIGHT.
STEP OUT OF THE CAR! HANDS ON YOUR HEAD!
BANG!
BANG!
BANG!

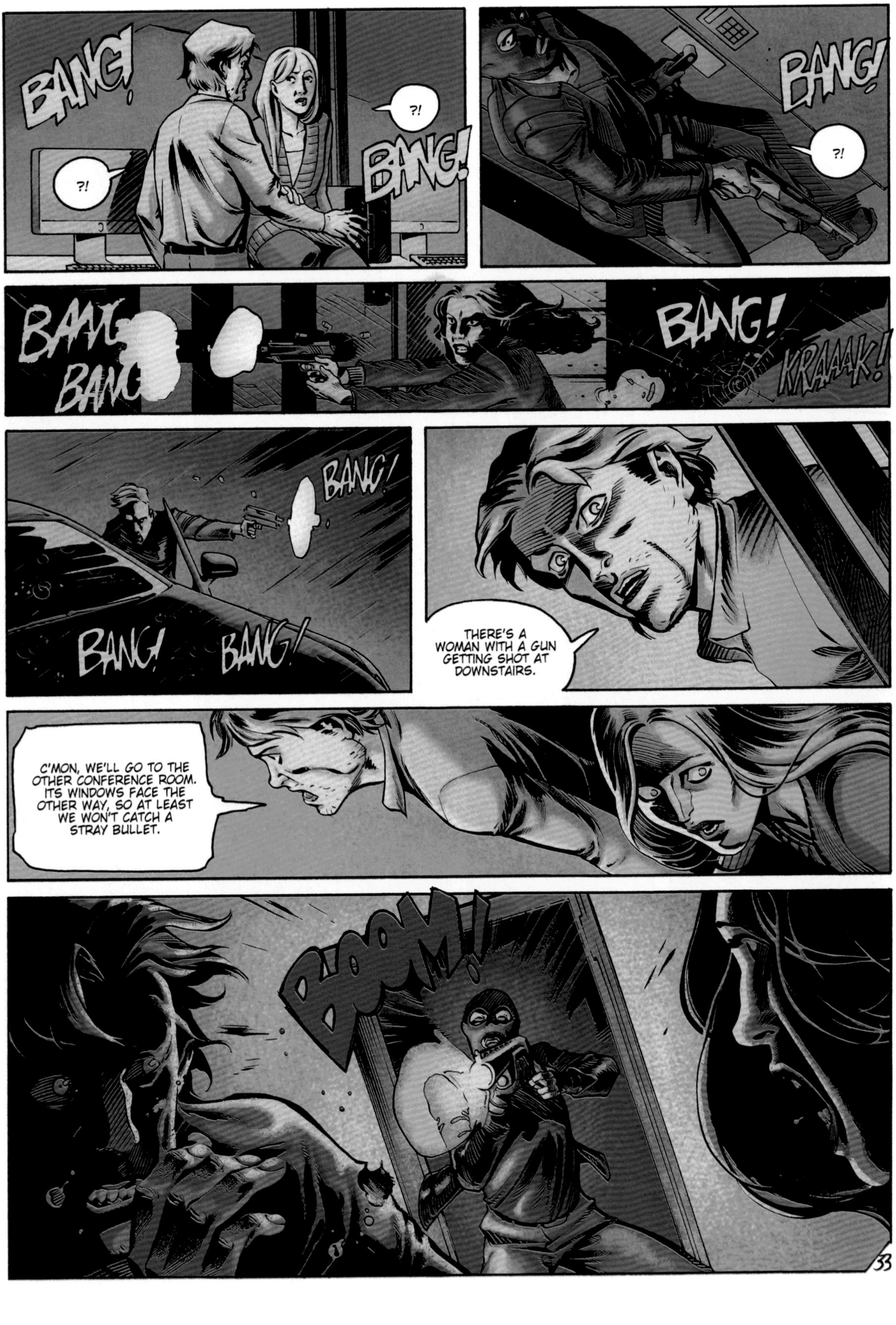
BANG!
?!
?!
BANG!
BANG!
?!
BANG
BANG
BANG!
KRAAAK!
BANG!
BANG!
BANG!
THERE'S A WOMAN WITH A GUN GETTING SHOT AT DOWNSTAIRS.
C'MON, WE'LL GO TO THE OTHER CONFERENCE ROOM. ITS WINDOWS FACE THE OTHER WAY, SO AT LEAST WE WON'T CATCH A STRAY BULLET.
BOOM!

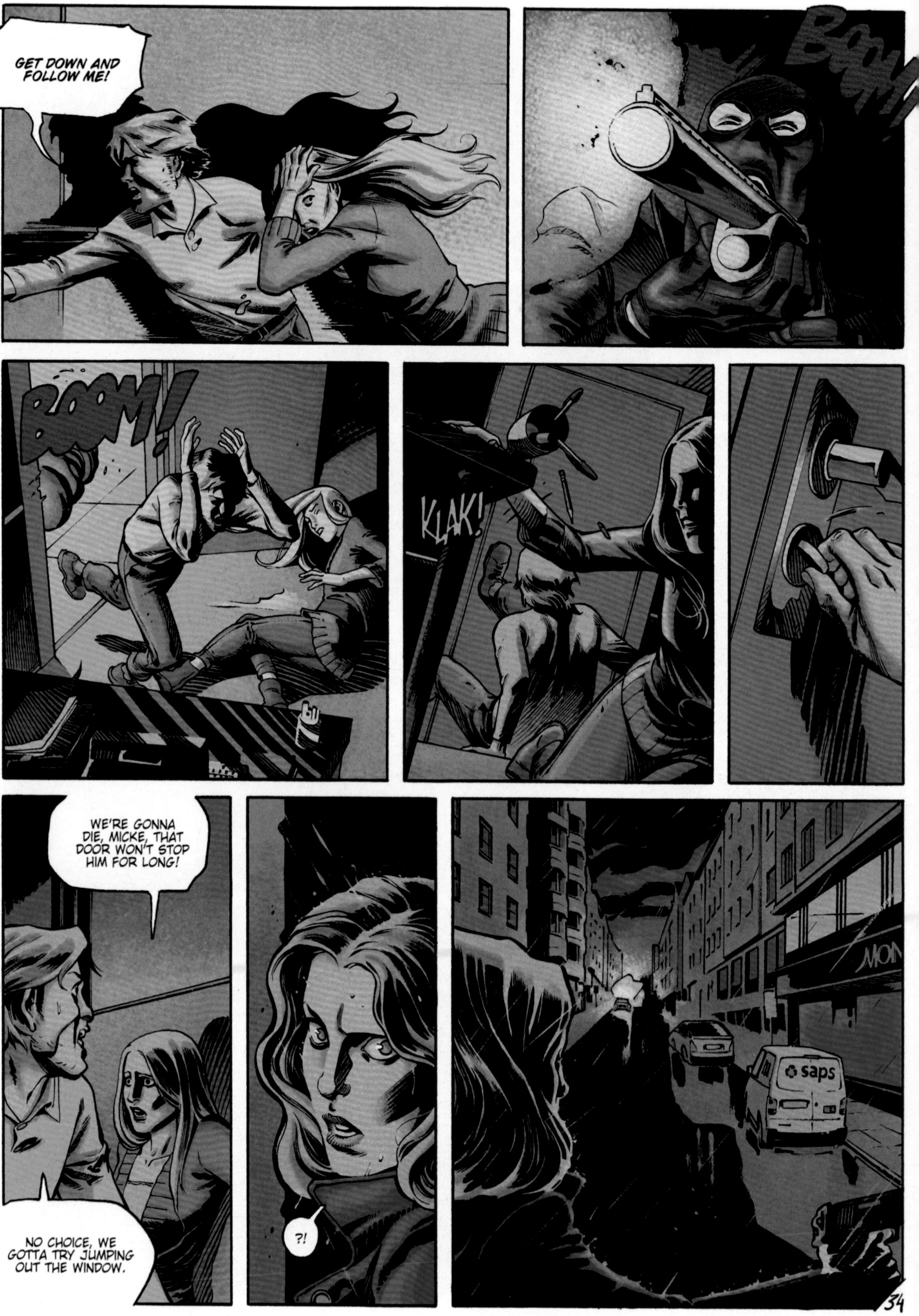

GET DOWN AND FOLLOW ME!
BOOM!
BOOM!
KLAK!
WE'RE GONNA DIE, MICKE, THAT DOOR WON'T STOP HIM FOR LONG!
NO CHOICE, WE GOTTA TRY JUMPING OUT THE WINDOW.
?!
saps
MON

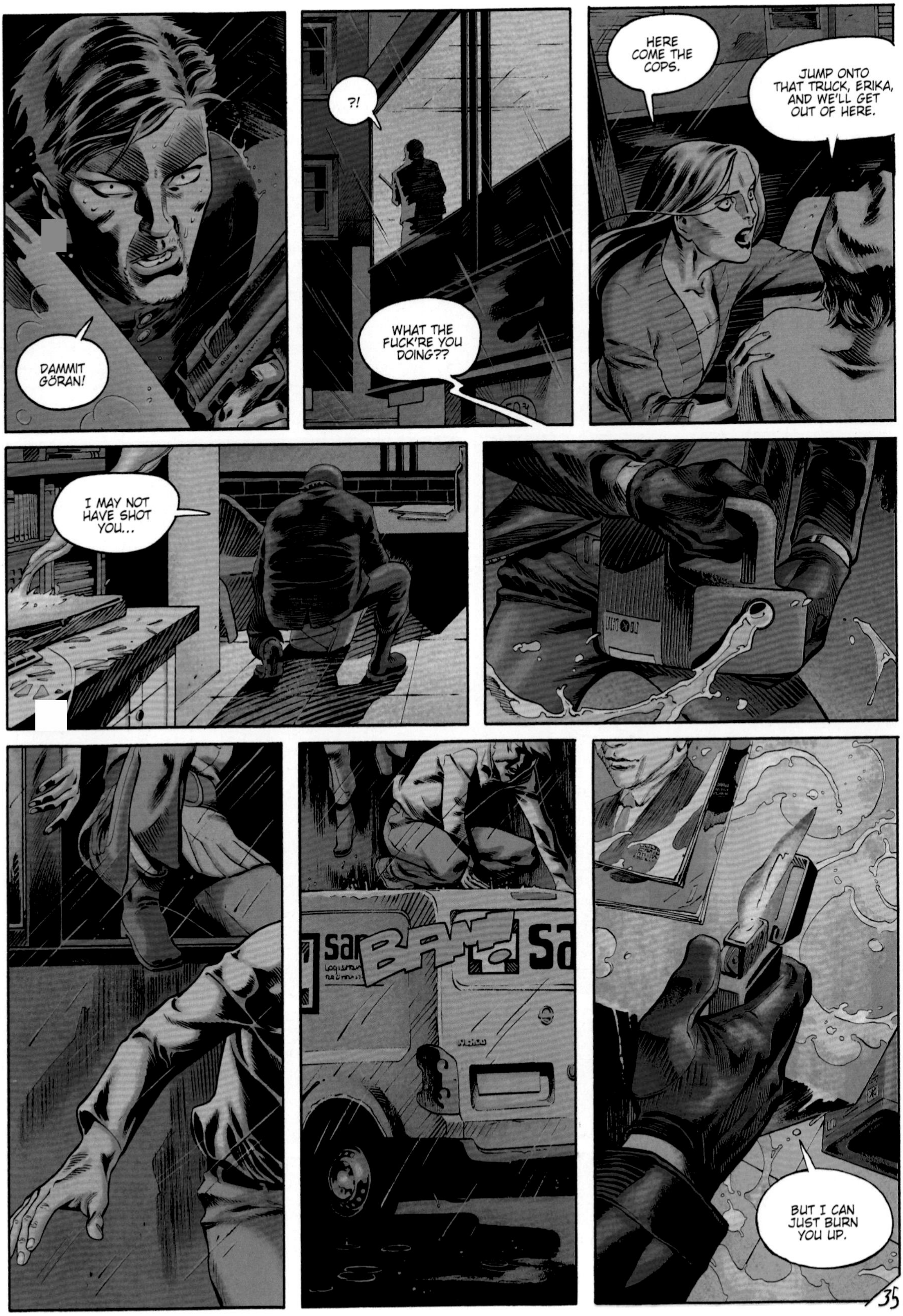
DAMMIT GÖRAN!
?!
WHAT THE FUCK'RE YOU DOING??
HERE COME THE COPS.
JUMP ONTO THAT TRUCK, ERIKA, AND WE'LL GET OUT OF HERE.
I MAY NOT HAVE SHOT YOU...
BAM!
BUT I CAN JUST BURN YOU UP.

HURRY UP! WE GOTTA GET TO THE COPS...

...BEFORE THOSE GUYS CATCH US.

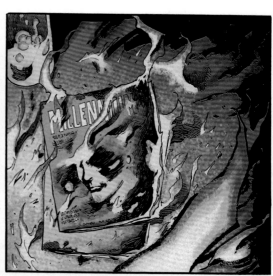

LET'S GET OUTTA HERE!

YOU GET 'EM?

I'LL EXPLAIN LATER!

MOVE IT!

?!

BANG! BANG!

36

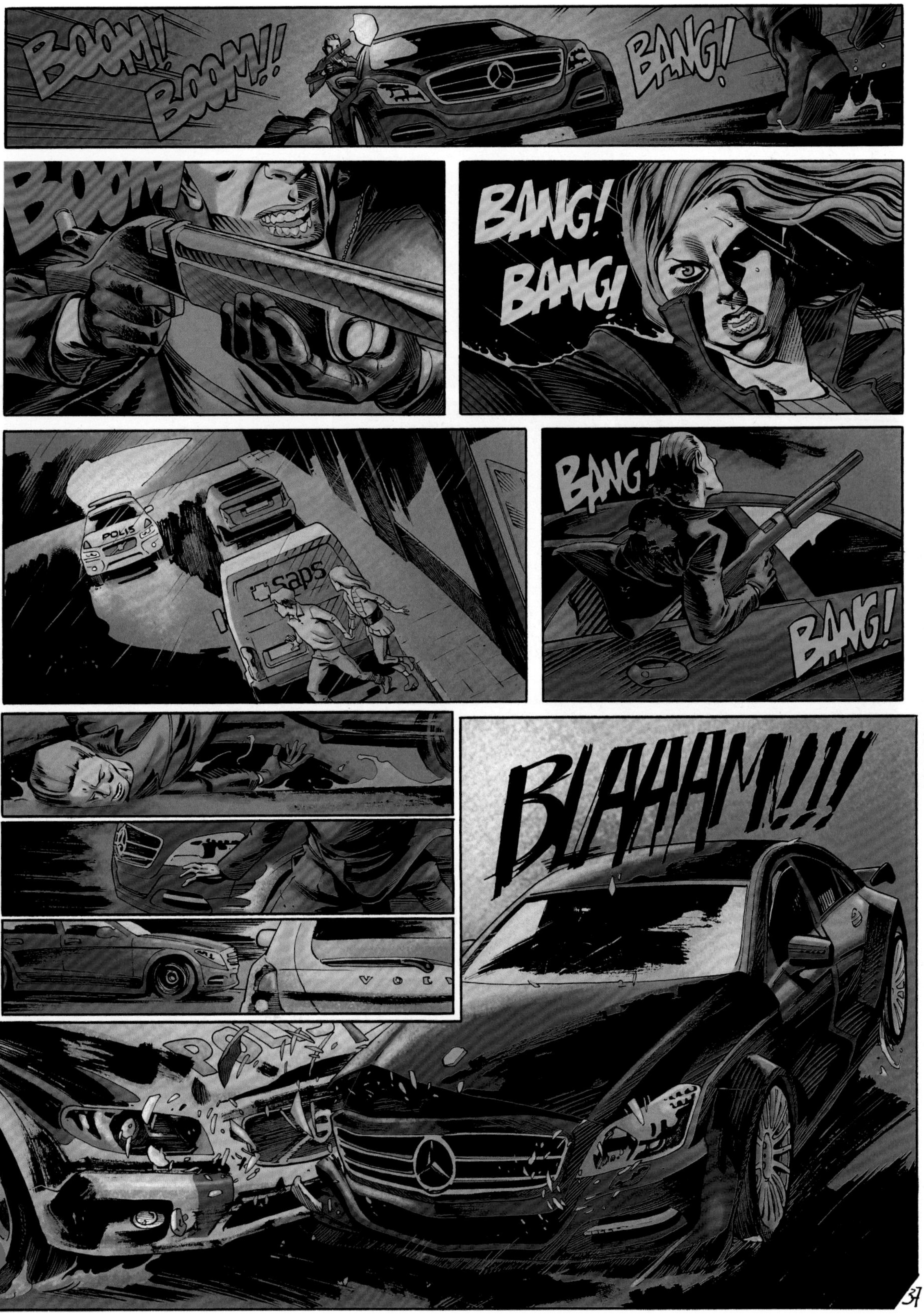
BOOM!
BOOM!!
BANG!
BOOM
BANG!
BANG!
POLIS
saps
BANG!
BANG!
BLAAAM!!!

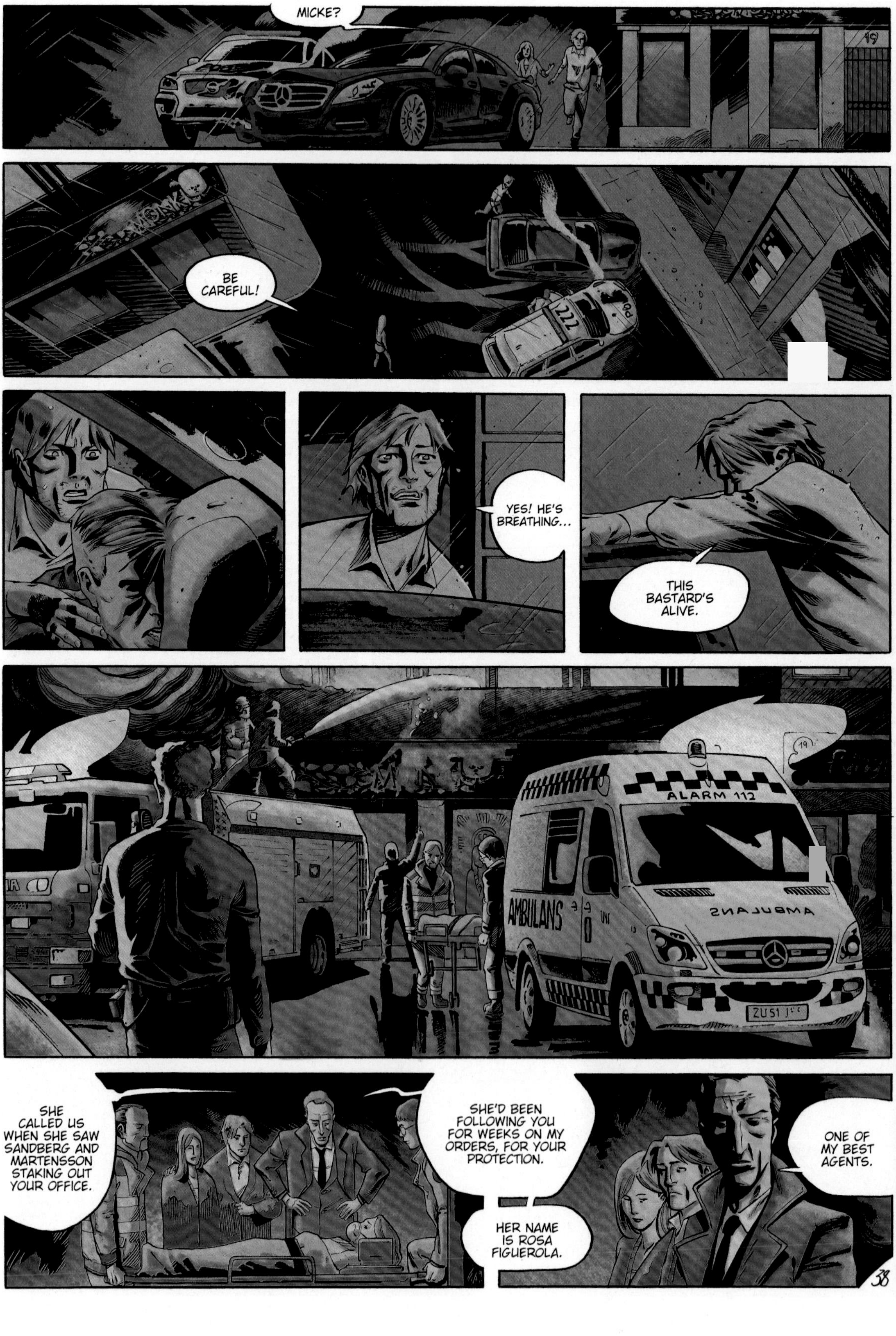
MICKE?
BE CAREFUL!
YES! HE'S BREATHING...
THIS BASTARD'S ALIVE.
ALARM 112
AMBULANS
SHE CALLED US WHEN SHE SAW SANDBERG AND MARTENSSON STAKING OUT YOUR OFFICE.
SHE'D BEEN FOLLOWING YOU FOR WEEKS ON MY ORDERS, FOR YOUR PROTECTION.
HER NAME IS ROSA FIGUEROLA.
ONE OF MY BEST AGENTS.

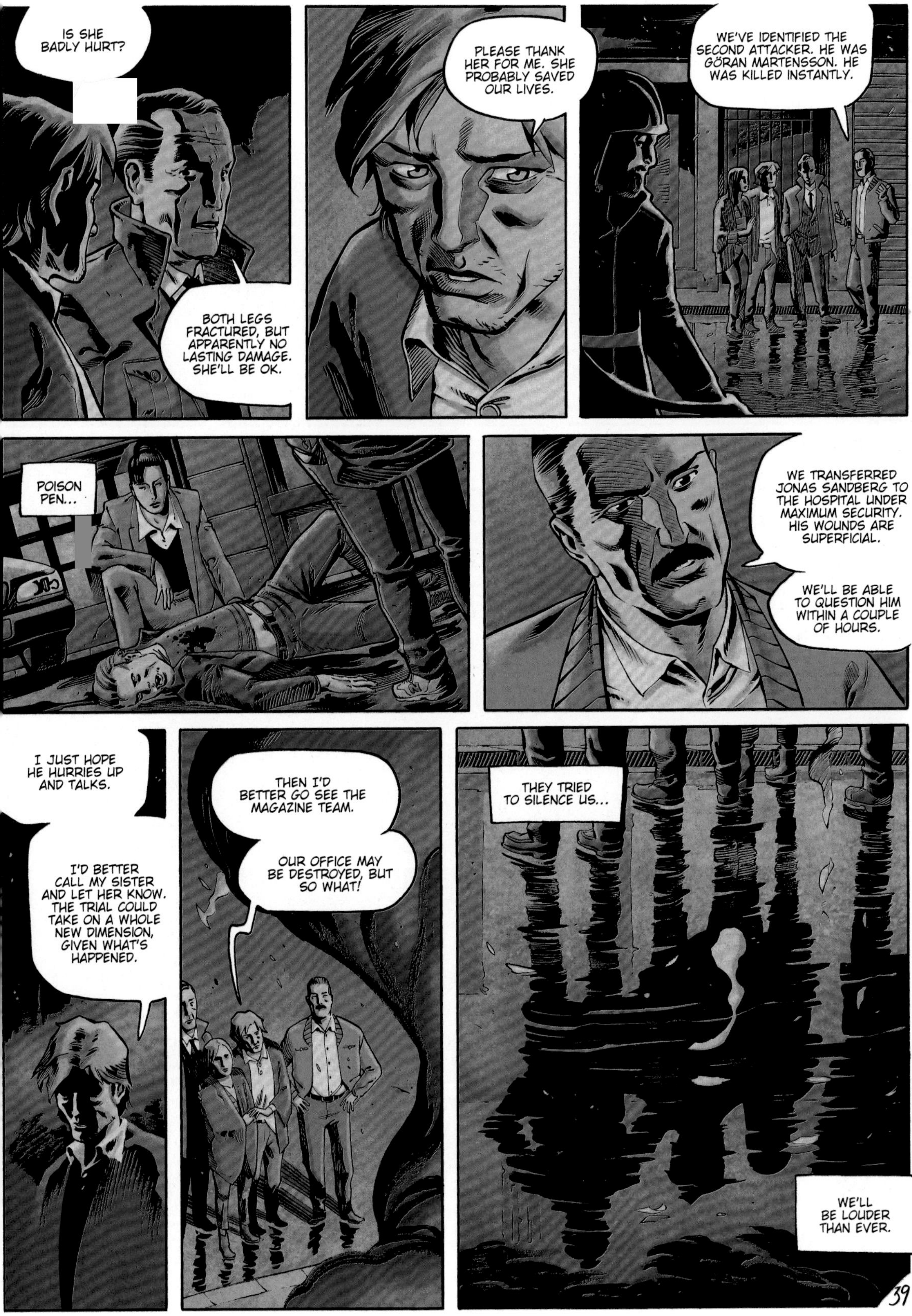
IS SHE BADLY HURT?
BOTH LEGS FRACTURED, BUT APPARENTLY NO LASTING DAMAGE. SHE'LL BE OK.
PLEASE THANK HER FOR ME. SHE PROBABLY SAVED OUR LIVES.
WE'VE IDENTIFIED THE SECOND ATTACKER. HE WAS GÖRAN MARTENSSON. HE WAS KILLED INSTANTLY.
POISON PEN...
WE TRANSFERRED JONAS SANDBERG TO THE HOSPITAL UNDER MAXIMUM SECURITY. HIS WOUNDS ARE SUPERFICIAL.
WE'LL BE ABLE TO QUESTION HIM WITHIN A COUPLE OF HOURS.
I JUST HOPE HE HURRIES UP AND TALKS.
I'D BETTER CALL MY SISTER AND LET HER KNOW. THE TRIAL COULD TAKE ON A WHOLE NEW DIMENSION, GIVEN WHAT'S HAPPENED.
THEN I'D BETTER GO SEE THE MAGAZINE TEAM.
OUR OFFICE MAY BE DESTROYED, BUT SO WHAT!
THEY TRIED TO SILENCE US...
WE'LL BE LOUDER THAN EVER.

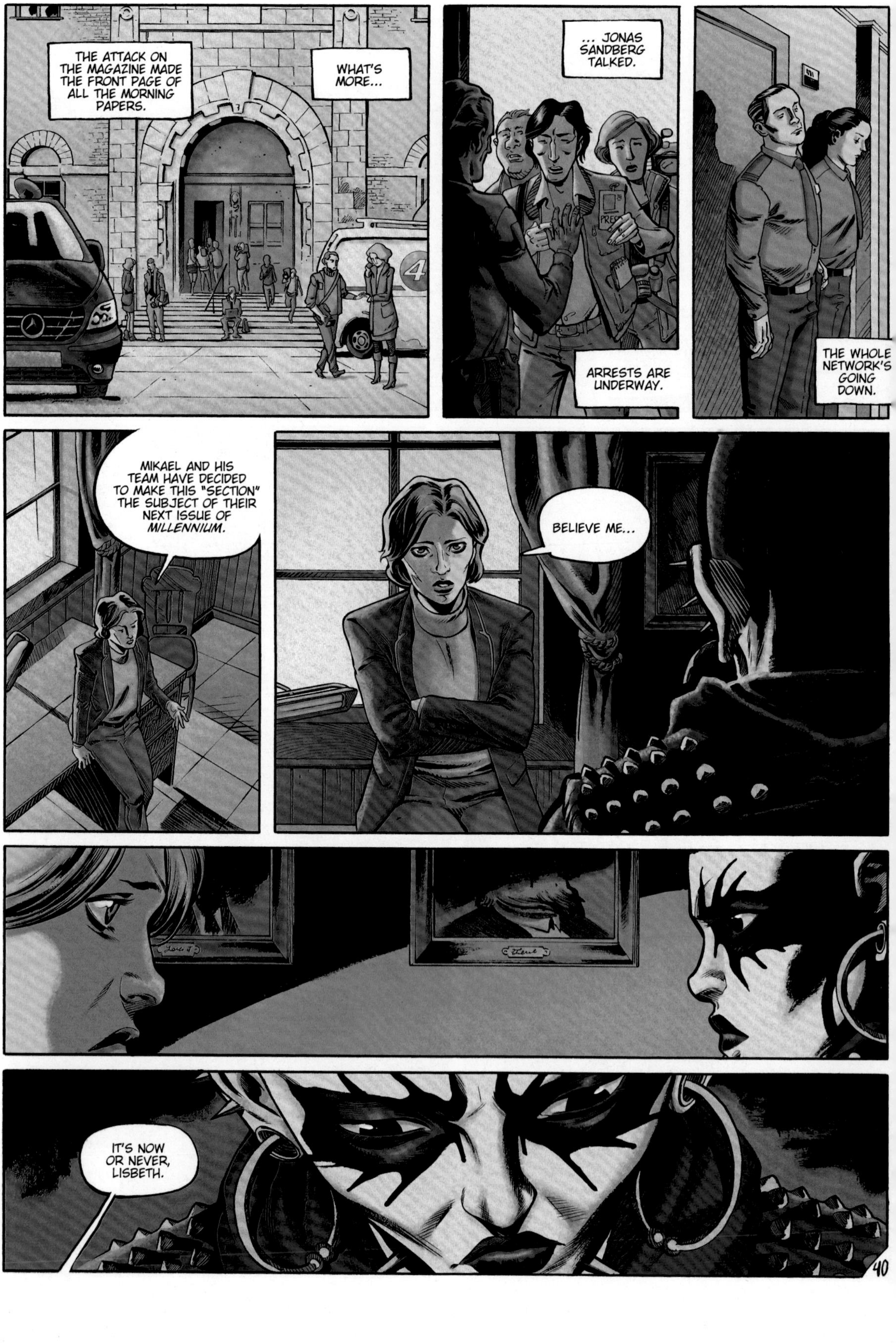
THE ATTACK ON THE MAGAZINE MADE THE FRONT PAGE OF ALL THE MORNING PAPERS.
WHAT'S MORE...
... JONAS SANDBERG TALKED.
ARRESTS ARE UNDERWAY.
THE WHOLE NETWORK'S GOING DOWN.
MIKAEL AND HIS TEAM HAVE DECIDED TO MAKE THIS "SECTION" THE SUBJECT OF THEIR NEXT ISSUE OF *MILLENNIUM*.
BELIEVE ME...
IT'S NOW OR NEVER, LISBETH.

YOU MUST TAKE THE STAND.

SINCE IT'S THE DEFENSE'S TURN TO BEGIN TODAY...

I'D LIKE YOU TO ENLIGHTEN ME, COUNSEL GIANNINI.

IS YOUR CLIENT GOING TO CONTINUE HER OBSTINATE SILENCE?

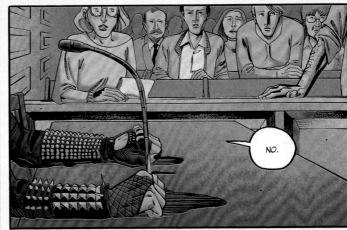

NO.

TODAY, I WILL NOT BE SILENT, BECAUSE I AM INNOCENT.

I AM THE VICTIM OF A PLOT THAT REACHES TO THE SWEDISH STATE'S HIGHEST SPHERE OF POWER.

AND I WILL PROVE IT.

I'LL PROVE THAT THE PSYCHIATRIST PETER TELEBORIAN WAS ONE OF THOSE WHO HATCHED THIS CONSPIRACY.

THAT HE IS A SADIST, EMPLOYED BY MEMBERS OF THE SÄPO BELONGING TO A SECRET CELL OF RIGHT-WING EXTREMISTS KNOWN AS THE "SECTION," AND THAT HE SOUGHT TO SILENCE ME TO PROTECT ALEXANDER ZALACHENKO.

MY FATHER. A DEFECTOR FROM THE RUSSIAN SPECIAL FORCES.

TURNED EXECUTIONER FOR THIS GANG OF SWEDISH NATIONALISTS.

41

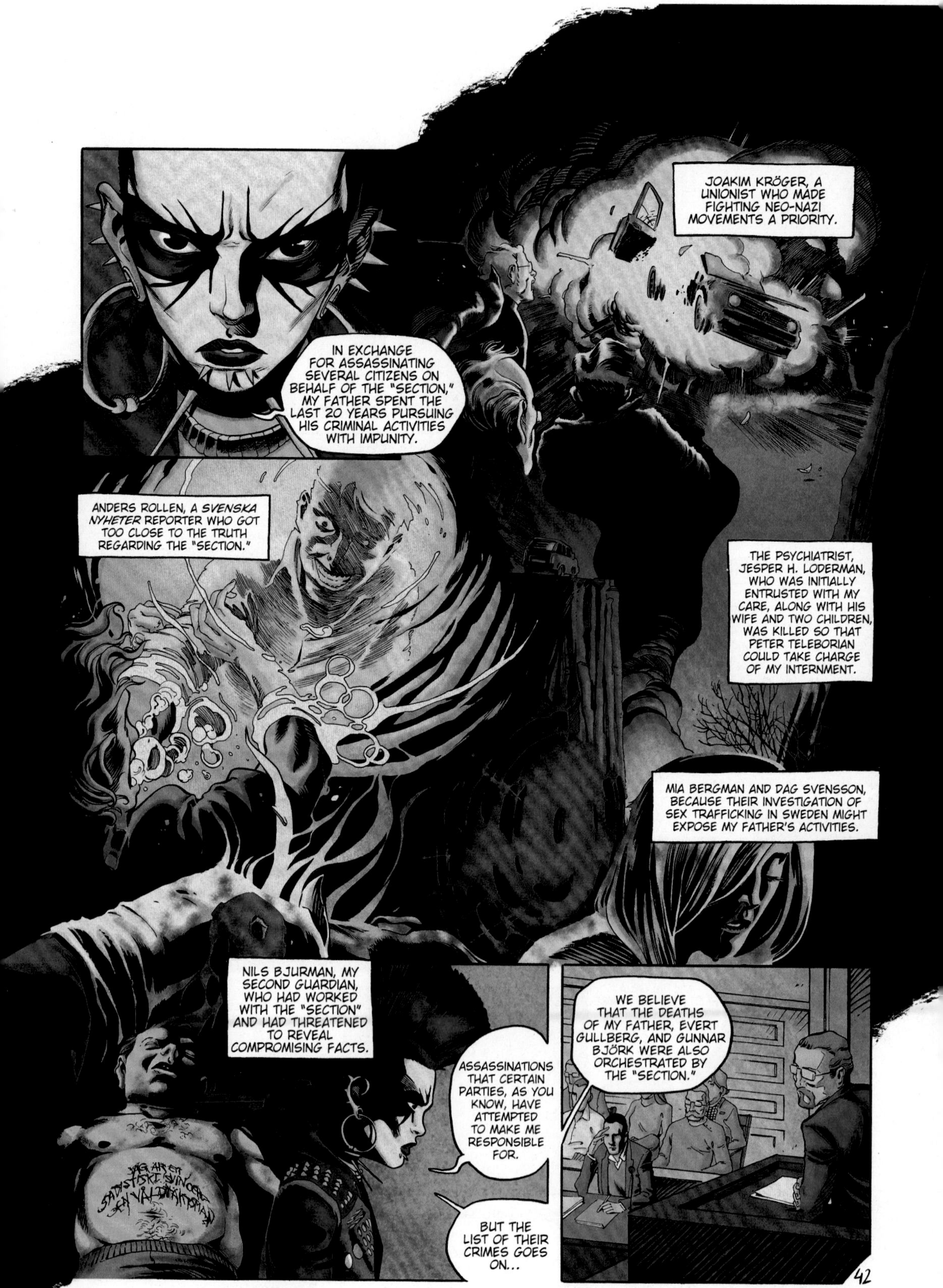
IN EXCHANGE FOR ASSASSINATING SEVERAL CITIZENS ON BEHALF OF THE "SECTION," MY FATHER SPENT THE LAST 20 YEARS PURSUING HIS CRIMINAL ACTIVITIES WITH IMPUNITY.
JOAKIM KRÖGER, A UNIONIST WHO MADE FIGHTING NEO-NAZI MOVEMENTS A PRIORITY.
ANDERS ROLLEN, A *SVENSKA NYHETER* REPORTER WHO GOT TOO CLOSE TO THE TRUTH REGARDING THE "SECTION."
THE PSYCHIATRIST, JESPER H. LODERMAN, WHO WAS INITIALLY ENTRUSTED WITH MY CARE, ALONG WITH HIS WIFE AND TWO CHILDREN, WAS KILLED SO THAT PETER TELEBORIAN COULD TAKE CHARGE OF MY INTERNMENT.
MIA BERGMAN AND DAG SVENSSON, BECAUSE THEIR INVESTIGATION OF SEX TRAFFICKING IN SWEDEN MIGHT EXPOSE MY FATHER'S ACTIVITIES.
NILS BJURMAN, MY SECOND GUARDIAN, WHO HAD WORKED WITH THE "SECTION" AND HAD THREATENED TO REVEAL COMPROMISING FACTS.
ASSASSINATIONS THAT CERTAIN PARTIES, AS YOU KNOW, HAVE ATTEMPTED TO MAKE ME RESPONSIBLE FOR.
BUT THE LIST OF THEIR CRIMES GOES ON...
WE BELIEVE THAT THE DEATHS OF MY FATHER, EVERT GULLBERG, AND GUNNAR BJÖRK WERE ALSO ORCHESTRATED BY THE "SECTION."

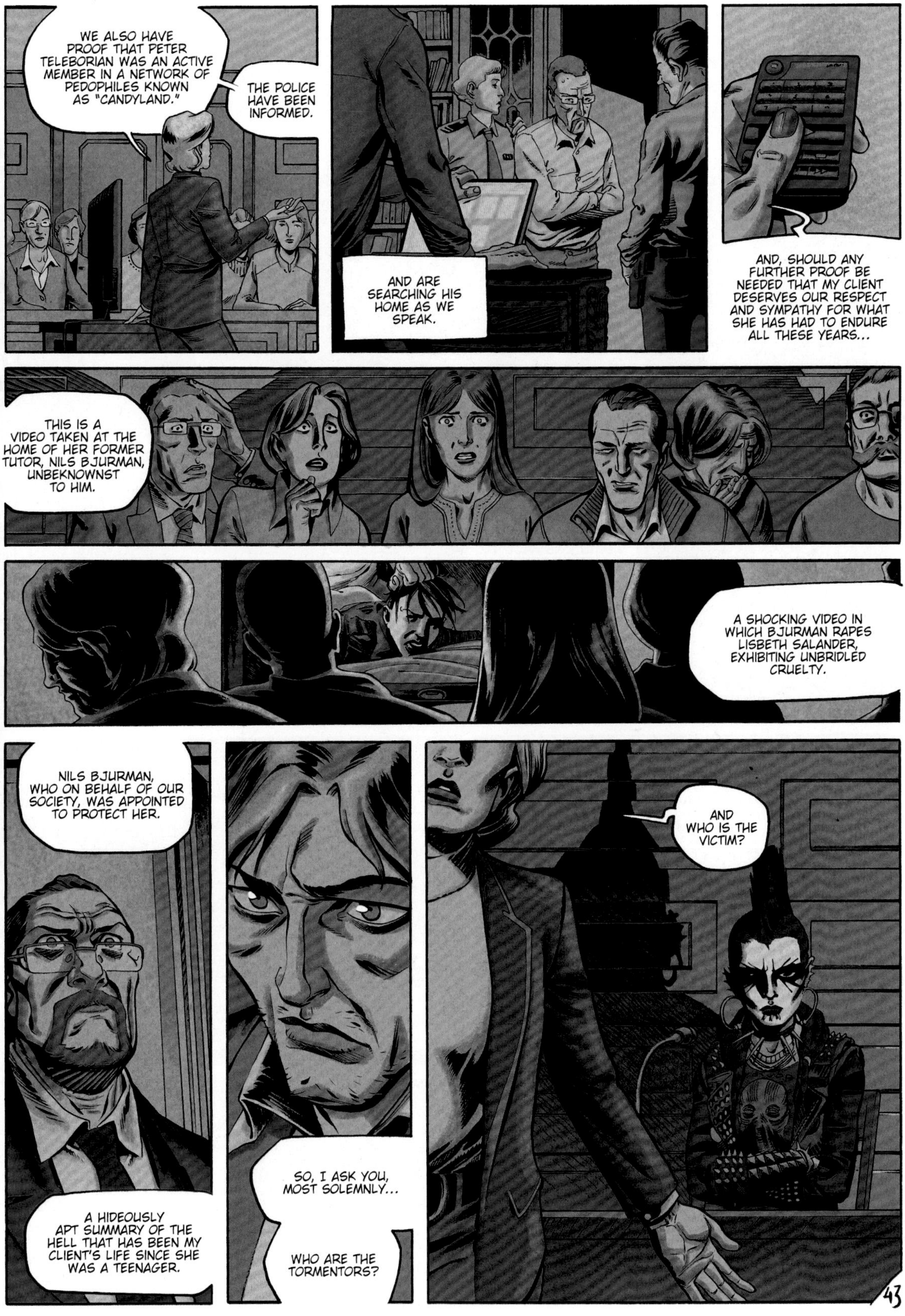
WE ALSO HAVE PROOF THAT PETER TELEBORIAN WAS AN ACTIVE MEMBER IN A NETWORK OF PEDOPHILES KNOWN AS "CANDYLAND."
THE POLICE HAVE BEEN INFORMED.
AND ARE SEARCHING HIS HOME AS WE SPEAK.
AND, SHOULD ANY FURTHER PROOF BE NEEDED THAT MY CLIENT DESERVES OUR RESPECT AND SYMPATHY FOR WHAT SHE HAS HAD TO ENDURE ALL THESE YEARS...
THIS IS A VIDEO TAKEN AT THE HOME OF HER FORMER TUTOR, NILS BJURMAN, UNBEKNOWNST TO HIM.
A SHOCKING VIDEO IN WHICH BJURMAN RAPES LISBETH SALANDER, EXHIBITING UNBRIDLED CRUELTY.
NILS BJURMAN, WHO ON BEHALF OF OUR SOCIETY, WAS APPOINTED TO PROTECT HER.
A HIDEOUSLY APT SUMMARY OF THE HELL THAT HAS BEEN MY CLIENT'S LIFE SINCE SHE WAS A TEENAGER.
SO, I ASK YOU, MOST SOLEMNLY...
WHO ARE THE TORMENTORS?
AND WHO IS THE VICTIM?

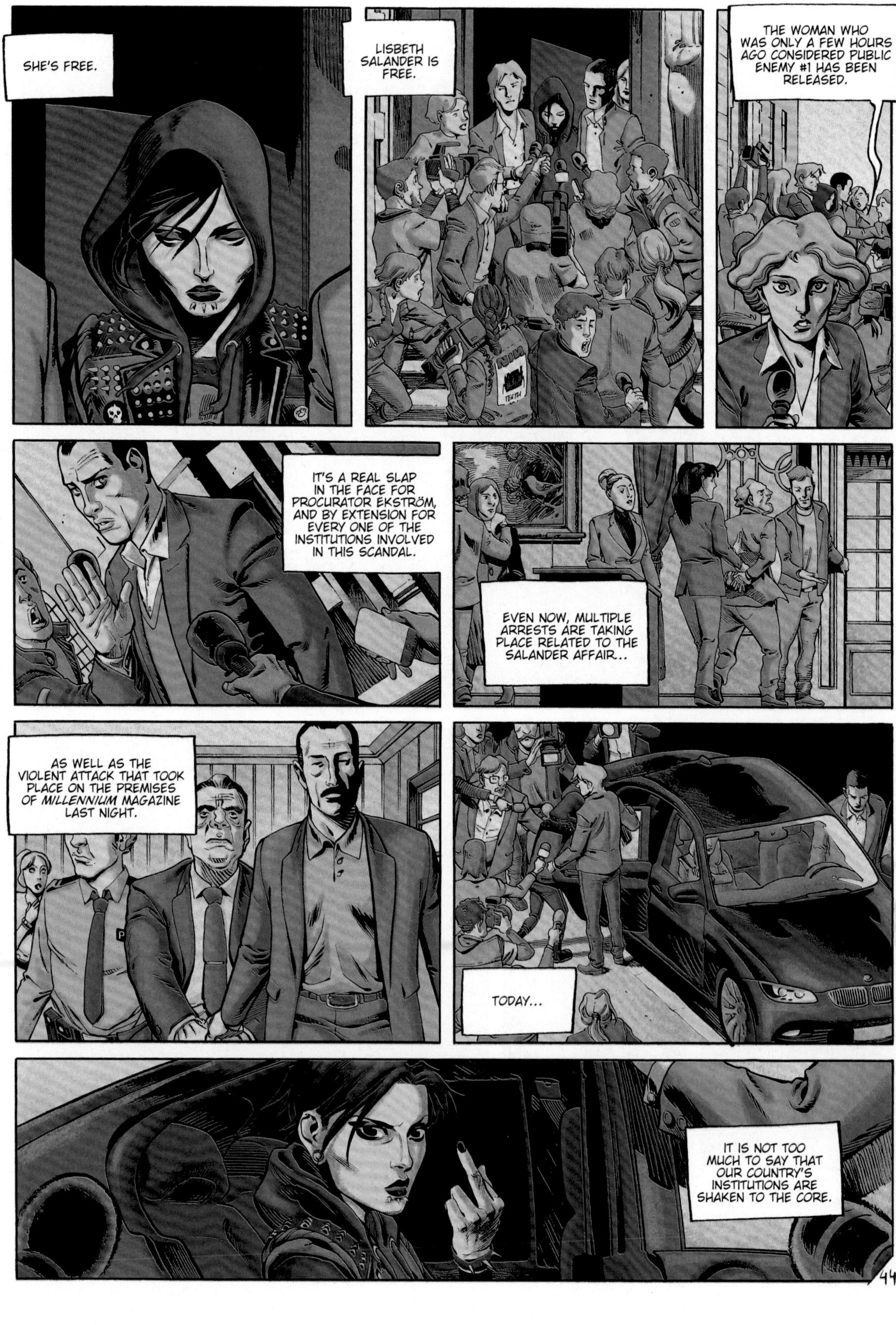
SHE'S FREE.
LISBETH SALANDER IS FREE.
THE WOMAN WHO WAS ONLY A FEW HOURS AGO CONSIDERED PUBLIC ENEMY #1 HAS BEEN RELEASED.
IT'S A REAL SLAP IN THE FACE FOR PROCURATOR EKSTRÖM, AND BY EXTENSION FOR EVERY ONE OF THE INSTITUTIONS INVOLVED IN THIS SCANDAL.
EVEN NOW, MULTIPLE ARRESTS ARE TAKING PLACE RELATED TO THE SALANDER AFFAIR...
AS WELL AS THE VIOLENT ATTACK THAT TOOK PLACE ON THE PREMISES OF *MILLENNIUM* MAGAZINE LAST NIGHT.
TODAY...
IT IS NOT TOO MUCH TO SAY THAT OUR COUNTRY'S INSTITUTIONS ARE SHAKEN TO THE CORE.

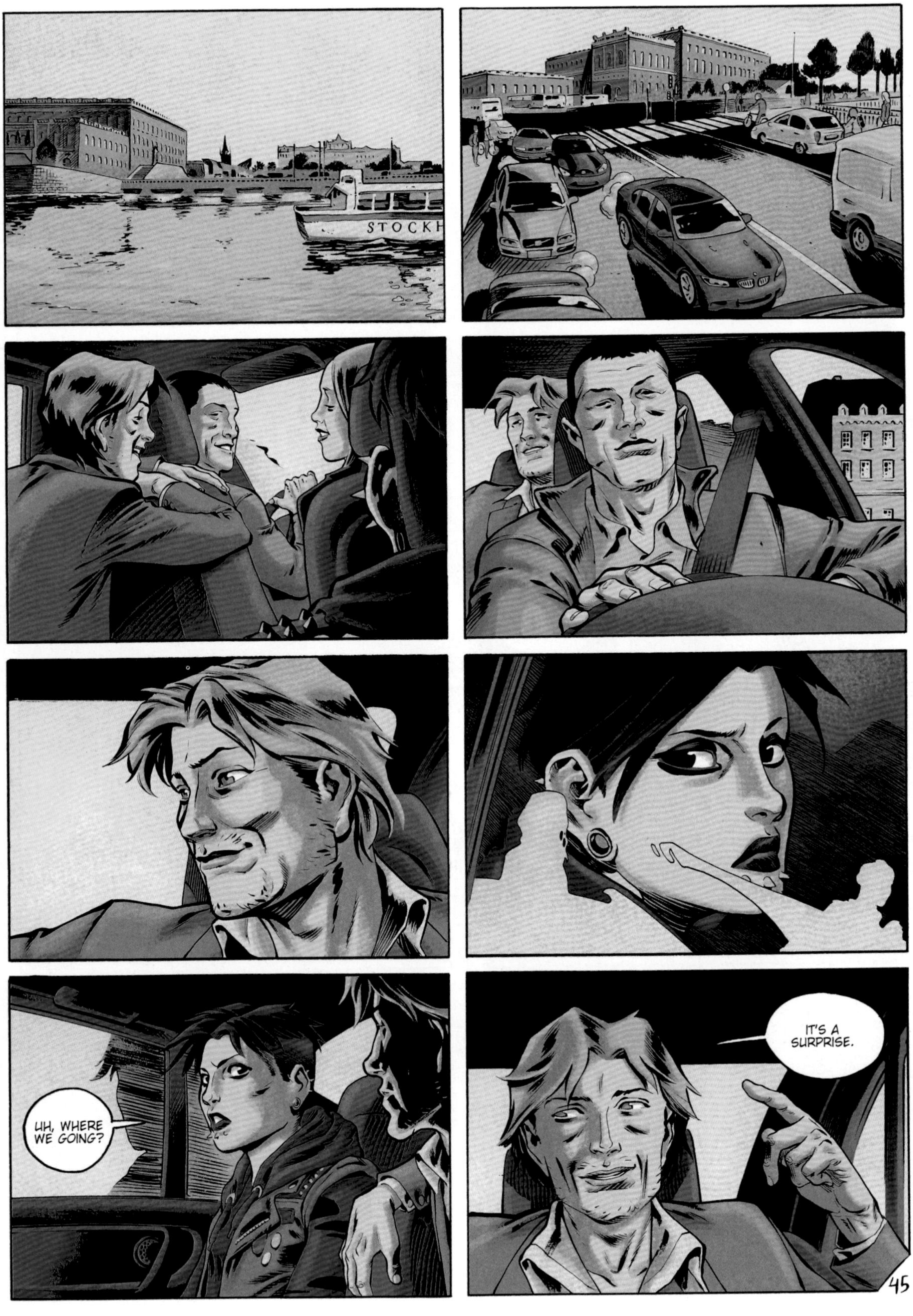
STOCKH
UH, WHERE WE GOING?
IT'S A SURPRISE.

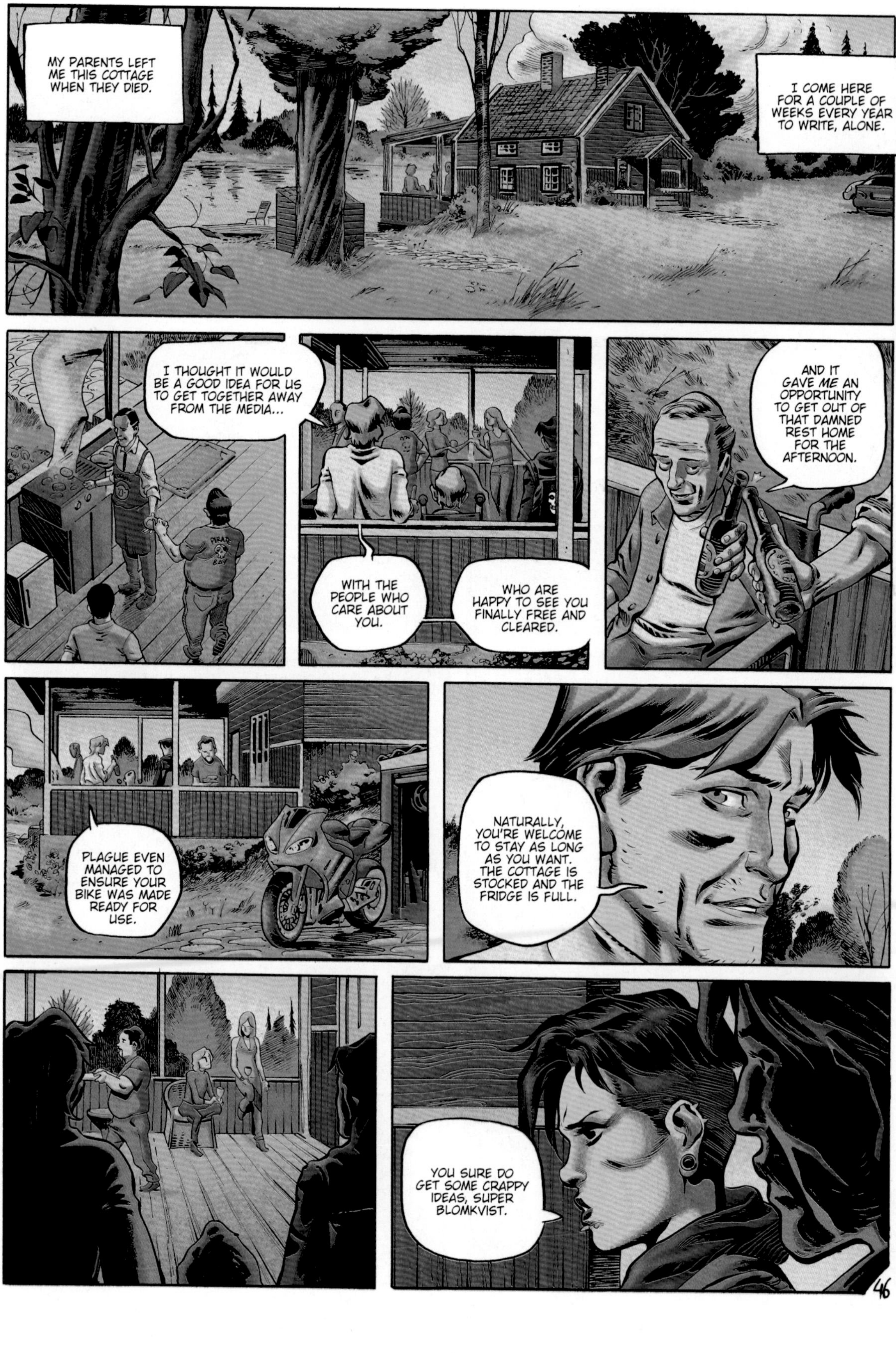

MY PARENTS LEFT ME THIS COTTAGE WHEN THEY DIED.
I COME HERE FOR A COUPLE OF WEEKS EVERY YEAR TO WRITE, ALONE.
I THOUGHT IT WOULD BE A GOOD IDEA FOR US TO GET TOGETHER AWAY FROM THE MEDIA...
PIRATE BAY
WITH THE PEOPLE WHO CARE ABOUT YOU.
WHO ARE HAPPY TO SEE YOU FINALLY FREE AND CLEARED.
AND IT GAVE ME AN OPPORTUNITY TO GET OUT OF THAT DAMNED REST HOME FOR THE AFTERNOON.
PLAGUE EVEN MANAGED TO ENSURE YOUR BIKE WAS MADE READY FOR USE.
NATURALLY, YOU'RE WELCOME TO STAY AS LONG AS YOU WANT. THE COTTAGE IS STOCKED AND THE FRIDGE IS FULL.
YOU SURE DO GET SOME CRAPPY IDEAS, SUPER BLOMKVIST.

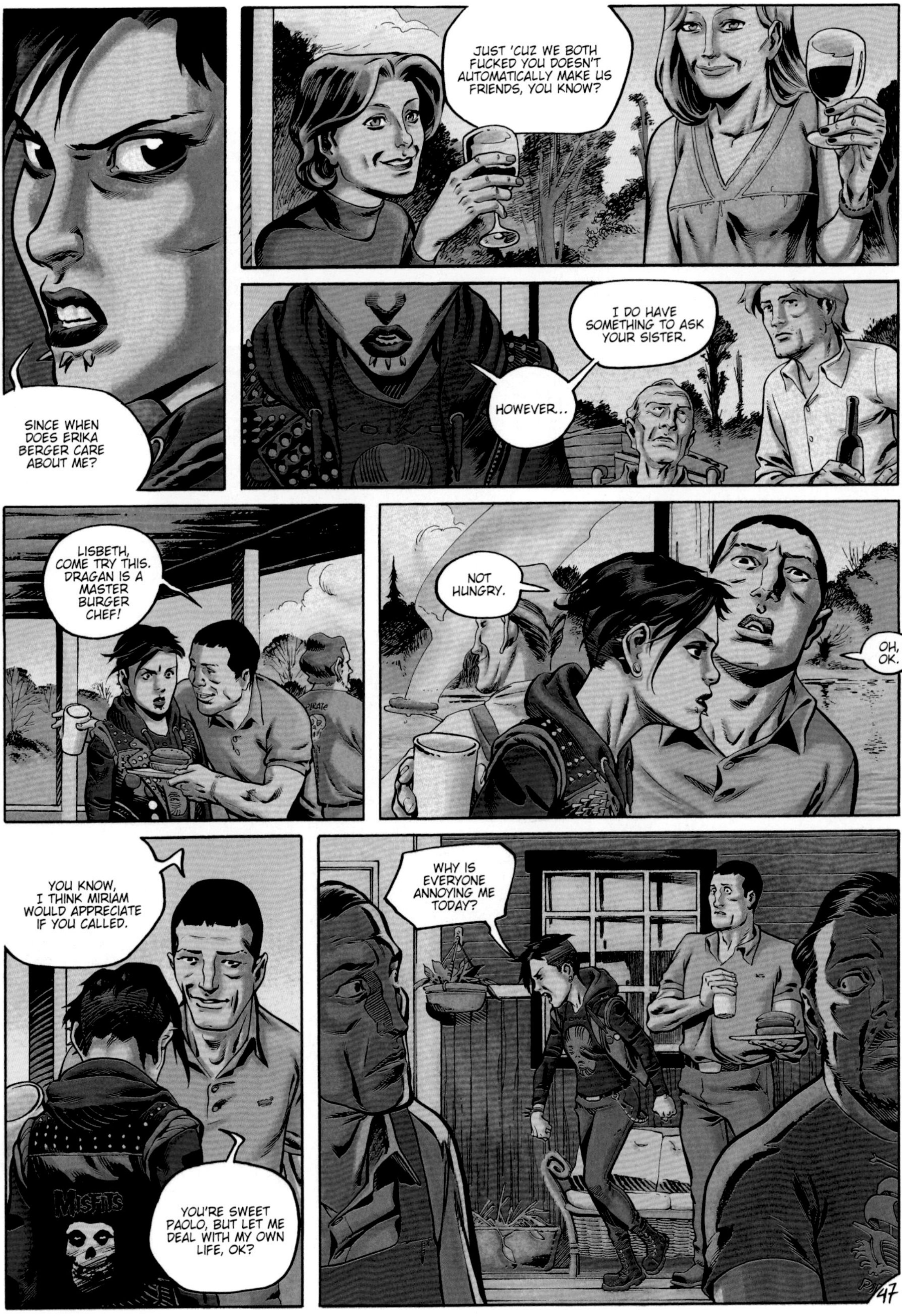
SINCE WHEN DOES ERIKA BERGER CARE ABOUT ME?
JUST 'CUZ WE BOTH FUCKED YOU DOESN'T AUTOMATICALLY MAKE US FRIENDS, YOU KNOW?
HOWEVER..
I DO HAVE SOMETHING TO ASK YOUR SISTER.
LISBETH, COME TRY THIS. DRAGAN IS A MASTER BURGER CHEF!
NOT HUNGRY.
OH, OK.
YOU KNOW, I THINK MIRIAM WOULD APPRECIATE IF YOU CALLED.
YOU'RE SWEET PAOLO, BUT LET ME DEAL WITH MY OWN LIFE, OK?
WHY IS EVERYONE ANNOYING ME TODAY?

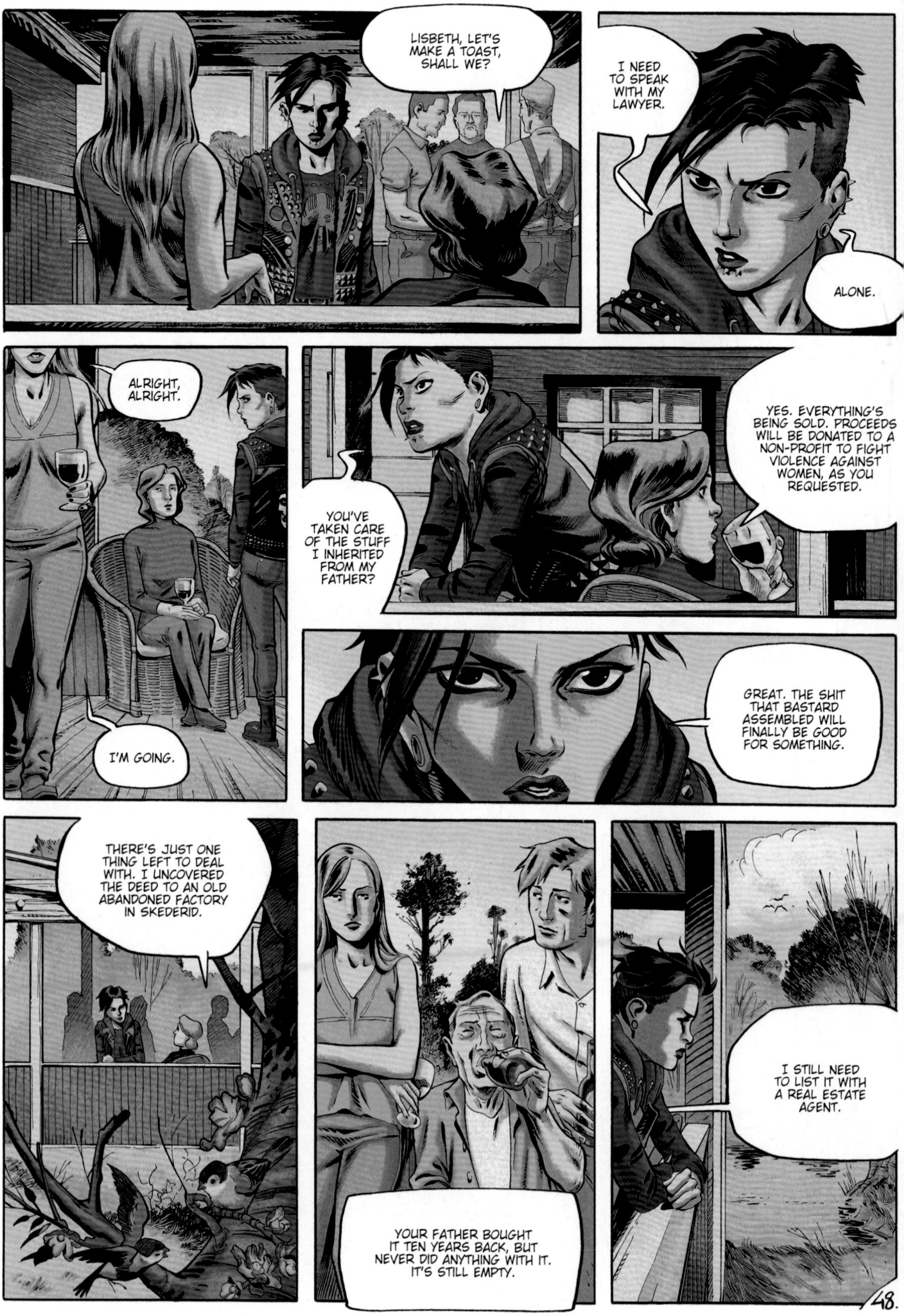
LISBETH, LET'S MAKE A TOAST, SHALL WE?
I NEED TO SPEAK WITH MY LAWYER.
ALONE.
ALRIGHT, ALRIGHT.
I'M GOING.
YOU'VE TAKEN CARE OF THE STUFF I INHERITED FROM MY FATHER?
YES. EVERYTHING'S BEING SOLD. PROCEEDS WILL BE DONATED TO A NON-PROFIT TO FIGHT VIOLENCE AGAINST WOMEN, AS YOU REQUESTED.
GREAT. THE SHIT THAT BASTARD ASSEMBLED WILL FINALLY BE GOOD FOR SOMETHING.
THERE'S JUST ONE THING LEFT TO DEAL WITH. I UNCOVERED THE DEED TO AN OLD ABANDONED FACTORY IN SKEDERID.
YOUR FATHER BOUGHT IT TEN YEARS BACK, BUT NEVER DID ANYTHING WITH IT. IT'S STILL EMPTY.
I STILL NEED TO LIST IT WITH A REAL ESTATE AGENT.

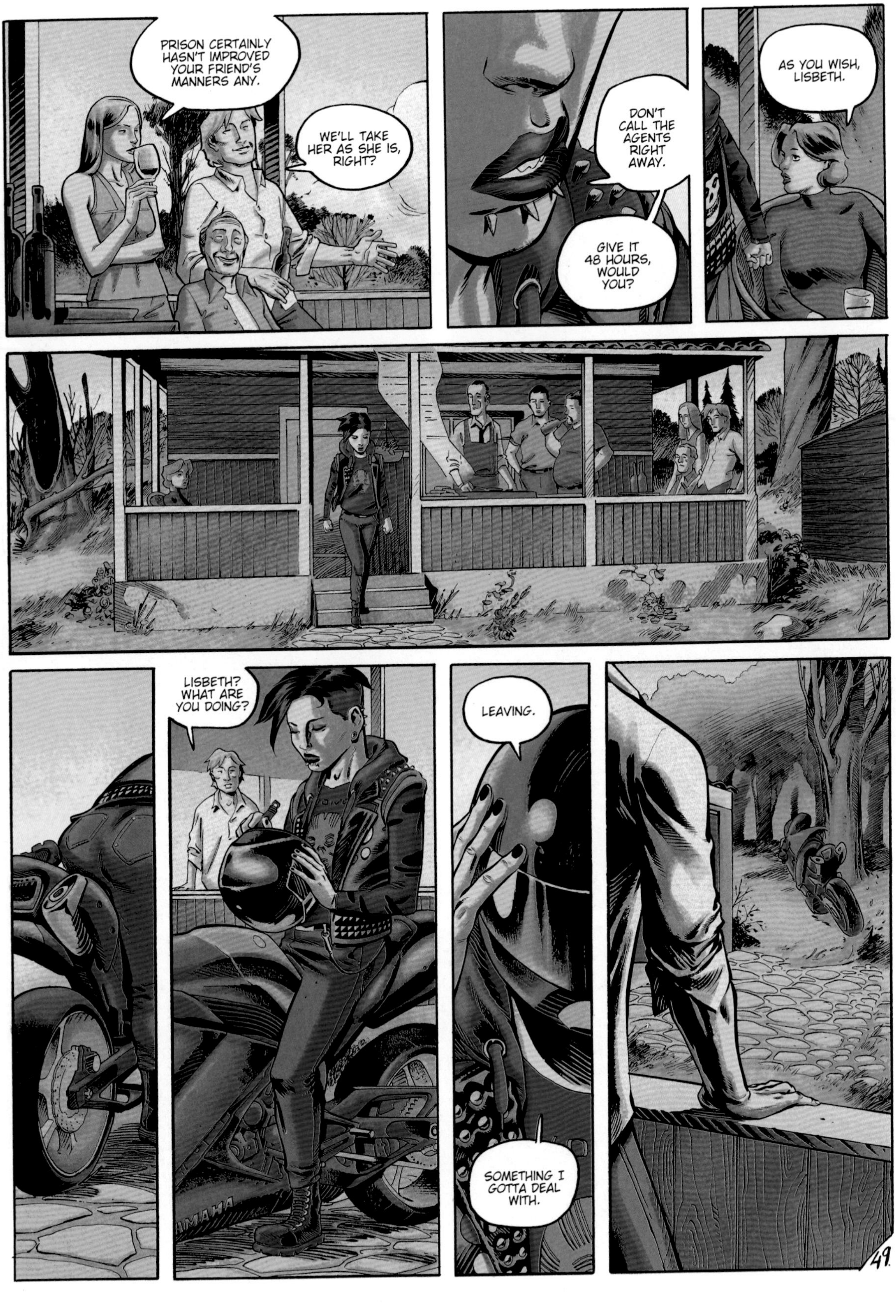
PRISON CERTAINLY HASN'T IMPROVED YOUR FRIEND'S MANNERS ANY.
WE'LL TAKE HER AS SHE IS, RIGHT?
DON'T CALL THE AGENTS RIGHT AWAY.
GIVE IT 48 HOURS, WOULD YOU?
AS YOU WISH, LISBETH.
LISBETH? WHAT ARE YOU DOING?
YAMAHA
LEAVING.
SOMETHING I GOTTA DEAL WITH.

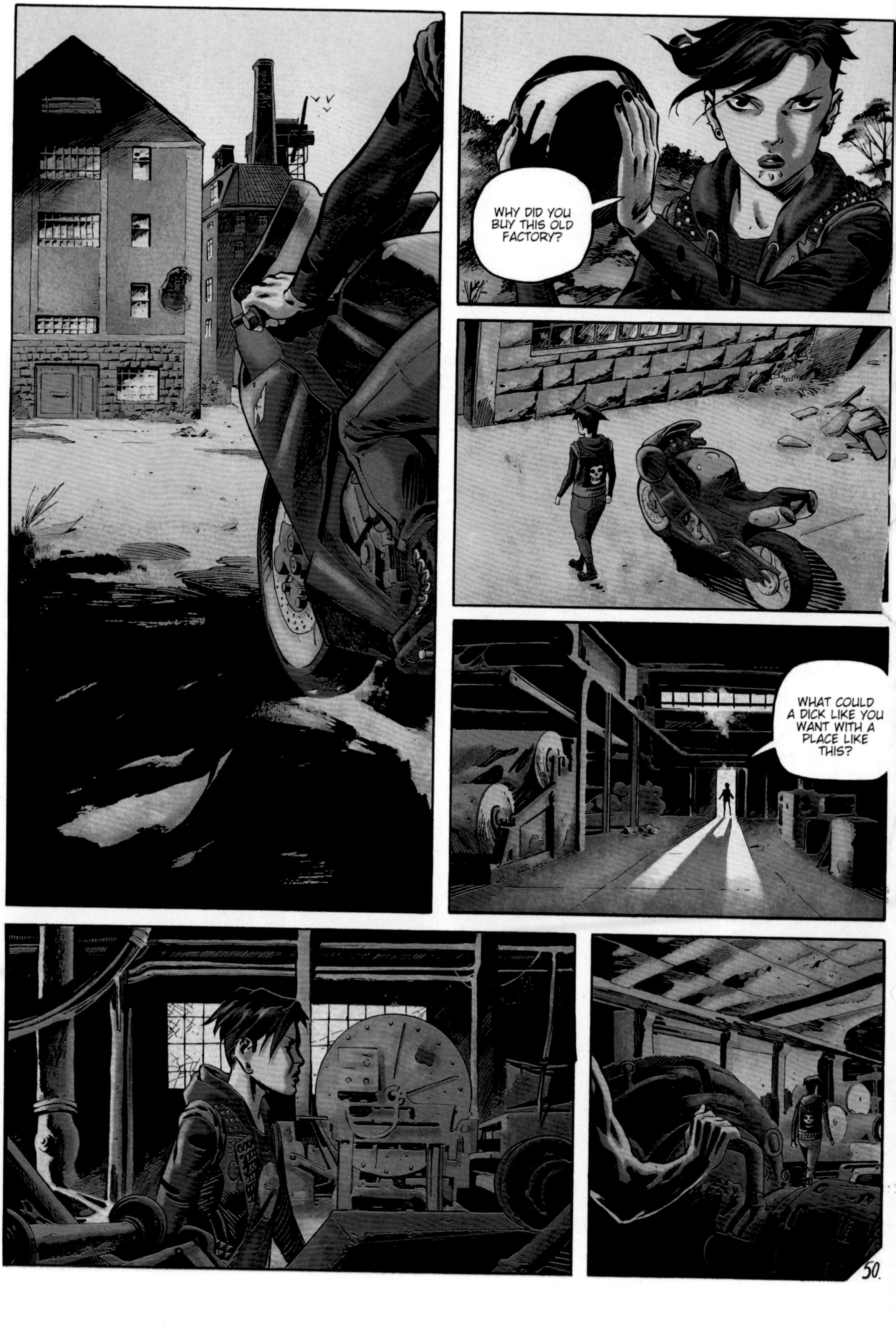
WHY DID YOU BUY THIS OLD FACTORY?
WHAT COULD A DICK LIKE YOU WANT WITH A PLACE LIKE THIS?

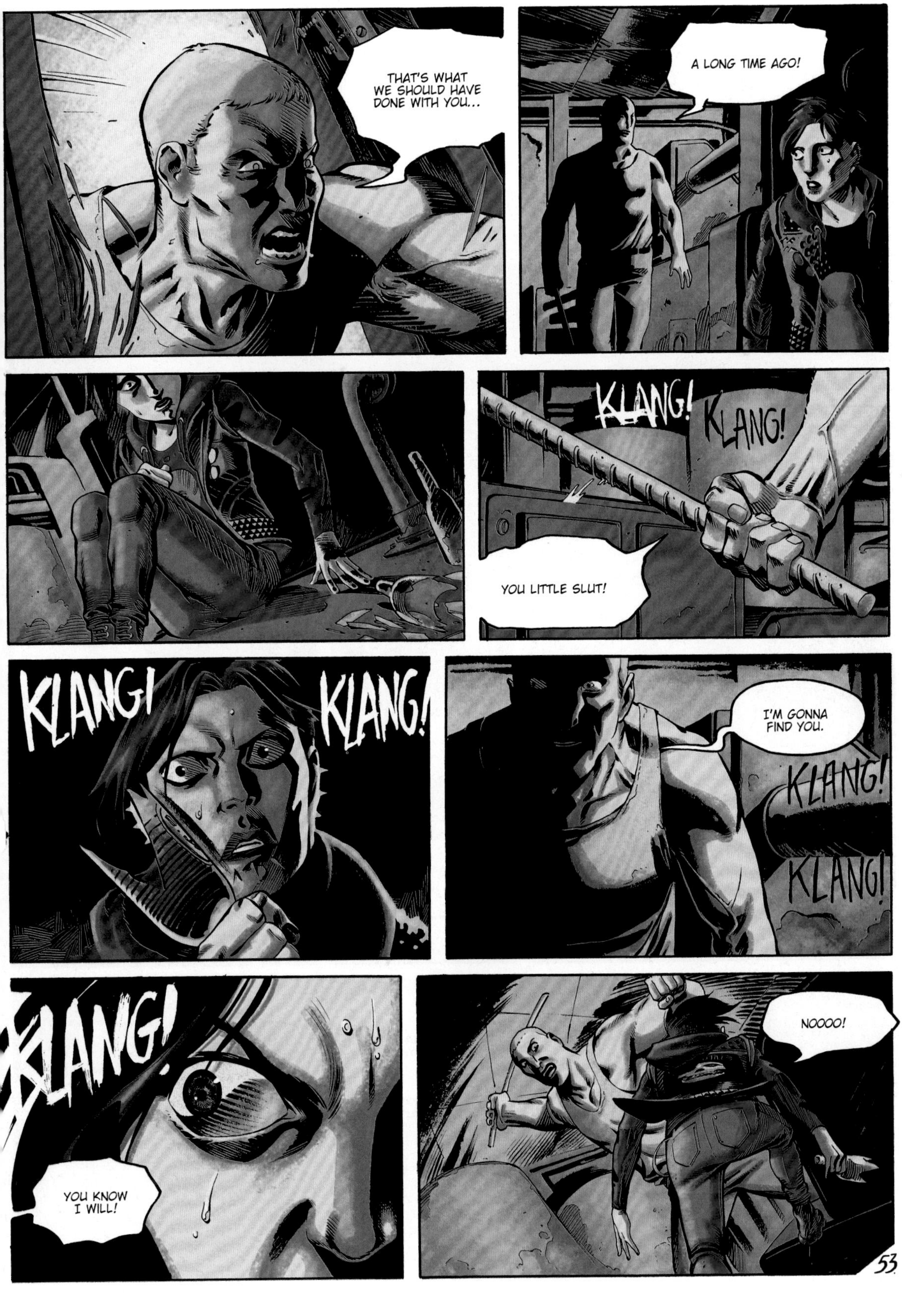
THAT'S WHAT WE SHOULD HAVE DONE WITH YOU...
A LONG TIME AGO!
KLANG!
KLANG!
YOU LITTLE SLUT!
KLANG!
KLANG!
I'M GONNA FIND YOU.
KLANG!
KLANG!
KLANG!
YOU KNOW I WILL!
NOOOO!

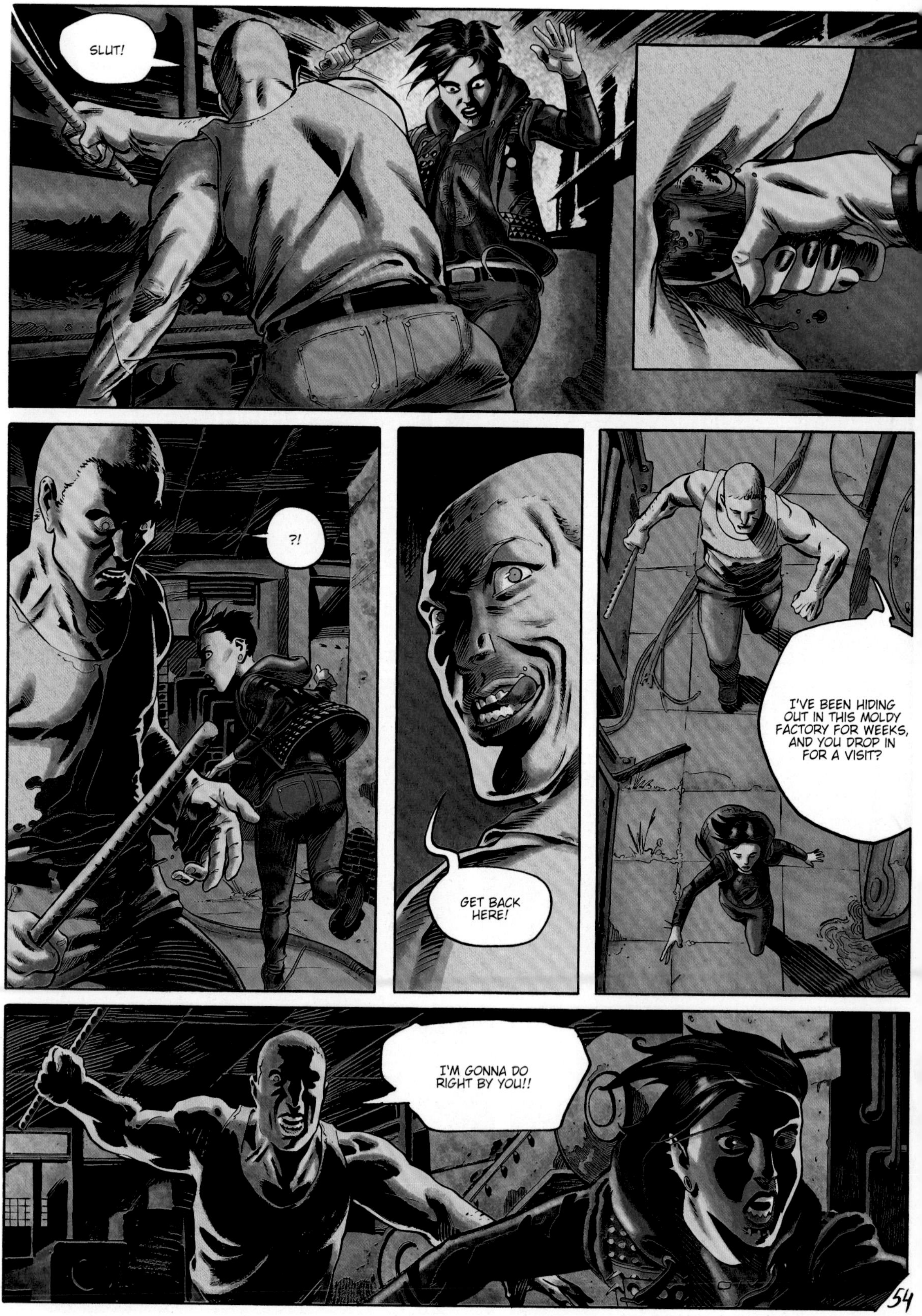
SLUT!
?!
GET BACK HERE!
I'VE BEEN HIDING OUT IN THIS MOLDY FACTORY FOR WEEKS, AND YOU DROP IN FOR A VISIT?
I'M GONNA DO RIGHT BY YOU!!

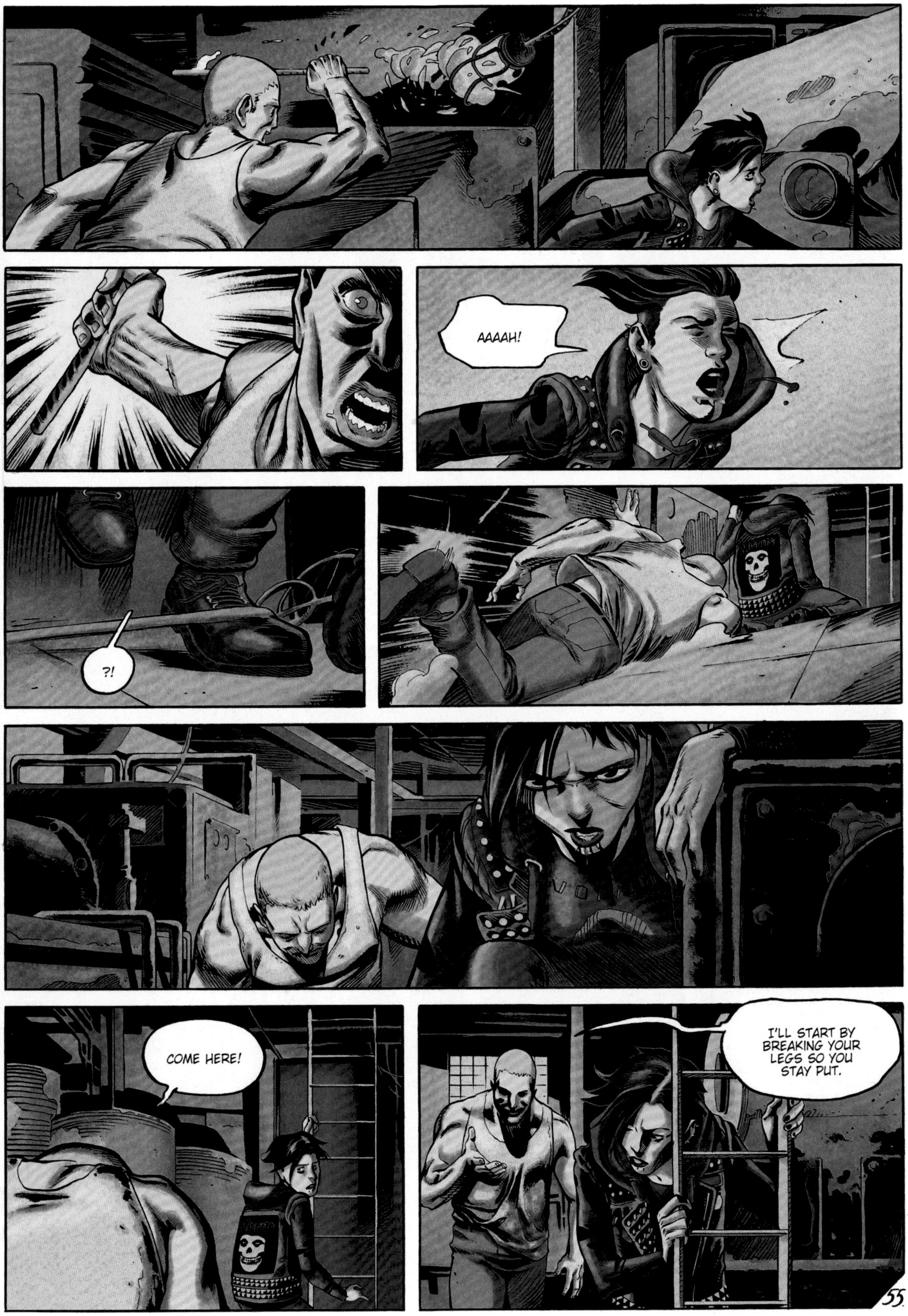
AAAAH!
?!
COME HERE!
I'LL START BY BREAKING YOUR LEGS SO YOU STAY PUT.

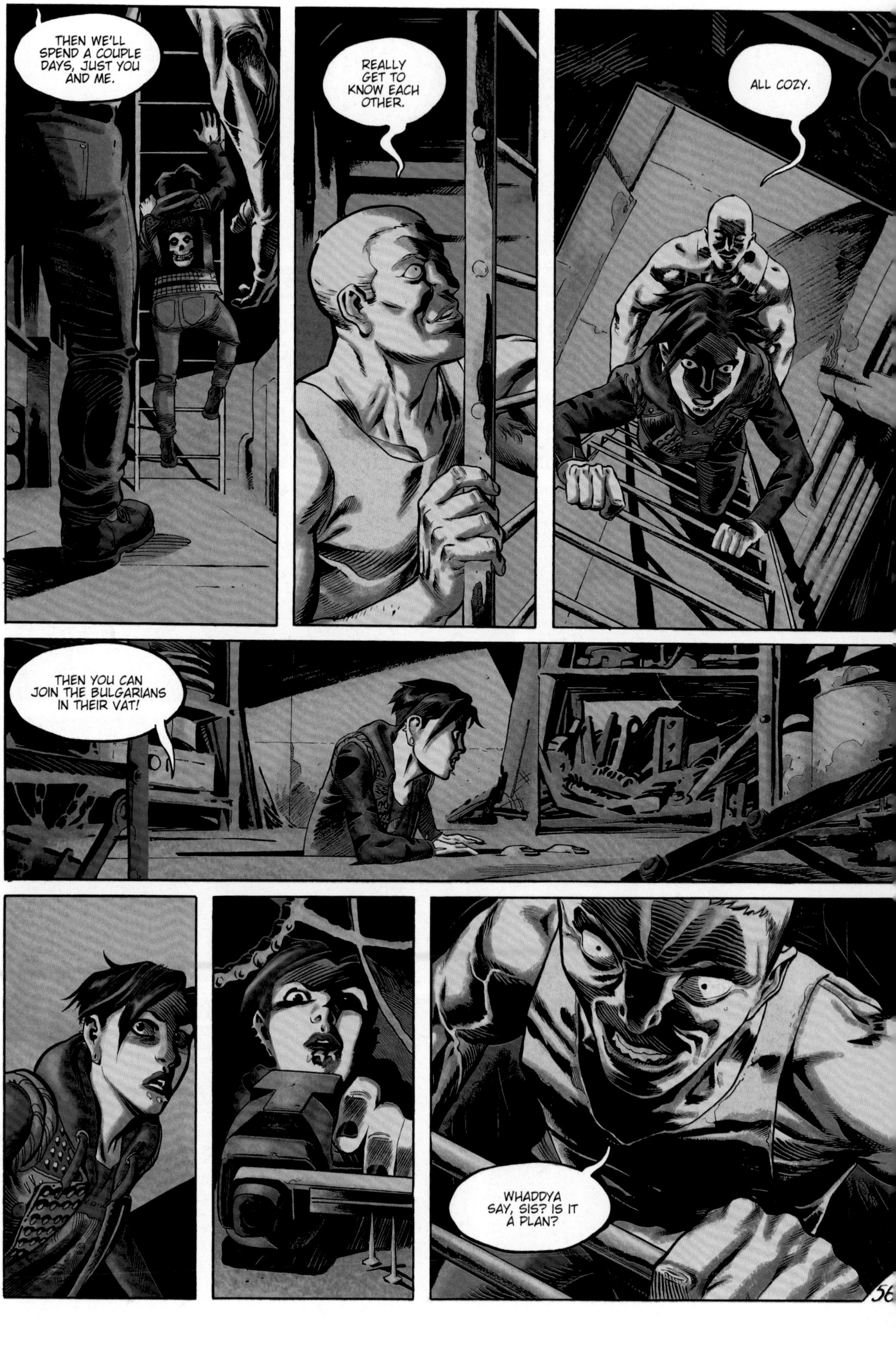
THEN WE'LL SPEND A COUPLE DAYS, JUST YOU AND ME.
REALLY GET TO KNOW EACH OTHER.
ALL COZY.
THEN YOU CAN JOIN THE BULGARIANS IN THEIR VAT!
WHADDYA SAY, SIS? IS IT A PLAN?

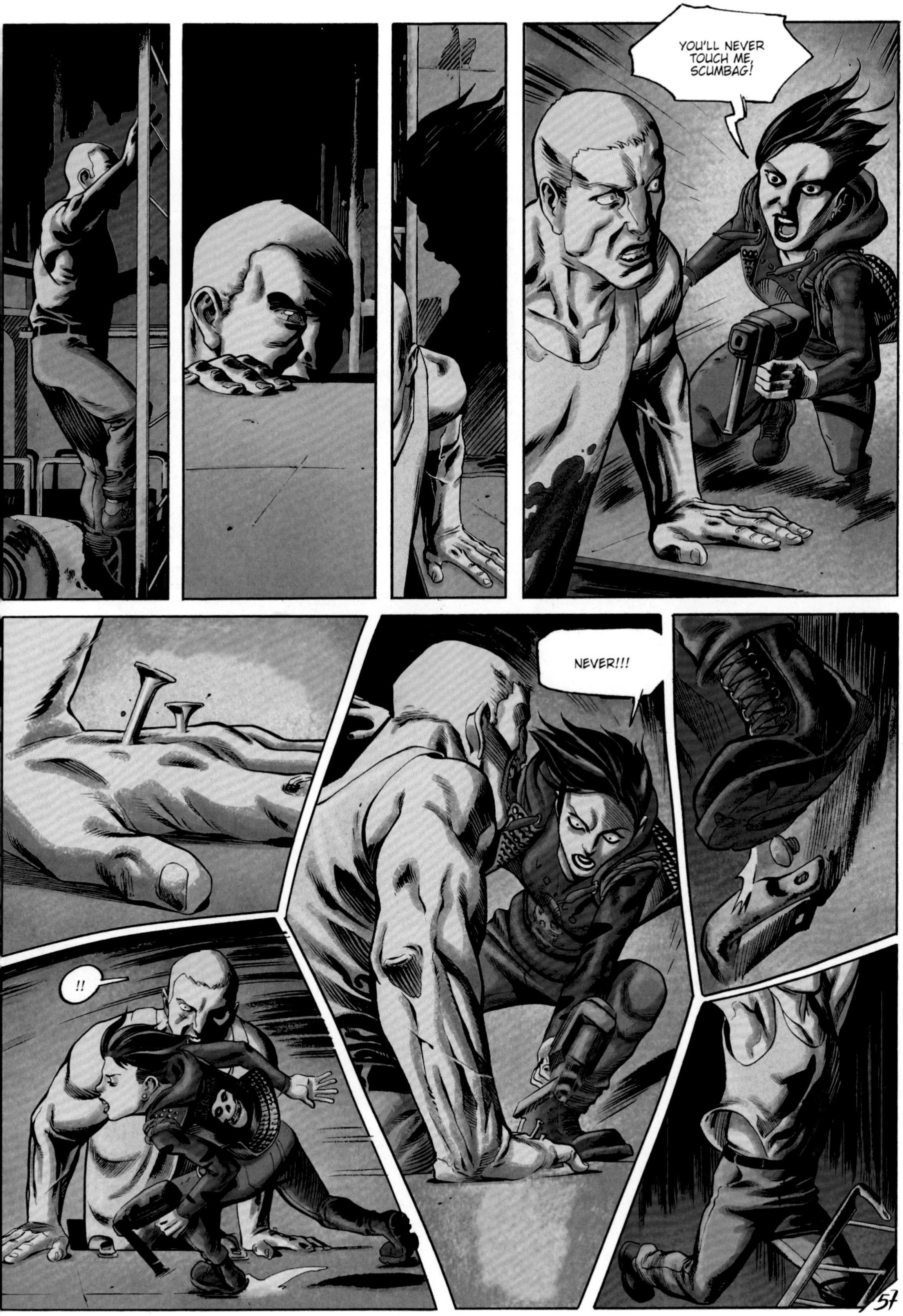
YOU'LL NEVER TOUCH ME, SCUMBAG!
NEVER!!!
!!

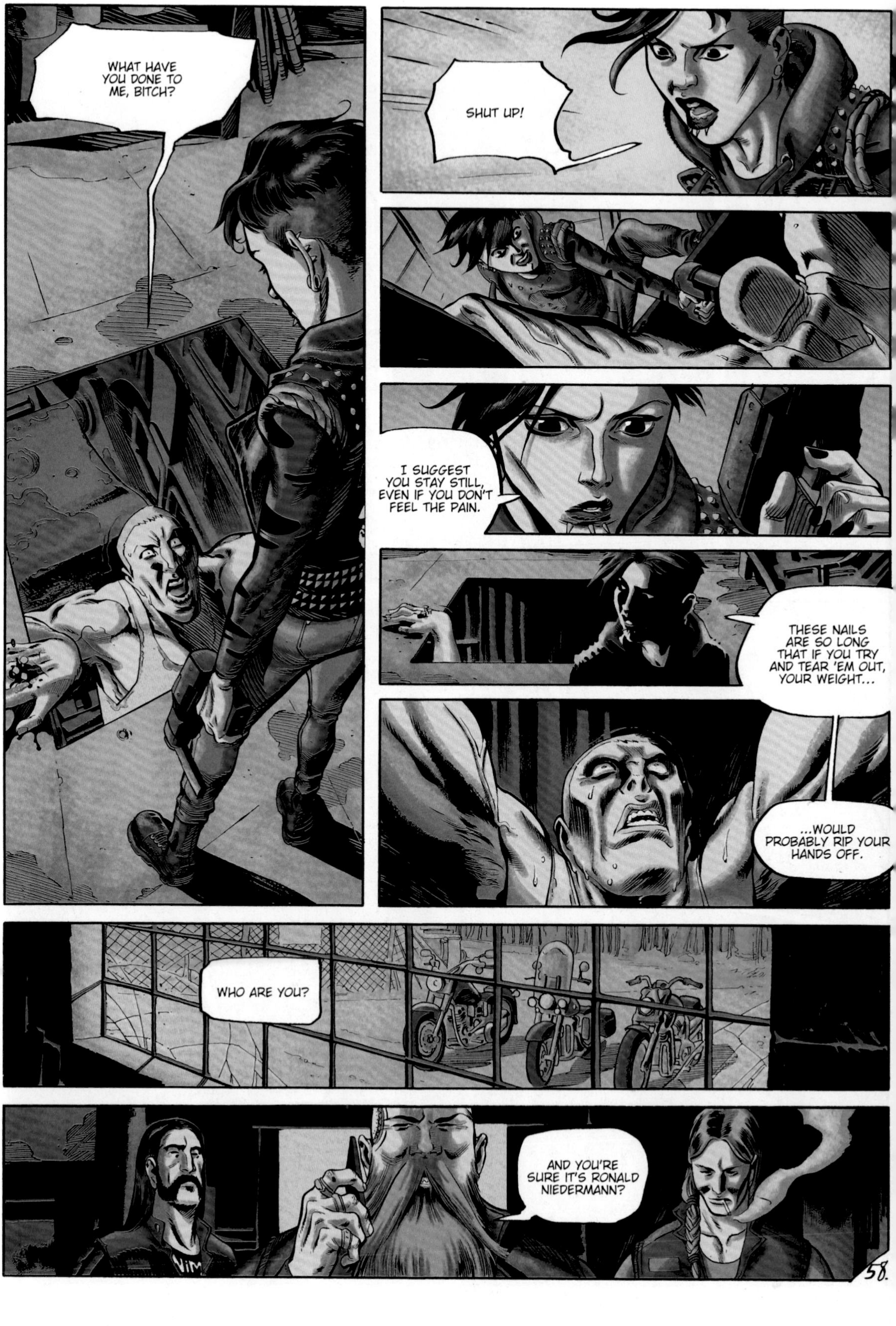
WHAT HAVE YOU DONE TO ME, BITCH?
SHUT UP!
I SUGGEST YOU STAY STILL, EVEN IF YOU DON'T FEEL THE PAIN.
THESE NAILS ARE SO LONG THAT IF YOU TRY AND TEAR 'EM OUT, YOUR WEIGHT...
...WOULD PROBABLY RIP YOUR HANDS OFF.
WHO ARE YOU?
AND YOU'RE SURE IT'S RONALD NIEDERMANN?

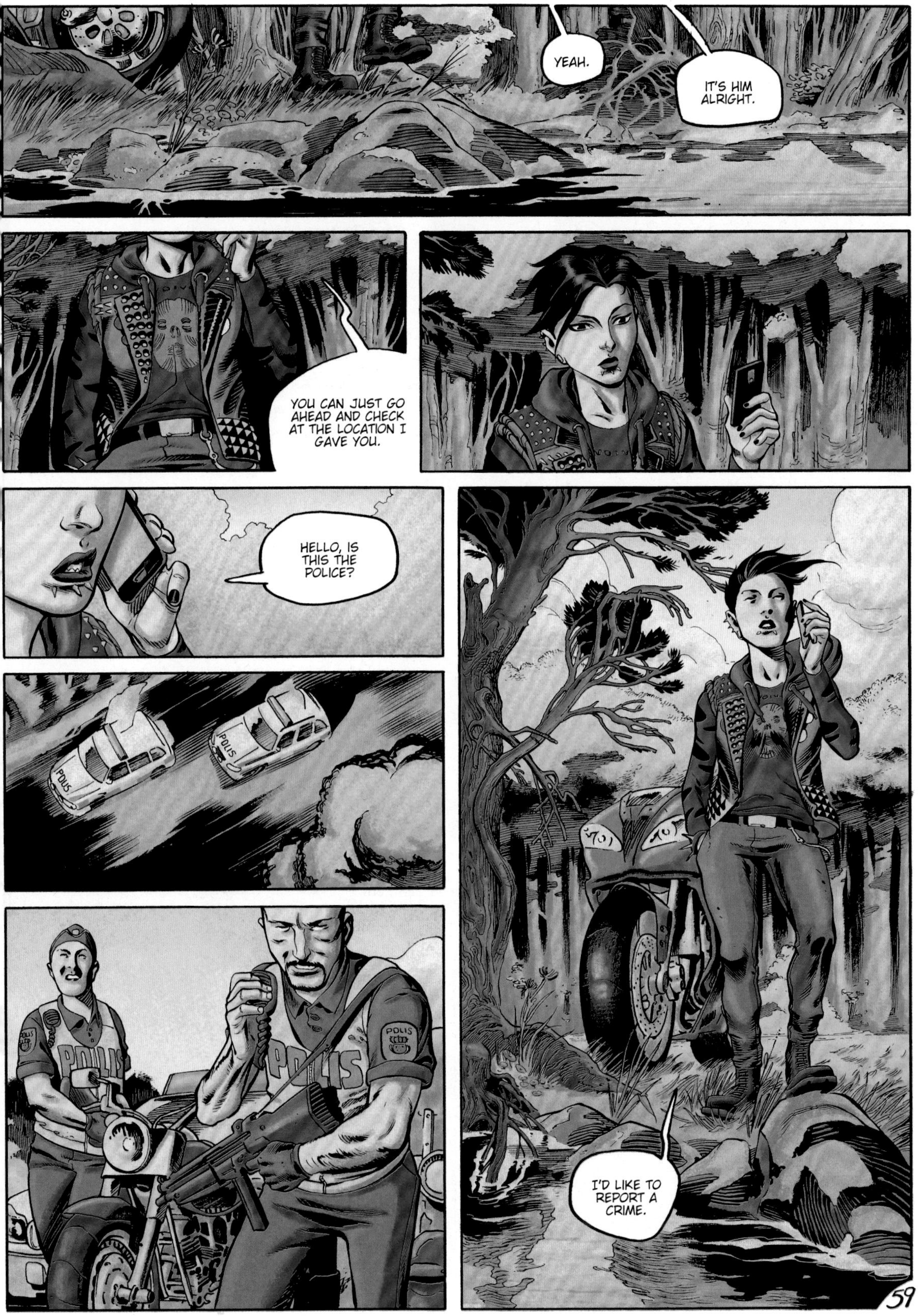
YEAH.
IT'S HIM ALRIGHT.
YOU CAN JUST GO AHEAD AND CHECK AT THE LOCATION I GAVE YOU.
HELLO, IS THIS THE POLICE?
I'D LIKE TO REPORT A CRIME.
POLIS
POLIS
POLIS
POLIS
POLIS

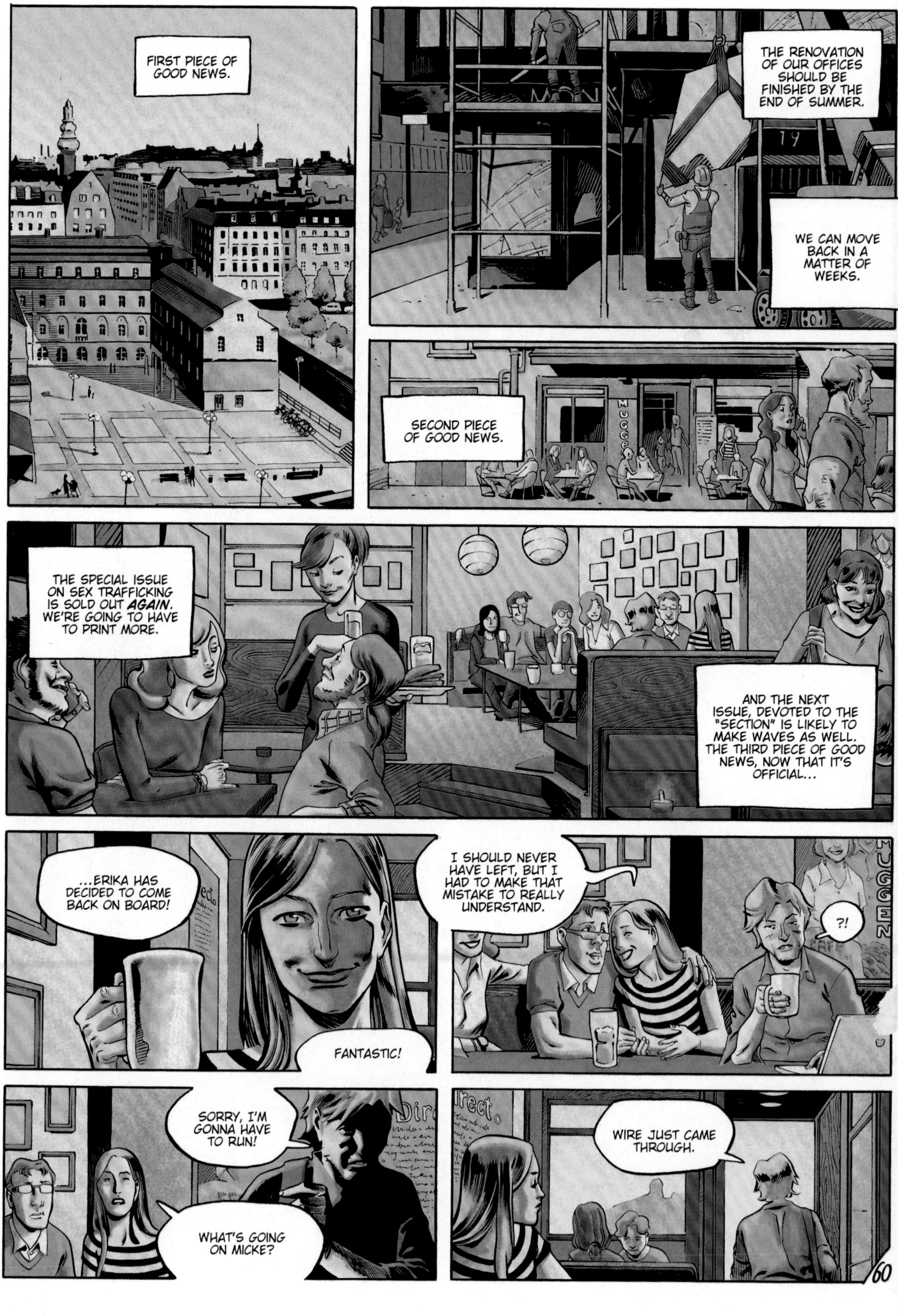
FIRST PIECE OF GOOD NEWS.
THE RENOVATION OF OUR OFFICES SHOULD BE FINISHED BY THE END OF SUMMER.
WE CAN MOVE BACK IN A MATTER OF WEEKS.
SECOND PIECE OF GOOD NEWS.
THE SPECIAL ISSUE ON SEX TRAFFICKING IS SOLD OUT AGAIN. WE'RE GOING TO HAVE TO PRINT MORE.
AND THE NEXT ISSUE, DEVOTED TO THE "SECTION" IS LIKELY TO MAKE WAVES AS WELL. THE THIRD PIECE OF GOOD NEWS, NOW THAT IT'S OFFICIAL...
...ERIKA HAS DECIDED TO COME BACK ON BOARD!
FANTASTIC!
I SHOULD NEVER HAVE LEFT, BUT I HAD TO MAKE THAT MISTAKE TO REALLY UNDERSTAND.
?!
SORRY, I'M GONNA HAVE TO RUN!
WHAT'S GOING ON MICKE?
WIRE JUST CAME THROUGH.

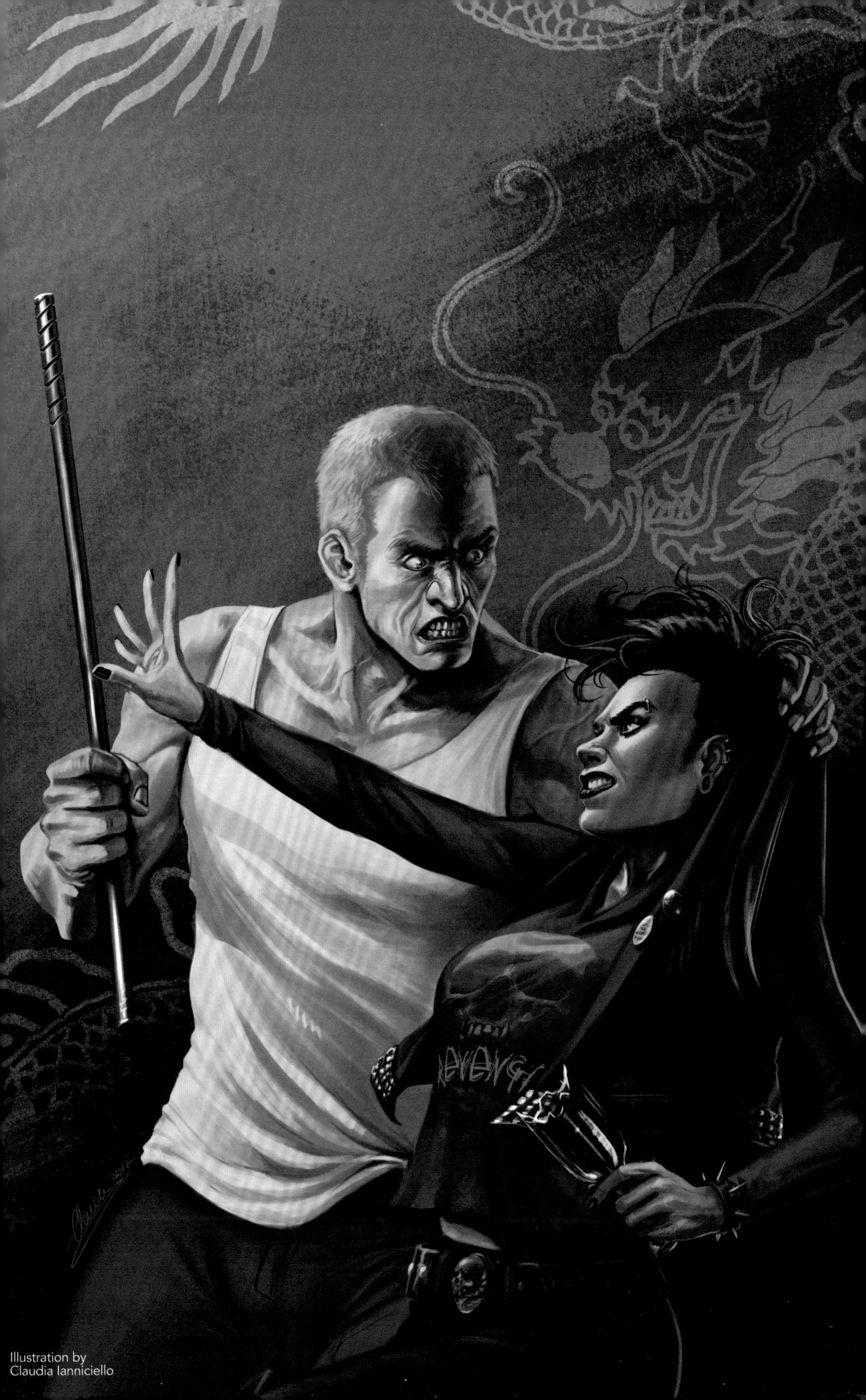

Illustration by
Claudia Ianniciello

MILLENNIUM

THE GIRL WHO KICKED THE HORNET'S NEST

COVERS GALLERY

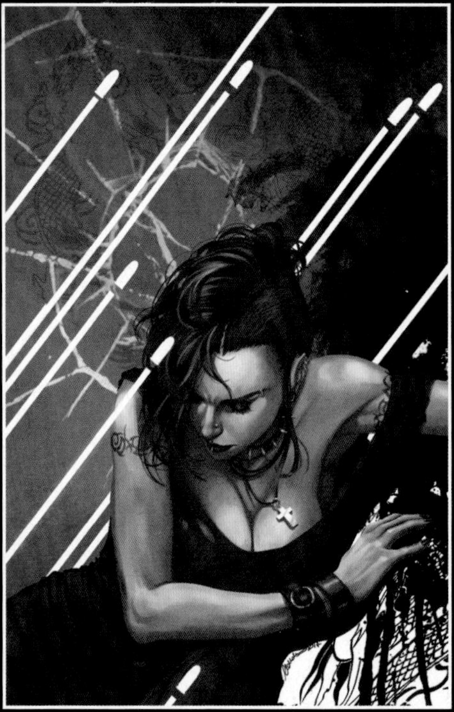

1 COVER A by **Claudia Ianniciello**

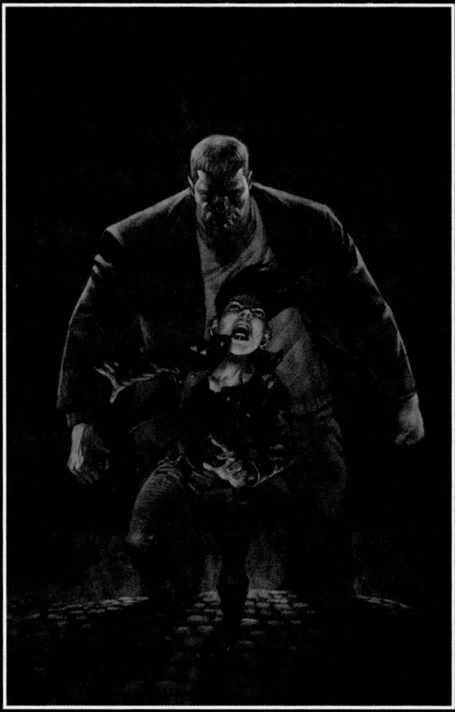

1 COVER B by **Homs**

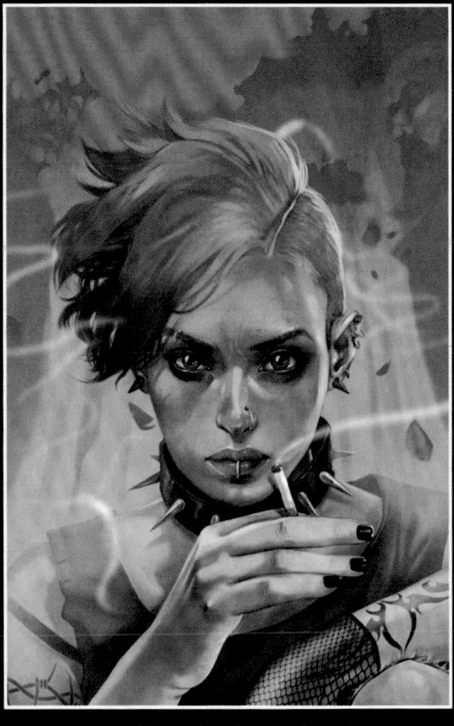

1 COVER C by **Claudia Caranfa**

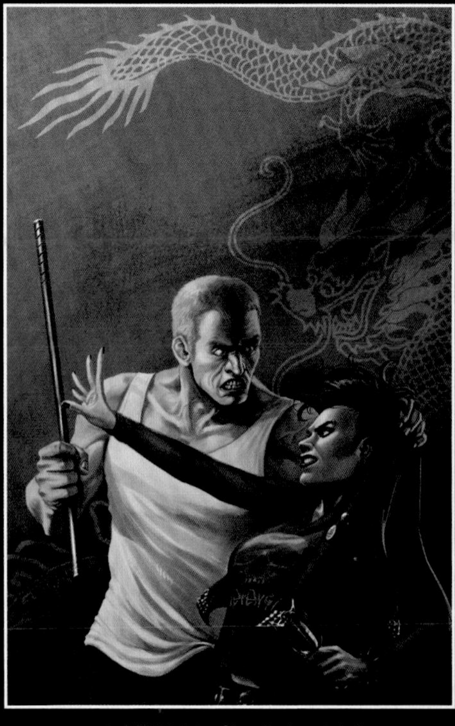

2 COVER A by **Claudia Ianniciello**

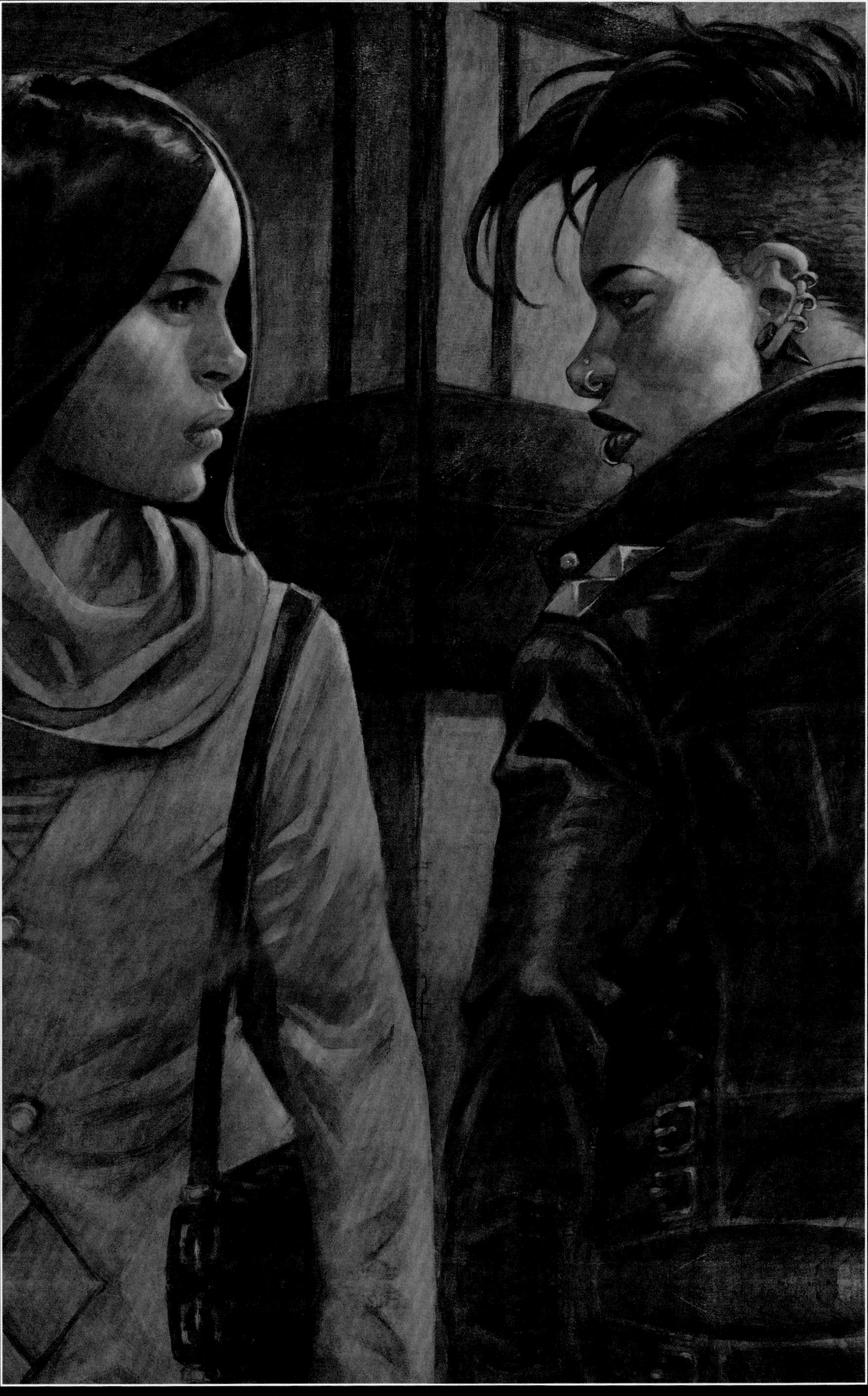

2 COVER B by **Homs**

HARD CASE CRIME COLLECTIONS!

"STEEPED IN THE GRIT AND GRISTLE OF THE GENRE AND NOT AFRAID TO WALLOW IN IT!"
BIG COMIC PAGE
HARD CASE CRIME
CHRISTA FAUST
GARY PHILLIPS
Peepland
ANDREA CAMERINI

$19.99 OUT NOW!

ISBN: 9781785851193

"HARD CASE MAY BE THE BEST NEW AMERICAN PUBLISHER TO APPEAR IN THE LAST DECADE."
- NEAL POLLACK IN THE STRANGER
HARD CASE CRIME
NORMANDY GOLD
MEGAN ABBOTT
ALISON GAYLIN
STEVE SCOTT
LOVERN KINDZIERSKI

$19.99 OUT NOW!

ISBN: 9781785858642

WRITERS:
CHRISTA FAUST
GARY PHILLIPS

ARTIST:
ANDREA CAMERINI

WRITERS:
MEGAN ABBOTT, ALISON GAYLIN

ARTISTS:
STEVE SCOTT, RODNEY RAMOS, LOVERN KINDZIERSKI

TITAN COMICS

For information on how to subscribe to our Hard Case Crime titles, or to purchase them digitally, visit:

WWW.TITAN-COMICS.COM

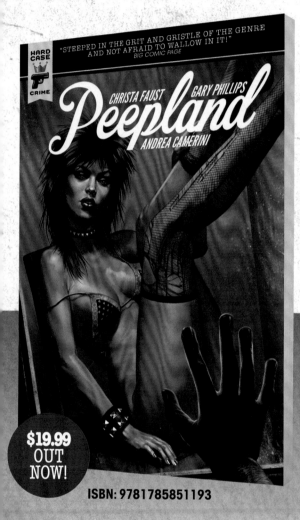

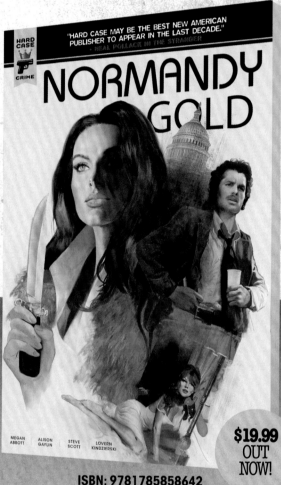

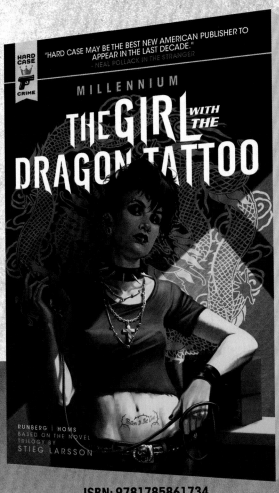

MILLENNIUM

THE GIRL WHO KICKED THE HORNET'S NEST

CREATOR BIOS

SYLVAIN RUNBERG

Sylvain Runberg is a French writer who divides his time between Stockholm, Provence, and Paris. He has a diploma in Plastic Arts and an MA in Political History. His first book was launched in 2004 and since then Runberg has had more than 70 books published by some of the largest French publishers (Glénat, Le Lombard, Dupuis, Dargaud, Casterman, Soleil, Futuropolis etc,...) and is now translated into 18 languages, having sold in total over a million copies worldwide.

Sylvain is best known for his comics adaptation of Stieg Larsson's *Millennium* trilogy. The adaptation has been acclaimed by both French and European media and readers and is already published in 13 other countries. Further to that success, Runberg has been trusted by Dupuis and the rights holders of *Millennium* to write an exclusive continuation of the comics series called the *Millennium Saga*.

Runberg is currently working on several new comics and TV projects that will be published in years to come.

JOSÉ HOMS

Homs is a Spanish comic artist who has worked for US companies like Marvel, but also for European publishers like Dupuis. Cutting his teeth on Marvel Comics titles such as *Blade, Red Sonja*, and *Marvel Westerns*, Homs' work has also appeared in magazine *Heavy Metal*, and in the Spanish anthologies *Barcelona TM* and *Revolution Complex*.

Since 2010 he has focused on work for the European market. Together with writer Frank Giroud, he was responsible for the 'L'Angelus' storyline in the *Secrets* series for Dupuis in 2010-2011.

MANOLO CAROT

Carot is a Spanish comic artist who sometimes works under the pen name Man. Born in Mollet les Vallès near Barcelona, he began his career in 1998 making illustrations for RPGs like *Aquelarre* and *Superhéroes Inc*, as well as Líder magazine of the publishing house La Caja de Pandora (1999-2001). He published his first comic stories for the erotic magazine *Kiss Comix of Ediciones La Cúpula*.